Shooter's Bible

GUIDE TO KNIVES

Shooter's Bible

GUIDE TO KNIVES

A Complete Guide to Hunting Knives, Survival Knives,
Folding Knives, Skinning Knives, Sharpeners, and More

ROGER ECKSTINE

SKYHORSE PUBLISHING

Skyhorse Publishing books may be purchased in bulk at special discounts for sales promotion, corporate gifts, fund-raising, or educational purposes. Special editions can also be created to specifications. For details, contact the Special Sales Department, Skyhorse Publishing, 307 West 36th Street, 11th Floor, New York, NY 10018 or info@skyhorsepublishing.com.

Skyhorse® and Skyhorse Publishing® are registered trademarks of Skyhorse Publishing, Inc.®, a Delaware corporation.

Visit our website at www.skyhorsepublishing.com.

10 9 8 7 6 5 4 3 2 1

Library of Congress Cataloging-in-Publication Data is available on file.
ISBN: 978-1-61608-577-3

Printed in China

CONTENTS

Foreword

Living on the Edge

Welcome to the first edition of *Shooter's Bible Guide to Knives*. If you're wondering why the name begins with a reference to firearms, it's because we wanted our knife bible to be immediately associated with the Shooter's Bible tradition. In a sense, it's our promise that this book will live up to the standards of the title that has earned the respect of enthusiasts worldwide.

My personal fascination with knives began in the backyard when I was still too young for Cub Scouts. My father introduced my siblings and me to the game of mumblety-peg. The game was played by balancing a knife in the palm of the hand and releasing it to the ground so that it entered the earth blade tip first. Actually, that first summer we used a long-handled screwdriver instead of a real knife. The winner of the game was the player who could produce the most graceful and intricate gyrations before it hit the ground. I remember trying to copy the cliff divers I had seen on ABC's *Wide World of Sports*. At the time I had no idea that the knife was actually one of the single most important inventions in the history of mankind.

When it comes to survival man is possibly the least physically able creature on planet Earth. Man's ability to develop weapons for defense and for harvesting food may be the only reason the species has survived. Long before gunpowder and firearms, it was the development of edged weapons that helped assure the evolution of man. Unlike blunt-force weapons that are swung or propelled, the knife is a lethal extension of the hand. I was reminded of this one day when working behind the counter of a local gun shop. A customer asked to see a combat folding knife on display inside the showcase next to a .357 Magnum revolver. I closed the knife and handed it to him. The man glared at me and handed it back without opening it. Then he asked to see one of the fixed-blade knives on display. Without making a move I asked him what he didn't like about the first knife. He said something under his breath and walked out of the store. Had he asked to see a handgun I would have gladly shown him several, handing them over after making sure they weren't loaded. Was I a poor knife salesman or simply living by the words "knives are always loaded"?

If knives are akin to guns in personal appeal, they certainly can be just as deadly. Barely minutes into one of the first concealed handgun license classes held in the state of Texas, the instructor, Tim Oxley, brought the class outside to demonstrate how anyone, no matter how out of shape they appeared to be, could defeat even an experienced shooter ready with a holstered gun. This exercise, known as the (Dennis) Tueller drill, proved that with just 21 feet between us and a knife-wielding assailant, it might be impossible to avoid being stabbed before we could draw and fire.

Aside from hunting and self defense, today's knives are designed to render many services. They can open packages, cut a seatbelt, cut away cloth to treat a wound, or merely serve the aesthetic desires of the collector. A knife can be a tool, a weapon, or an object of art. Some makers specialize in a single category. Some manufacturers are so prolific they might beg a separate volume of their own, prompting us to favor the latest designs. If the number of guns displayed in our sister publication *Shooter's Bible* is a daunting task, just remember that while guns in one form or another have been around for hundreds of years, edged weapons may predate the discovery of fire. Listing and describing every knife or knife maker in a single publication is likely an impossible task. But that won't keep us from trying.

Roger Eckstine
2012

Acknowledgments

To begin with, I feel honored to have been chosen to author the first edition of *Shooter's Bible Guide to Knives*. The desire to expand the Shooter's Bible series to include a study of edged weapons speaks volumes about the publisher. Thank you to Jay Cassell for drawing the first sword and starting the good fight. Thank you to my editor Julie Matysik for making it a reality. I'd like to thank Todd Woodard for his professional guidance throughout my writing career. I'd like my wife and family to know how much I appreciate their support. But there would be no story to tell if it weren't for the people inside the knife industry. I would like to thank the designers, whether they've contributed only a handful of ideas or a generation of blades and machines. And shake the rough-hewn hand of every machinist that knows the cost of a fine edged blade. I recognize that some makers were born directly into the trade, and I thank them for honoring the pact of their traditions. I would also like to thank the makers that came to the knife industry out of necessity or to help out a friend or two in bringing to life their vision of what a knife should be. Once that first knife was made they were hooked, like we all were. I'd like to thank shops, like Beckwith's Blades in Houston, Texas, that make a go of selling knives by offering quality products and expertise. I'd like to thank the special operators for lending their knowledge and experience to the development of edged weapons as a viable option for the civilian as well as the professional. I'd like to thank the personnel at each knife company, large and small, who share their passion and commitment to making good knives. There is much more to be written about knives. So, to you the reader, I'll just say thank you, until the next time.

About the Author

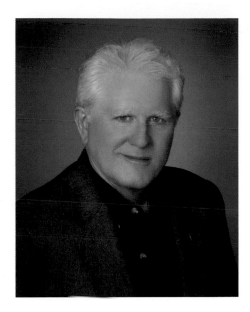

*R*oger Eckstine is arguably the most prolific writer of in-depth tests and evaluations of firearms to emerge over the past twenty years. Eckstine brings his eye for function and detail to the *Shooter's Bible Guide to Knives* after a lifetime connection with edged weapons. Born in New York when much of Long Island was still rural, Eckstine grew up at a time when knives were commonplace but demanded respect. Instruction by his father, a decorated World War II veteran who himself bore the scars of edged weapons, had a lasting effect on a young Eckstine. A natural writer and musician, Eckstine chose first to follow his passion for music—becoming a successful recording artist—which included a stint in Europe. Returning to the States, his interest in competitive shooting and martial arts led to a career in writing, after his experiences on the national competitive shooting circuit began to appear in magazines such as *Gun Games* and *Performance Shooter*.

Roger Eckstine is currently a Contributing Editor with *Gun Tests Magazine* and lives with his wife and family in Houston, Texas.

Knife Anatomy

Fixed Blades and Folders

The knife is a simple tool, yet it is possible to walk into a store with the intention of buying "the best" knife in the house and end up leaving totally confused without making a purchase. The fact is there may not be such a thing as the best knife. More likely there is the best knife for the job. Over the course of time you may end up buying dozens of knives for a variety of purposes. If you are fascinated with knives and buy simply out of curiosity and admiration, that should be reason enough. The more the merrier. But to pick the correct knife for a specific job, you have to be able to identify the features of each prospective knife and weigh them in relation to your needs.

Despite the wide variety of knives large and small, economical or extravagant, all knife designs are closely related. Perhaps the easiest way to understand the different types of knives is to first cut the field in two. There are fixed-blade knives and there are folding-blade knives. The fixed-blade knife can be traced back to prehistoric times, while the first evidence of folding knives leads us to believe they existed as far back as 500 BC to 600 BC. In our discussion of knife anatomy ("the separating or dividing into parts for detailed examination," definition number 6, Webster's New College Dictionary), let's begin with the older of the two designs: the fixed-blade knife.

The two most prevalent fixed-blade designs available today are the half-tang design and the full-tang design. Half-tang designs go by a variety of names, but the key is that the blade is thinned and either glued, tapped, and turned in to the handle, or molded around it. You may find them referred to as a Rat tang or a Push tang. A through-handle tang passes completely through the handle. The end of the tang is threaded and connected to the pommel.

⌄ This fixed-blade knife utilizes a through-handle tang. The guard is slipped over the tang and seated forward against the blade. The handle would be next. Once the pommel has been drilled and tapped, it screws onto the tang, capturing the handle. Kits such as this one are available from texasknife.com.
Photo courtesy of R. Eckstine.

⌃ The RAK from Ontario Knife Company, located in Franklinville, New York, is a full-tang knife. The blade length is sharpened and serrated. The handle offers finger grooves and a full wrap of paracord with lanyard. The cord can be removed in favor of hard panels that are bolted into place. The pommel is pointed for aggressive striking. Photo courtesy of OKC.

Although the through-handle tang is longer, it still may be referred to as a half tang because it measures much less top to bottom than the blade itself. The full-tang design is based on maintaining approximately the full height of the blade from end to end.

The front half of the blank is cut and sharpened, and the rear half serves as a frame for the handle. The rear section can then be sandwiched by two opposing plates or wrapped with material to form the handle. The full-tang knife is widely considered to be stronger, because the blade and the handle are one continuous piece of metal from point to pommel. Half-tang knives can also be very strong, but the method of attachment is critical. If glue is used then there is always a danger of shrinkage. The material used for the handle must also be stable and not susceptible to changes in temperature or humidity.

At the opposite end from the point of the blade is the pommel. The pommel finishes the contour of the handle and can offer the additional benefit of creating a striking surface. The striking surface can be blunt or pointed depending whether it is meant as a tool to drive in a tent stake or to break glass during the course of a rescue. It can also be shaped more aggressively to serve specifically as a weapon for close quarters fighting. The pommel may also offer a hole through which a connecting cord or lanyard may be attached. A lanyard can be used to connect the knife to the belt or sheath for the purpose of retention. Rawhide is the traditional material for making a lanyard. The popularity of rawhide lanyards has recently given way to paracord, a very strong multifilament cord used in parachute construction. Aside from retention, a current trend is to attach a braided cluster of cord to the lanyard hole for the purpose of storing a significant length of emergency rope in a small space. The lanyard can also serve as a pull handle for deployment from the sheath.

Whether or not a knife is constructed with a half-tang or full-tang design, the top ridge of the handle will commonly present an index point for the thumb. Some knives will feature a raised section ahead of the grip area on the bare spine itself or the index point will bridge both the blade and handle areas. On half-tang knives this point is generally limited to the handle. Index cuts on a full-tang knife may be continued into the grip panels. A variation of the full-tang design is the exposed tang handle. In this design the edges of the grip panels stop short of meeting the edges of the tang. This design can offer a more direct index to the tang and provide greater radial leverage in order to twist the knife. Twisting the knife can be part of a more aggressive attack, but its more common use will likely be to help remove it, should it become stuck in wood, sheet metal, and so forth.

In the case of most fixed-blade knives, the lower edge of the grip will introduce a surface distinct from the upper ridge, usually in the form of finger grooves. Finger grooves are applied to not only strengthen one's hold but also to allow the user to distinguish when the sharpened edge (or primary edge in the case of double-edged knives) is facing downward. There may be a complete set of grooves or just one or two in order to accommodate the first and second fingers, which are the strongest digits found on the human hand. Or immediately ahead of the finger grooves a small portion of the blade may be left unsharpened. This area is referred to as the choil. The choil may be your last indication before a finger ventures onto the sharpened edge. However, the forward or index finger groove is commonly integrated with a sudden widening of the tang referred to as the guard. This is the section of the knife that divides the blade from the handle in order to protect the user's hand, especially when the knife is driven into harder material. The guard may be machined into the blade and consist of a sudden widening in front of the handle. The guard may also include a flare outwards towards the sides. Or the guard may consist of a separate piece altogether slipped over the tang and seated in front of the handle. In what is likely a carryover from the sword, the hand guard is sometimes referred to as the hilt. Some knives

offer a smaller secondary guard as well that divides the index and middle fingers. This is called a double guard.

※

The folding knife is an invention that allows the user to carry a given amount of edge in a smaller space than a comparable fixed-blade knife. Whereas a 5-inch fixed-blade knife may take up nearly a foot of vertical space, a 5-inch folding knife will take up approximately half as much. The most common design connects the handle to the blade with a hinge or pivot that allows the two components to overlap in the closed position. The folding knife can be pocketed and handled safely because the edge, once folded, is blocked and guarded. Does this make a folding knife safer and more convenient than a fixed knife? Easier to carry and conceal, yes. Whether or not it is safer than a fixed-blade knife can depend on its design, quality of construction, and how it relates to the user. For a folding knife to be operated safely it must be maintained in good working order. For example, since the blade is designed to be movable, its ability to stay open or remain closed is subject to wear and should be monitored continuously. The level of safety and convenience of a folding-blade knife may also be relative to the method of deployment and recovery; in short, the way the knife opens and closes. Does it work as intended or is it too complex? The user must understand and adhere to a strict operating protocol specific to the design and be able to perform it comfortably.

Samples of early folding knives show an inability to lock the blade in the open position. Exerting linear or upward pressure on the handle and downward pressure to the blade while cutting was likely enough to keep the blade open to perform work. But the hinge is the weak point of a folding knife and this should limit what it is asked to do. This speaks to the theory of the best knife being the best knife for the job. The methods of keeping the blade open are perhaps the key issue in bringing strength to the design and greater confidence to the user. Let's continue the discussion with descriptions of common mechanisms used to either hold or lock the blades in the open position. The slip-joint is a spring-tension hold method found on traditional pocket knives or what some refer to as camp knives. The spring consists of a piece of steel riveted to the handle. When the blade is rotated, the spring pushes itself into a notch at the back of the blade. This is not a true locking device because folding the knife requires only that the user overcome the spring pressure in order to rotate the blade back into the handle. Another spring-loaded action activated by the blade being opened is the clasp lock. This utilizes a tension-loaded piece of metal located on the spine of the blade at the pivot. This is considered a true locking action because it requires pushing a lever or pulling on a ring to remove the clasp from a notch in the pivot in order for the blade to pass. The ring lock, or twist lock, is a simple guard device. This concept uses a ring or what could be referred to as a collar to surround the pivot. The ring has a notch in it through which the blade can pass to achieve the open position. The ring is then twisted to prevent the blade from folding.

Columbia River Knife and Tool (CRKT) makes the Glide Lock knife that offers a true bolster lock design.

The bolster of a folding knife is found on the outside of the handle usually at both the front and rear. Whereas the knife blade is housed between two liners that create a frame for the mechanism, the bolsters provide additional mass for structural support including the pivot and support pins. Invention of the bolster lock is credited to Charles Kain of Indianapolis, Indiana. Barry Gallagher is the designer who created the current models for CRKT. On the CRKT Glide Lock knives the upper left side bolster is pushed forwards away from the handle. Since the bolster rotates with the blade, the protruding edge of the bolster can now be used as a lever to rotate the blade out from the handle. Sliding the bolster back into its place locks the blade in the open position.

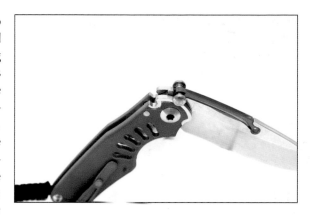

⩔ The Ti-Lock knife from Chris Reeve Knives of Idaho is unique. By removing the lock from the body of the knife, the maker has more freedom in designing the handle and frame. The locking mechanism is entirely visible, lending itself to the added decoration of a blue, anodized lock rail. Titanium construction, sandblasted and cut, makes for a handsome knife that offers light weight and superior grip.
Photo courtesy of R. Eckstine.

Another original locking mechanism is the Ti-Lock knife from Chris Reeve Knives.

The design was brought to Chris Reeve by its inventor, Grant Hawke, of Idaho City, Idaho. The Ti-Lock mechanism was originally conceived as a means to isolate the lock from the body of the knife in order to allow more freedom in designing the handle and frame. Undeniably unique, the locking stud is

⩔ The frame-lock knife does away with bolster and scales. One side of the frame is cut and tensioned against the end of the blade. When the blade is rotated to its fully open position, the support side falls into a notch, locking the blade in place. Friction between the blade and the support is minimized by using a ball bearing for direct contact. This Chris Reeve Sabenza knife utilizes a ceramic ball bearing to limit wear and provide a smooth action.
Photo courtesy of R. Eckstine.

《 The Glide Lock knife from CRKT utilizes a sliding bolster to lock the knife blade into position. With the top bolster moved forward the knife is free to rotate with the bolster itself used as a lever. Once the bolster is slid back into position the blade is locked.
Photo courtesy of CRKT.

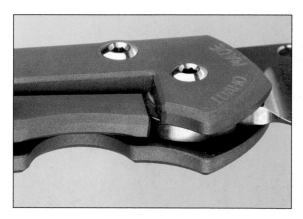

tensioned from above the blade. Once opened the stud locks into a notch on the upper ridge of the handle. Since the locking mechanism is exposed, it is not only decorative but easily accessible from either the right or left side of the knife. The Sabenza is not only another Chris Reeve product, but he in fact lays claim to its frame-lock design.

The frame lock does away with bolsters and scales, vastly reducing the amount of moving parts. Instead, the two sides of the handle combine to create a robust frame that not only contains the blade but locks it into place. This is achieved by cutting one side of the handle so that a section of the handle is under tension and set to move into position behind the blade locking it open. Since the sides of frame-lock knives are necessarily heavier, the extra width of the handle material provides broad support, making this design quite strong. Movement of the locking section is smoothed by a ball bearing to reduce friction against the side of the blade. High end knives, such as those in the Chris Reeve Sabenza series, utilize a ceramic rather than steel ball bearing for greater lubricity and less wear on the blade. Since the handles also serve as the frame, frame-lock knives tend to be heavier than other designs. But the Sabenza knives are formed from titanium, which keeps them remarkably light. The sandblasted finish of the Sabenza offers a natural non-skid grip, making the application of additional material unnecessary.

A lock-back knife, or back lock, is easy to spot by the relief in the top portion or spine at or near the end of the handle. The relief provides access to the locking

⌃ The Benchmade AXIS lock provides a locking bar that rides between the handle and the liners. When the knife is opened, two omega-style springs, one on each side, push the locking bar into a slot at the rear of the knife. Release is by sliding the locking bar rearward and folding the knife. Since the bar rides fully through both sides of the knife, operation is ambidextrous.
Photo courtesy of R. Eckstine.

arm that runs along the handle spine. When the blade is rotated into the open position, the locking arm connects under spring pressure into a notch on the back of the blade behind the pivot. Once in place the locking arm essentially forms an extension of the blade into the handle. That's why the lockback is considered one of the stronger designs found in folding knives.

The mid lock is a variation on the lockback, with the release located at or near the middle of the handle spine rather than at the rear. The intent of this design is to make the locking arm shorter and more rigid, offering greater strength. Many of the knives made by Cold Steel utilize the mid lock. Strength has always been a goal of the Cold Steel knife company and their demonstration videos featuring mid-lock knives are well known. What is less well known is the locking mechanism found in one of the first folding knives offered for sale by Cold Steel, the Pocket Bushman. The Ram Safe™ lock was designed by Andrew Demko. The Ram Safe™ lock works off a self-adjusting ram that moves forward as the knife is opened and wedges itself tightly between the tang cut away and the U-shaped roof of the handle. (The handle is closed on top, constructed from a sheet of stainless steel folded over to surround the blade on three sides.) The Ram Safe™ lock is released by pulling on the lanyard. This takes some practice as the spring that secures the ram is

⌄ Nathan's Knife Kit, from CRKT, provides an excellent example of a lock-back knife. The locking action takes place at the rear of the blade where the lug in the locking bar falls into a notch at the rear. Powered by a torsion bar spring seated in the back spacer, the lock is released by pushing down on the locking bar accessed through a relief located at the rear of the handle. Mid-lock knives position the relief further forward, about midway between the hinge and the rear of the handle.
Photo courtesy of R. Eckstine.

formidable. But this very economical design (about $40 suggested retail price), may come closer to offering the strength of a fixed-blade knife than any other folder.

The Axis lock was designed by a team at Benchmade Knives.

Considered to be among the strongest, the Axis lock can be operated with only one hand and it is ambidextrous. Its strength is due primarily to the fact that the blade is fully blocked by a heavy stop pin held in place by the liners and crossing the entire width of the frame. Positioned over the rear of the blade, it engages a ramped tang portion of the blade when opened. According to Benchmade: "Two omega style springs, one on each liner, give the locking bar its inertia to engage the knife tang. As a result the tang is wedged solidly between a sizable stop pin and the AXIS® bar itself." The Axis lock is used in manual, assisted manual, and automatic opening knives. Setting of the lock is automatic upon opening. The release buttons are located on either side of the handle just rearward and above the line of the pivot point. Sliding just one of the release buttons to the rear will unlock the blade.

Probably the most common locking mechanism is the liner lock.

Reportedly it was invented by Michael Walker in 1980 and was originally known as the Walker lock. In this design a section of the liner on one side is cut away and bent so that it angles inwards, applying pressure to the blade in its folded position. Once the blade is rotated out of the handle, the portion of the liner that rests against the side of the blade moves towards the center. The tip of the liner comes to rest at a flat spot machined into the rear of the blade behind and somewhat below the pivot point. To close the blade the liner must be manually pushed aside. The liner lock was a great advancement in knife lock technology and hastened the evolution of the tactical knife. Knives that can be opened and closed with one hand are favored by tactical operators and rescue personnel because they may not have a second hand to spare in hand-to-hand combat or while applying pressure to a wound. A knife in the hand opposite one's holster can also be vital in preventing a gun takeaway. The strength of the liner lock is largely dependent on the quality if not the strength of the individual components. The spring action of the liner lock must be active enough to trap the blade in the open position before it can bounce back and retract towards the handle, endangering the

≫ Originally referred to as the Walker lock for its renowned inventor Michael Walker, the liner lock is one of the most popular and versatile designs used today. In this design a section of the liner on one side is cut away and bent so that it angles inwards, applying pressure to the blade in its folded position. Once the blade is extended, the liner moves into a notch cut into the rear of the blade, supporting it in the open position. Release is by shifting the liner towards the outside of the handle.
Photo courtesy of R. Eckstine.

≫ Nail nicks provide a groove for the thumbnail so the blade can be pulled from between the liners.
Photo courtesy of R. Eckstine.

user's hand. The spring action must also be durable and retain a functional amount of tension, while the liner is wide enough to distribute the weight of force. One characteristic to look for is a liner lock that covers at least 50 percent of the blade notch when it is locked in the open position. In addition, the bearing surfaces of the blade and the tip of the liner must engage and disengage smoothly without catching.

The safest way to open or close a folding knife is by using both hands with one hand at the spine of the handle and the other along the spine of the blade. Traditional folding knives often provide a groove called a nail nick.

The method for opening a traditional folding knife is to pinch the blade with the thumbnail inside the nail nick and pull the blade from between the liners. Nail nicks are still in use today but they have been joined by several more designs to help the user open the blade. One of the most common is the thumb stud.

The thumb stud can be as simple as a screw head threaded directly through the blade. A thumb stud may only protrude on one side or evenly on both sides of the blade, making it ambidextrous and equally available to both the right- and left-handed user. The studs are removable so the user can choose how long the stud or studs need to be to fit the hand. Another method of opening that is inherently ambidextrous is the thumb hole.

⌃ Thumb hole opening knives provide ambidextrous operation but add a telltale bump to the contour of the spine. Whereas the bump can be used to provide greater downward pressure from beneath the thumb, it can also interfere with the draw. For example, if the knife is carried by a pocket clip with the spine of the blade facing the outer seam, a prominent bump may cause it to snag on the corner of the pocket when the knife is drawn directly upwards.
Photo courtesy of R. Eckstine.

⌄ Thumb studs vary in size and shape. They can be fitted to only one side, both sides equally, or one thumb stud can be larger than the other. The size of the stud is generally in relation to the width of the knife in the closed position. If the studs are too large they can catch on clothing and make it difficult to draw the knife quickly.
Photo courtesy of R. Eckstine.

The thumb hole is a round or oval cut fully through the knife blade just ahead of the pivot. Some thumb holes introduce an upward curve to the spine of the knife. This is generally found in blades that are narrower from top to bottom and serve as an indexing point for the thumb. Other thumb hole designs do not interfere with the natural profile of the blade. In both cases the design of the thumb holes and the size or placement of the studs can have a bearing on how the knife is carried. Regarding pocket clip knives, where the knife itself is inside the pocket and the clip loops over the edge of the pocket, a stud that is too large can catch on the pant material. A thumb hole that introduces an extra contour or hump to the blade spine can also get caught inside a tight pocket. If the draw technique cannot be modified to avoid this problem, then the answer might be to carry the folder in a belt-mounted pouch designed specifically for the knife.

Many Emerson brand knives offer a disc seated across the top of the blade to provide the leverage for a thumb opening. This design offers less drag than thumb studs and still provides ambidextrous operation. If catching on pocket material is interfering with your draw, then this problem can be an advantage when it comes to Emerson Wave knives. The Emerson Wave knives include a hook along the rear of the blade spine.

This hook is designed to grab the material edge of the pocket as the knife is withdrawn. As the knife leaves the pocket the blade is forced to unfold. Not assisted by gravity or a spring, this is a clever opening device that should confound the anti-knife crowd that want to disarm their fellow citizens.

Another mechanical device to assist manual opening is the flipper.

This is an outcropping along the outer edge of the pivot area of the blade. With the handle clasped between the thumb, forefinger, ring finger, and pinkie, the index finger can open the knife by pressing or rolling back the flipper. Most flipper knives also have a thumb stud, so this type of opening is optional. Some buyers choose this type of knife because once open, the back profile of the flipper creates a raised area that can serve as a thumb index or partial hand guard depending on the design.

Assisted-opening knives can be very helpful in terms of one-handed opening. After the opening movement is begun a spring action takes over and brings the blade to its fully open and locked position. This necessarily speeds deployment and can be helpful

« The Emerson Wave design adds a hook along the rear surface of the blade spine. The purpose of this small wave-shaped hook is to affect automatic opening of the blade. There is no other mechanical assistance, such as a spring, so the hook simply catches on the corner of the pocket and pulls open the blade. The Wave knife can also be drawn without opening simply by avoiding contact with the edge of the pocket. Normal thumb opening also can be achieved from either side by using the edges of the disc that is mounted across the spine of the blade. Photos courtesy of R. Eckstine. ⌄

⌃ The flipper can be used as an alternative to pushing on a thumb stud to open a folding knife. The flipper is a lever machined as one with the blade that protrudes from behind the hinge when the knife is in the closed position. With the hand moved away from the liners, the index finger is used to push inward on the flipper and rotate the blade to its fixed position. Once the blade is locked open, the flipper acts as a guard between the handle and the edge. Photos courtesy of R. Eckstine.

in a situation where hand or wrist movement may be limited. But there is also the danger that the knife can open as a result of incidental contact or friction. This is where design and quality play a part in the safety of an assisted knife. Some assisted-opening knives have a safety to lock the blade in the closed position. Use of this type of lock is highly recommended, especially when the knife is carried loose in a pocket or inside a bag. The irony is that whatever time is saved using an assisted-opening knife may be negated by the need to release the safety. The answer might be to choose an assisted model that requires greater manual action before the blade is propelled by the assist mechanism. Also, limit your assisted-opening knife to fixed carry, such as inside a sheath, not loose in a pocket or bag. Bear in mind that the same spring pressure that releases the blade will have to be overcome to close the knife as well. If one-handed operation is a necessity, the ability to close as well as open the knife should be taken into account.

Automatic-opening knives are generally only available to law enforcement personnel. Some are opened with a button and then folded manually. Others feature automatic retraction of the blade as well as deployment. Most automatic opening knives unfold from the handle in a pivoting motion but there are some where the blade deploys forward straight through the tip of the handle. Almost all automatic knives utilize a safety to keep the knife open, closed, or both. Perhaps the key appeal, aside from the appreciation of a remarkable machine, is that manipulation can be simplified. If the operator typically wears gloves, an auto-opening knife can be a lifesaver. With modern technology the construction of auto-opening knives is at a higher level of quality than ever before. However, many seasoned operators continue to recognize concerns such as the complexity and expense of automatic knives. The abundance of pins, springs, cams, and other moving parts can leave the professional operator wary of malfunction.

THE BLADE

The blade is the heart and soul of the knife. It is the reason the knife exists. Everything else is a means to adapting it to the human hand or a way to keep it at the ready. Early blades were made from stone, wood, bone, or igneous matter such as lava. Sometimes the piece of bone or wood could be used as it was found merely because it already had a pointed, sharp, or jagged edge. Some stones could be given a cutting edge by impact. Struck in just the right manner, the rock would fracture, leaving a thin, narrow edge. Struck repeatedly, the edge could be fashioned with a series of highs and lows creating a coarse serration.

It is difficult to say how many times an ancient knife made from rock or animal bone could be sharpened or reused. But once carbon steel entered the picture not only did it become possible to sharpen a worn blade, but steel once used for other purposes could be recycled or transformed. An excellent example is the railroad spike knife. Railroad spikes are sledgehammered into hardwood ties that have been treated with creosote or tar, which makes the wood more difficult to penetrate. The spikes had to endure not only the pounding of a sledgehammer but the weight, heat, and pressure of freight cars and locomotives, so they were plenty tough. Able to heat and transform even the toughest metals, blacksmiths are famous for turning out knives from scrap material such as railroad spikes.

Yet what is it really that we expect from the blade? To be sharp, hold an edge, not break at the edge line, or snap in two. We want to be able to sharpen it when it gets dull and in the meantime the blade should not rust, corrode, or stain. Simple. Well, not really. If the metal is soft it may not produce an edge as sharp as one that can be achieved using a harder metal. But the softer steel will probably allow you to sharpen the blade yourself with a common stone. Harder metals require machinery, and the best option for sharpening such knives may be to send them back to the manufacturer. In terms of toughness or ductility, if the metal is too hard it can become brittle and the edge can break off. Or under stress, such as when the knife is twisted, should it become jammed in media that tends to grip, such as moist wood, low tensile strength may allow the blade to snap. Some metals offer more porous surfaces than others. This can be solved with an exterior coating, but any work knife exposed to chemicals will require more regular cleaning and oiling to protect the surface. Exposure to salt water further increases the danger of corrosion.

Some of the challenges of making a sharp, durable knife can be addressed by using laminate steel. Laminate steel places a layer of hard metal sandwiched between two layers of softer metal. The intent is to benefit from the fine edge capability of the hard steel and protect its brittle nature from rearing its ugly head. This method is not always successful and laminate lines can, in the eyes of some, spoil its ascetic value. The better solution to all of the above lies in understanding the definition of the words "alloy" and "alloy steel." An alloy is the degree of mixture with base metals. Think of it as a recipe. To begin with, steel is an alloy of iron and carbon. Alloy steel is carbon steel to which various elements such as chromium, cobalt, copper, manganese, molybdenum, nickel, tungsten, or vanadium have been added in sufficient amounts to obtain desirable physical and chemical properties. For example, steel can be made more stain resistant by increasing the nickel content.

We've all heard the term "stainless steel." This means that the composition of the steel contains no less than 10.5 percent chromium. Stainless steel is not impervious to corrosion or stain but such maladies are less likely to occur. Other elements can be added to adjust or enhance the performance requirements of the knife blade. Carbon content provides edge retention, hardness, tensile strength, and resistance to general wear and abrasion. Chromium not only adds corrosion resistance but also hardness, toughness or ductile strength, tensile strength (the ability to withstand torque), and

abrasion resistance. Adding manganese is another way to ensure hardness, tensile strength, and resistance to wear. Nickel not only enhances corrosion resistance but also hardness. Silicon adds tensile strength by increasing its ability to flex without breaking and return to shape. Vanadium also increases hardness and tensile strength and offers the added benefit of increasing the blade's ability to withstand impact. One of the latest innovations is the addition of nitrogen by 1 percent. This is proving especially effective in combating the challenges of salt-water immersion.

Whereas the actual content by percentage can vary or be as closely guarded as any industrial secret, the components of popular blade steels are more widely available. But, as we see in the accompanying table, hardness is not an absolute. The most commonly used standard for hardness is the Rockwell Scale C (HRC). Blade steel is awarded an HRC rating based on a test measuring the depth of penetration produced by a 120-degree diamond cone indentor under the weight or pressure of weight of 150 kgf, (kilogram force). Few knife makers specify an exact HRC rating. Theoretically, this would be possible if each individual blade was tested and marked. But, due to the organic nature of the components and the somewhat fluid process of producing a blade, most makers publish a range rather than an exact rating. In the accompanying table we can see the components of some of the more widely used steels and their approximate hardness rating:

Knife Blade Hardness
Rockwell Scale C (HRC)

Steel	Components	HRC
154CM	Carbon, Chromium Molybdenum	58–61
CPM-S30V	Carbon, Chromium Molybdenum, Vanadium	58–60
X15T.N	Carbon, Chromium, Manganese, Molybdenum, Nickel, Nitrogen, Silicon, Vanadium	58–60
M2	Carbon, Chromium, Manganese, Molybdenum Nickel, Silicon, Tungsten, Vanadium	58–60
D2	Carbon, Chromium, Vanadium, Manganese, Molybdenum Nickel, Silicon, Vanadium	60–62
M390	Carbon, Chromium, Manganese, Molybdenum, Silicon, Tungsten, Vanadium	60–62
N680	Carbon, Chromium, Manganese, Molybdenum, Silicon, Vanadium	57–59

Steel	Components	HRC
N690	Carbon, Chromium, Cobalt, Manganese, Molybdenum, Silicon, Vanadium	58–60
440C	Carbon, Chromium, Manganese, Molybdenum, Phosphorous, Silicon, Sulfur	58–60
8CR14MOV	Carbon, Chromium, Manganese, Molybdenum, Nickel, Phosphorous, Silicon, Sulfur, Vanadium	57–58
AUS-8	Carbon, Chromium, Manganese, Molybdenum, Nickel, Phosphorous, Silicon, Sulfur, Vanadium	58–59
1095	Carbon, Manganese, Phosphorous, Sulfur	57–60
9CR13COMOV	Carbon, Chromium, Cobalt, Manganese, Molybdenum, Vanadium	58–60
CPM-M4	Carbon, Chromium, Manganese, Molybdenum, Silicon, Sulfur, Tungsten, Vanadium	60–62
VG10	Carbon, Chromium, Vanadium, Molybdenum, Cobalt	59–60
420HC	Carbon, Chromium, Manganese, Silicon, Vanadium	60–62
4034	Carbon, Chromium, Manganese, Silicon	54–55
X-15 TN	Carbon, Chromium, Manganese, Molybdenum, Nickel, Nitrogen, Phosphorous, Silicon, Vanadium	54–55
12C27	Carbon, Chromium, Manganese, Phosphorous, Silicon	59–61
1.4116	Carbon, Chromium, Manganese, Phosphorous, Silicon, Vanadium	55–57
H-1	Carbon, Chromium, Manganese, Molybdenum, Nickel, Nitrogen, Phosphorous, Silicon, Sulfur	57–58

Damascus Steel

What if the list of available component elements was very short? How could the cutting ability of a blade or its ability to bend and not break be enhanced? Without being able to isolate and combine the necessary elements, the simple answer might be to take two or three of your best blades and bind them together. Maybe that's going too far, but it does introduce a method of producing blades that goes back centuries. Damascus steel blades are the result of the physical joining of more than one steel alloy to create a pattern. Sometimes referred to as pattern steel, the process begins with rods or sheets of steel that may vary in hardness from mild steel of less than 50 HRC to the hardest tool steels that register more than 60 HRC on the Rockwell scale. The parts are forge welded and fused together under a hammer. The steel is drawn out, cut, folded, and welded again. This process is repeated to create the desired amount of layers. The finished blank may then be altered with grooves or shallow holes. When the blank is hammered to pre-blade thickness these marks

are lifted to the surface, creating a pattern. The process requires patience and skill and each blade is a work of art. The layering produces a natural serration wherein exposure of the hard and soft steels alternate along the edge. This makes Damascus blades ideal for cutting on fibrous materials such a rope. Today, with the availability of high performance alloy steels, Damascus blades are valued primarily for their stunning appearance.

⌃ The Elishewitz Tank offers a 3.75-inch Damascus steel blade with 4.75-inch handle that features walrus tusk scales and titanium bolsters. Damascus steel is a complex work of art, physically melding more than one alloy steel in a manner that produces an edge of multiple characteristics and a stunning visual grain.
Photo courtesy of Elishewitz Custom Creations.

EDGES AND BLADE SHAPES
Basic Blade Shapes
Courtesy of Case College, W. R. Case & Sons Cutlery

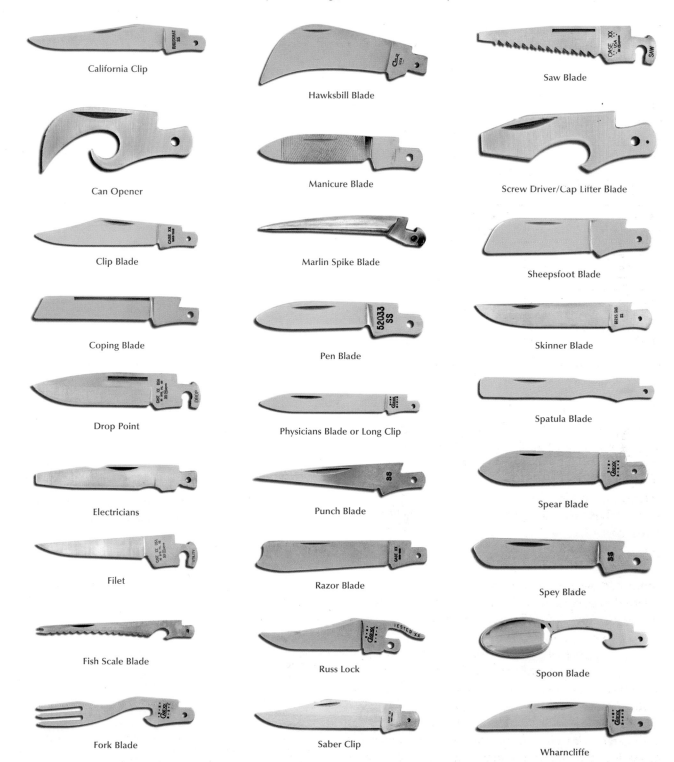

California Clip

Hawksbill Blade

Saw Blade

Can Opener

Manicure Blade

Screw Driver/Cap Lifter Blade

Clip Blade

Marlin Spike Blade

Sheepsfoot Blade

Coping Blade

Pen Blade

Skinner Blade

Drop Point

Physicians Blade or Long Clip

Spatula Blade

Electricians

Punch Blade

Spear Blade

Filet

Razor Blade

Spey Blade

Fish Scale Blade

Russ Lock

Spoon Blade

Fork Blade

Saber Clip

Wharncliffe

⌃ Dagger-shaped blades, such as the one found on the Gerber Guardian, are not only symmetrical in shape but both edges are sharpened. Thus, there is no "safe" side to a dagger. Photo courtesy of Gerber Legendary Blades.

⌃ Currently out of production, this spear-point knife was designed for one of the original Navy Seals. It offers a combination edge blade and a symmetrical shape much like a dagger. But spear-point blades leave the upper edge of the blade unsharpened. Photo courtesy of R. Eckstine.

The three most popular edges used today are the plain or smooth edge, the serrated edge, and a blade that offers both. The smooth, or plain, edge blade offers one continuous cutting surface. The serrated-edge blades have teeth. This allows for a back and forth saw-like cutting. There are many styles of serration but the teeth are rarely offset from side to side in order to provide space as found on a wood saw, for example. The combination or combo-edged blades usually offer more plain edge with at most the rearward quarter length of the blade finished with serrations. Some fixed blade knives also offer a serrated surface on the spine, which is opposite or above the primary edge. Double-edged knives are available and they typically offer a plain-edge blade along the entire upper and lower edges of the blade. In this regard there is no "safe" side to the blade. A dagger is a good example of a double-edged blade.

But this type of blade is illegal in most jurisdictions for anyone other than law enforcement personnel. Despite its aggressive-sounding name, a spear point differs from the dagger. The top and bottom of the knife may also rise and fall equally in profile, but the edge above the tip and along the spine is left unsharpened. Despite its name, a spear point may also form a blunt outline rather than a sharp narrow point.

Aesthetics and artistic license play a part in blade design, and just about any knife can be used for any number of tasks. But, traditionally, blade shapes vary with the job they were designed for. If we were to visualize the knife as a lever, the shape of the blade will offer one or more key points where force can be applied. For example, let's say the job is to cut through a length of hide along one continuous line. For this job leverage is applied from beneath the handle and downward on the tip against the hide. The lever must be strong enough not to flex and the girth of the blade should not block the operator's view of any predetermined line. The amount of contact with the hide is going to be limited to a small area from the tip rearward. For this cut a sheepsfoot blade would be a good choice because it is very strong and the blade thins down at the tip, making it suitable for detailed work. The spine runs parallel to the edge but slopes down to the point in a lazy round curve. A coping blade is similar to the sheepsfoot but the blade is typically not as massive or as great from top to bottom. The spine and edge are parallel in ruler-like fashion, then turn downward at about a 45-degree angle to the tip. This abrupt drop adds definition to the point. Patternmakers who must follow a complex set of lines commonly favor the coping blade for its nimble handling. The edge of the wharncliffe is straight and the spine rises and falls in a graceful, round arc producing a small, natural point, so it, too, offers a well-defined point of contact. However, it might not be the first choice for hard use or repeatedly cutting fine lines or rendering a pattern. The wharncliffe is more often called upon to cut using the length of the blade rather than its sharp point because, should it become dull, the point can become peg-like and tear the material.

The drop point and the clip point are among the most commonly seen blade shapes. The drop-point blade offers a gentle downward curve along the spine, giving the blade a "humpback" appearance. The tip can be pointed or blunt. Like the drop point, the clip-point blade has many variations. But the clip can be identified by a rise in the spine towards the back and a downward sweep to the tip. The cutting edge also sweeps upwards to a well-defined point. Returning to our example of cutting a sheet of hide, it is along the arc of this upward sweep where the greatest amount of leverage can be applied. The sabre point is similar in its upward sweep of the cutting edge from back to front and the way the spine slopes downward towards the tip. But the sabre offers an aggressive swedge or false edge on the forward top portion of the blade. Of the three the sabre is generally considered to offer the more weapon-like appearance. In comparing the thrusting characteristics of the sabre to the dagger or spear-point blades, the sabre (or its relatives the clip and drop point blades) tends to move off line when it enters media in response to its asymmetrical profile. The thrust of a dagger or spear-point blade is much more likely to stay in line with the direction of the thrust.

One blade style that combines the thrusting ability of a spear point with the well-defined edge of a sheepsfoot is the American tanto.

According to the brilliant knife designer and manufacturer Chris Reeve, the American tanto was developed from the European tanto. The European tanto has a body of full height and the blade sweeps upward, making a wide, full turn. Some say this shape mimics the machete. The American tanto squares off this

upward turn. This creates a well-defined secondary edge for slashing or cutting and a heavily reinforced tip in line with the bore of the handle.

Blades for skinning or filleting seek to distribute pressure evenly along the edge. Skinners tend to be heavier for power and wider to spread the skin away from the knife. Fillet knives are almost surgical. They must be more exact and take up less space so as not to disturb more delicate meat and tissue. A bird-hook blade is for removing the entrails of a freshly killed bird. More of a hooking tool than an actual blade, the bird hook is inserted into the anus, wound to capture the entrails, and pulled out to clean the carcass. A caping knife is more of an all-around knife, similar to a drop point used for field dressing or preparing game in the kitchen. A gut hook knife is used on larger game where skinning is a necessity. The outside of the hook is smooth but the inner radius is razor sharp. Fixed-blade gut hook knives often share the same handle or general ergonomics of a hunting knife, but the blade finishes

⌃ The American tanto, bottom, offers two distinct points as well as a heavy gauge blade to back them up. Two variations are shown, including the Zero Tolerance SpeedSafe (middle) and the Ka-Bar FIN knife, which combines the tanto with a hawksbill profile. Photo courtesy of R. Eckstine.

⌃ The Case Changer Set 6004 consists of a sturdy lock-back knife with three extra blades that can be carried in the covered leather pouch and changed out at any time. The saw, drop point blade (center), and clip point blade (shown mounted) offer an enhanced groove for thumbnail opening. The hooked blade is known as a gut hook and can be used to quickly remove hide. Many consider the gut hook to be a forerunner to the seatbelt cutters found on today's rescue knives. The knife handle includes amber bone scales between polished brass bolsters.
Photo courtesy of W. R. Case.

with the hook rather than a point. Folding gut hook knives often hinge from between the liners opposite another second folding blade. Some gut hook knives are little more than a sharp hook and finger loop. Once a cut has been made in the animal skin, the gut hook is inserted and pulled in a zipper-like fashion. The "seat-belt cutter" found on many of the new rescue knives is comparable in many ways to the gut hook blade.

The hawksbill features an aggressively shaped blade with a sharp downward turn much like its namesake. It can serve as a pruning tool or as a weapon. The karambit, an Indonesian knife that doubles as a farm implement and fighting knife, is a good example of a hawksbill shape.

The spey blade was originally designed for neutering cattle. The spey is a good, all-around cutter, short and blunt, offering good linear strength.

The hoof pick and the marlin spike are two more working tools. Neither is actually a knife per se but are often found packaged in concert with folding knifes. The hoof pick is for cleaning the mud from a horse's hooves. A golfer or hunter wearing cleats might find this useful. The marlin spike is a mariner's tool used to loosen knots, especially when the rope is wet.

A long-time favorite, the spike is pushed into the knot to loosen the lines. The pen blade got its name from when it was used to sharpen writing quills. A mild-looking knife, it remains popular as a secondary blade found on folding pocket knives. One other blade with a relatively sedentary purpose is the spatula blade. Commonly found as part of a doctor's knife set, the unsharpened blade consists of a flat piece of steel with a round or round-edged square tip. The spatula blade can be used to stir medicine, act as a grain stick to measure a prescription, or as a tongue depressor.

The scimitar and the Bowie-style blades are each linked to their own measure of legends or myth. The scimitar is a word that means "sword" in Arabic.

A number of different scimitars described as medieval or the style belonging to pirates can be purchased from sellers dealing in "movie swords." The prevailing shape is a bold upswept curve with both the blade edge and spine ending in a needle point. Its strength is cutting along the edge rather than thrusting. This makes it an excellent choice for the draw cut, slice, or slash. This type of knife is not illegal to own, but it could prejudice a jury as easily as it could scare off an attacker. The Bowie knife was designed to be equally effective for the thrust and the slash but it can easily do the work of a camp/trail knife.

It could be described as a heavy blade with much of its edge parallel to its spine after which it scallops downward in a long arc. The edge sweeps upward to a point closer to the center of the blade. Some might define it simply as a heavy clip point fixed-blade knife,

⌃ The Indonesian Karambit is sometimes referred to as having a hawksbill blade. The Emerson Super Karambit takes this age-old farm implement into the modern tactical arena. The Super Karambit is a folder with liner lock and Emerson's wave-shaped pocket hook for one-hand opening capability.
Photo courtesy of Emerson Knives.

⌃ The Camillus folding knife number 18670 offers a 2.75-inch coping blade and a marlin spike. The marlin spike is the mariner's friend. The spike is used to pierce through the bonds of the wet, tightly knotted rope enabling the user to free the line.
Photo courtesy of Camillus Knives.

⌃ The word "scimitar" means sword in Arabic. The Spyderco Warrior offers the bold curves of a scimitar plus a serrated spine. Pirates would like this knife because it has the added corrosion resistance of high nitrogen content H-1 stainless steel. A portion of the sales of this knife goes to the Spec Ops Warrior Foundation.
Photo courtesy of Spyderco Knives.

⌃ If any blade in American legends can rival that of England's Excalibur, it is the Bowie knife. Colonel Jim Bowie was renowned for his hand-to-hand combat skills even before the 1827 Sandbar fight that made Bowie and his knife a legend. Bowie's reputation drew challengers, but he survived to fight to the death at the Texas Alamo in 1836. The Bowie knife is currently available in a number of forms and fashion including this fancy presentation Bowie from W. R. Case (left) and the Schrade SCOR (right) that features a double guard.
Photos courtesy of W. R. Case and Taylor Brands.

and the shape can be found in a number of configurations tagged with the name of a famous fighter who served heroically at the Alamo. The legend of Colonel Jim Bowie and the knife that bears his name began after Bowie's ferocious capitulation in the famous Sandbar Fight that is reported to have taken place in Natchez, Mississippi in 1827. Acting as a second at a duel that ended with unsatisfactory results, Bowie was attacked on multiple fronts where he suffered a gunshot wound as well as being beaten and stabbed. The brawl ended when, after the thrust of a sword at the hands of Major Norris Wright bounced off Bowie's sternum, Bowie used his knife to kill Wright, stabbing him in the chest. If popular accounts of this fight are correct, a comparably dramatic ending can be seen in the 1995 motion picture *Rob Roy*. Subsequently, Bowie became the target of several more men, much like a gunslinger whose fame drew challengers seeking to make their reputation by killing Jim Bowie, the man with the mighty blade. In some circles the Bowie knife is referred to as owning the power and mystique rivaled only by the sword Excalibur in the time of King Arthur.

Grinds

The shape of the cross section of the blade is referred to as the grind. The grind is determined at the very beginning when the greatest amount of metal is removed from the stock. Which grind is applied can be determined by the material and what the knife will be used for. The six most commonly used grinds are the hollow grind, convex grind, flat grind, sabre grind, chisel, and Scandinavian grind.

The hollow grind removes material from both sides in almost a scooping motion. This produces a very thin profile favored for slicing. The hollow grind is typically less suitable for impact, such as chopping or other outdoor duties. The convex grind, sometimes referred to as the Moran edge, for Bill Moran who popularized it, is much the opposite of the hollow grind. The cross section of the blade can be seen bulging outward symmetrically above the edge like a U-shape with a point at the bottom. This creates a type of secondary bevel that can require extra attention when sharpening.

The flat grind combines elements of both the hollow and convex grinds. The flat grind shows a continuous bevel from the spine to the final edge. It is called a flat grind because the line from the spine downward is very nearly flat. In comparing the two, the flat grind could be described as a narrow V-shape with a slight secondary bevel as it turns in towards the edge. But this secondary bevel is more linear than the one found on the convex grind, making it easy to sharpen. Sharp and strong, the flat grind is extremely versatile.

The sabre grind is much like the flat grind but instead of the V-shape beginning at the spine, the angle to the blade edge begins about halfway down or further along the side of the blade. Sometimes referred to as a V-grind, this type of blade can carry more weight, prove more rigid front to back, and still offer much of the sharpening capability of the flat grind.

The chisel grind is sharpened essentially on one side only. This makes the knife fairly strong for chopping and easy to sharpen. But the offset of the blade can make it difficult to use when trying to cut a straight line, because the unsharpened side offers more friction than the sharpened edge.

The Scandinavian grind is much like the flat grind, in that the bevel describes one continuous line in a V-shape from the spine to the edge. But whereas the flat grind requires working the secondary bevel for sharpening, the Scandinavian grind is sharpened with the blade laid flat upon the stone. Not having to present an exact angle to the stone can make the Scandinavian grind easier to sharpen. In the opinion of many knife makers, what a Scandinavian grind blade may give up in strength is made up for in its sharpness.

Handle Materials

The very first handle materials were made from whatever was immediately available and whatever worked. Through time what natural materials were available continued to change with trade and transportation until they bumped up against external forces such as tariffs, politics, trade agreements, and conservationists concerned with endangered species. Some of the forces that change the way knife handles are made have been ruled by nature. For example, at the time of this writing abalone is particularly difficult to get.

Knife handle materials can range from decorative to strictly functional. Natural materials tend to be more decorative if not functional. Synthetic or manmade materials lean more towards being functional. They either allow the manufacturer to keep costs down, or they do a superior job of creating an effective contact surface. But that doesn't rule out trying to make the latest super material attractive, either.

To begin our review of materials used to form knife handles, let's try to differentiate between handles and scales. Scales may add structural integrity but are more often applied to enhance appearance and/or improve the ability to hold on to the knife. Whereas some handles may consist of one solid mass or two framed

⤊ Abalone is a shell-born material that produces unique patterns and colors with every piece. A treat for the eye, abalone handle scales require care and can be easily damaged with hard use.
Photo courtesy of W. R. Case.

⤊ Mother of Pearl is harvested from the interior of mollusk shells. Handle scales made from a thick layer of Mother of Pearl can be quite durable, but expect to pay more. Less expensive knives utilize only thin sheets of the material, making the handle more prone to cracking or chipping when dropped.
Photo courtesy of W. R. Case.

panels, scales are a component of the handle that may be as complex as a combination of liners, bolsters, and scales. We've already mentioned abalone. Abalone scales are made from the shell of a large, rather tasty sea snail.

Its shell can be polished to reflect iridescent hues of pinks, blues, silvers, and greens. Highly decorative, abalone shell needs to be cared for and if dropped can be seriously damaged. Another shell-born material is Mother of Pearl.

This consists of the inner lining of mollusks and it presents a deep glowing look. Mother of Pearl can be expensive and should add significantly to the price. As tough and as resilient as the inner coating of a shell can be, a cheaper knife utilizing only a thin layer of Mother of Pearl will be more susceptible to cracking or chipping if it is dropped.

Bone may not only be one of the earliest handle materials but may have provided some sort of point or edge as well. Today, bone is still widely used, most notably as the scales for traditional pocket knives. Jigging, or notching a pattern into bone, is a common practice to provide extra grip and ornamentation.

Bone can also be colored with stain. The source for bone ranges from the shin bone of cows to that of the giraffe.

Ivory-gripped knives are rare because ivory is now contraband. Often advertised as Mammoth Ivory, it can be difficult to tell if the material came from a mammoth elephant (now extinct in any event) a hippo, or a walrus. Knife handles advertised as ivory may actually be fashioned from teeth as well as tusks. Easily chipped or cracked, such knives are pursued more widely for

collection rather than for field use. But, natural horn material from rams, buffalo, and impala are also materials that have been used to fashion knife scales and complete handles. Rugged and attractive, they can provide years of service before cracking becomes a problem. The antlers of stag, most notably Sambar stag, are often coveted for their rustic look and durability.

At a time when available material runs the gamut from traditional to space age, the connection to nature continues to make mammal-based materials immensely popular.

Wood is a natural material that has had mixed results as the basis for a knife handle. Wood is a wonderful medium because it can be easily shaped and drilled. But even after sealing and refinishing, most woods are still susceptible to moisture, shrinking, and drying out especially when used in a variety of climates. Unless the wood is particularly dense or exhibits a high level of elasticity, it tends to react to changes in humidity. Nevertheless, bamboo has been used with success. It also affords a natural pattern of adhesion. African snakewood is an example of exotic hardwood that knife makers, accustomed to working with metal, have come to appreciate.

Used in violin bows, African snakewood is also marketed as letterwood.

Cocobolo is a tropical hardwood with a number of characteristics that make it desirable for a knife handle. For one, its multicolored layers are decorative and

Jigging is the practice of notching a pattern into the handle material for the purpose of decoration or to enhance grip. Jigging can be used to produce a regular geometric pattern, such as a grid or a more abstract decoration. The jigging shown on this F&W Sowbelly from Queen Cutlery is a worm groove pattern in bone.
Photo courtesy of Queen Cutlery.

Antler material, such as the stag handle on this Case Deer Hunter, remains as popular as it is traditional.
Photo courtesy of W. R. Case.

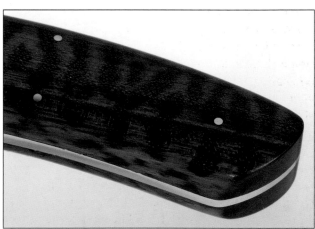

African snakewood is one the very hard woods that are naturally resistant to drying and cracking. Often used to make violin bows, it is sometimes sold as flooring under the name of letterwood.
Photo courtesy of R. Eckstine.

easily exposed. The grain is fine and cocobolo is rich in natural oils that keep it from cracking over a long period of time. Burlwood is not actually a wood but a sort of mutation generated by certain trees when the trunk is attacked by fungus or insects. Some people refer to the growth as a cancer. Burlwood is not only tough but its patterns are unique, ranging from growth rings to dots. Burlwood is also milled for flooring, Commonly sold in billets used by instrument makers, it remains a favorite with wood sculptors. Quince wood shares some of the same visual aspects as burlwood. When machined or sculpted it offers a blunt petrified wood pattern.

We might list stabilized wood as a separate material altogether. Primarily, what makes wood unstable is the moisture that loads its fiber, leaving it subject to shrinking, warping, and cracking. Stabilized wood has had its moisture removed, usually by a vacuum process, and replaced by resin. Blocks of stabilized wood, pre-cut to the approximate size of a knife handle, can be purchased from suppliers such as texasknife.com. You can also buy evacuated wood ready for the resin process. In comparison to the "dried" wood, the resin-laden stabilized wood weighs more, offers brilliant highlights along its natural grain, and can be worked to provide a hard, well-defined edge.

Another way to produce a stabilized wood is the practice of binding layers of wood veneer with a phenolic resin under heat and/or pressure. Laminate wood composite handles, such as Staminawood and Pakkawood, are partly wood and partly resin. One of the key characteristics of laminating wood with resin is that the finished product is impervious to water. The end product can be carved, machined, and polished.

⌄ Wood has always been a natural choice for making a knife handle. Wood is easy to come by and enjoyable to work with, but wood is also prone to drying, shrinking, and cracking. One way to avoid this problem is to evacuate the moisture from the wood and replace it with phenolic resin. This is referred to as stabilizing. The block of pecan wood on the right has had the moisture content removed. It is ready to be treated with resin. The block of ambrosia spalted maple on the left has been fully stabilized. Note the bold colors, smooth surface, and sharp edges. Photos courtesy of R. Eckstine.

Visually, laminate wood-composite handles feature enhanced grain patterns and vivid colors bursting from each layer.

Aluminum, titanium, and stainless steel are the three most widely used metals for knife handles. Titanium and stainless steel are most widely found on frame-lock knives where the frame and the handle are one. Back-lock and mid-lock knives are another type of folding knife wherein metal handles are used, primarily stainless steel. Each of these metals offers great linear strength, and titanium has the added benefit of being very lightweight. In addition, sandblasted titanium offers a gritty non-skid surface that is rather handsome. Stainless steel can prove slippery when wet, but we rarely see it machined with a grip pattern. Instead, the edges of stainless-steel-handled knives are more often curved to provide extra contours, such as finger grooves, to aid grip. The most widely used aluminum is 6061 with a T6 temper. Sometimes 6061-T6 is referred to as aircraft aluminum because it was developed for use in aircraft wings and fuselage. Whereas titanium is sometimes used as liner material to save weight, aluminum, which is softer, is more often used as a handle scale to cover and reinforce the liner. Aluminum and titanium are each highly corrosion resistant but readily lend themselves to electrochemical coloring processes, such as anodizing, so these materials can also be highly decorative.

Paracord, short for parachute cord, is a nylon kernmantel rope that was used for support in World War II parachutes. The word is derived from German *kernmantle*, which means "coat-protected core." Also known as 550 cord, it consists of a core rope, the kern, and a braided sheath, the mantel. The core provides tensile strength, and the sheath protects the core from abrasion. Very durable, somewhat elastic, and non-abrasive paracord can be used to wrap the handle end of the full tang of a knife. To review, a full-tang knife can be described as metal bar of equal height and width with one end sharpened and the other left unsharpened with some accommodation for holding in the hand. The unsharpened end can be covered with solid materials, or wrapped with material such as paracord. To save weight, and more importantly space in a rucksack, the knife might be stowed without any cover on the handle. A paratrooper, for example, once downed, can use the cord from his parachute to wrap the handle for greater comfort. Conversely, a knife with a paracord handle can also serve as a source for emergency cord should the need arise for repair or even a tourniquet. Paracord is very inexpensive (less than 15 cents per foot) and can be found in different colors and weave patterns. Its only downside is when wet the resulting grip can prove mushy or unstable. Nevertheless, its rugged utilitarian look is growing in popularity.

Given the ways that leather is used to create a knife handle, it can sometimes go unrecognized. Leather strips or thong can be used to wrap the handle much like paracord, but most people think of leather in terms of hide or in sheets. More effectively, the leather is cut into rings and stacked like washers over the tang. Once compressed, the rough side out offers very good grip. Epoxy resin can be added for bonding and toughness. Once bonded, the leather grip can also be worked and shaped as if it were a solid, producing the desired contour and a distinguished visual texture.

Dating back to the turn of the twentieth century, celluloid is one of the oldest synthetic or manmade materials used for knife handles. It has the look and feel of modern acrylic. Celluloid handles can be clear or opaque and come in a number of colors. But the material was later recognized to be unstable, subject to shrinking, cracking, and discoloring. Perhaps worst of all, as the celluloid deteriorates it gives off a corrosive gas that can corrode the blade. Knives with celluloid

This full-tang knife with tanto-style blade can be carried on the belt or vertically on a chain around the neck. The Kydex sheath (top left) offers an exact formfitting mold of the knife blade for positive retention. The accessory to the right is for belt carry. The handle is wrapped in paracord to provide a better grip than bare metal. The lanyard serves as a pull handle. The braid is not only decorative but serves as a supply of emergency rope.
Photo courtesy of CRKT.

⌃ Cut into washer-like rings, leather can be stacked, bonded, and compressed to form an attractive, durable handle. Photo courtesy of Ontario Knife Company.

⌃ Carbon fiber begins with turning fibers into yarn. The yarn is woven into mats, treated with resin, and laminated under tremendous heat and pressure. Thin layers of carbon fiber can be used for decoration or applied in multiple layers to provide weight-saving structural integrity. Photo courtesy of R. Eckstine.

handles are strictly collector's items but must be stored separately in order not to affect other knives.

CPL composite is more commonly recognized as the material used to make bowling balls. It can be produced with a swirl pattern that is unique from batch to batch. Durable enough to withstand hard use, CPL composite can also be textured and colored. Fiberglass Reinforced Nylon, or FRN, is an excellent material for making knife handles. As its name implies, FRN consists of a nylon material reinforced with fiberglass filament. FRN will not swell, it's shrink resistant, and can easily be textured and shaped.

Kraton is generally considered to be a synthetic replacement for rubber. The advantage of kraton over rubber is increased resistance to heat and wear while retaining a degree of flexibility. The kraton handle also offers a degree of compression and a tacky feel that offers additional traction.

Zytel is another nylon-based material that has proven durable and cost effective to manufacture. It is impervious to shrinking, rotting, or warping and can be textured to add grip. Zytel handles actually vary in strength and toughness, because the formula each manufacturer uses can be slightly different. The determining factors are the amount of fiberglass it contains and the quantity and type of resins that are used. Grivory is sort of a next generation Zytel. Grivory is favored for its ability to withstand higher temperatures and greater impact. Perhaps the most cost-effective material currently being used is polypropylene. Its molecular formula is $(C_3H_6)_n$ but you will recognize it as plastic (actually a thermoplastic). Polypropylene is used in a wide variety of products and applications, including everything from bags to synthetic medical devices. It's not fancy but it will provide a long service life.

Carbon fiber is as tough and as complex as it is attractive. One of the strongest materials known, it also weighs very little. Carbon fiber begins with filaments less than the width of fine human hair. These filaments are woven into yarn. The yarn is then woven into mat-like sheets. The sheets are then bonded with epoxy resin and subjected to baking under very high temperatures. Knife handles may feature an inlay of only a couple of sheets for decoration or utilize slabs many layers thick for primary structural integrity.

One of the most popular and dense epoxy/fiberglass laminates is G10. Formed by placing glass-woven fabric impregnated with an epoxy resin binder under high pressure, G10 offers superior mechanical and dimensional stability. It will not shrink and its tendency to absorb moisture is absolutely minimal. These characteristics have made it a mainstay in the electronics industry, most commonly used for printed circuit boards. Dependable and economical, its stability and strength are what makes it a favorite among knife makers.

Micarta is also formed by laminating fabric plus a bonding agent under pressure. Micarta can be made with fiberglass fiber, but green canvas and black linen micarta have become the favorites. The simple formula is to laminate sheet after sheet and take advantage of the natural adhesion offered by the texture of the sealed fabric. Another method is to create a more

G10 is an epoxy fiberglass laminate that is widely relied upon in the making of circuit boards. It's easy to manufacture, will not transmit electricity, and can be readily machined. Note the smooth bevel along the edge and the fabric-like texture that offers a non-skid grip. Photo courtesy of R. Eckstine.

Micarta can be laminated in parallel sheets to produce a hard, attractive surface that is durable and offers good skid resistance when wet. But micarta can also be cut and shaped at angles to expose the ends of the cloth fiber. This adds to adhesion especially when it is wet. The fibers drink in the moisture and temporarily expand the grip into the user's hand. Note how the grip panels do not fully reach the edge of the tang on this Chris Reeve Pacific knife. This slight undercut affords the user greater radial leverage. Photo courtesy of R. Eckstine.

massive block of micarta and machine it to shape, exposing the fiber. The result is a softer, more organic surface. In wet conditions the exposed fiber tends to drink in surface water and actually expand the grip, making the knife easier to hold on to.

Sheaths

Since the knife is basically a loaded gun, there has to be a way of making it safe to carry or otherwise safe to handle. This means covering the blade and retaining it in a covered position. Folding knives allow the user to simply rotate the blade into the protection of the handle. There also needs to be a safe hands-free method of carry. Enter the sheath. The sheath of a fixed-blade knife must cover both the point and the edge of the blade. It must also retain the knife through adequate friction, a crossing strap, or a mechanical lock. The sheath should not attract, draw, or retain moisture. It should also not be so thin that the blade can wear through. Unlike a handgun holster that can be made to fit a variety of guns of the same approximate size, a sheath should be made specifically for the knife.

Since the advent of the pocket clip, the use of a sheath for folding knives is becoming less prevalent. Especially since more and more knife handles are offering the option of placing the clip on either side of the knife handle and at either end. Yet there are basically only two types of sheaths made specifically for folding knives, both of which are looped for carry on the belt. The two types are open top and covered. The open top sheaths are almost always made from leather, because leather offers a natural adhesion especially when the sheath has been slightly undersized or shrink fit by wet molding. There are also leather sheaths with covered tops, and the latching device is usually a snap. Velcro is more widely found on the nylon-covered top sheathes. Nylon sheaths almost always utilize a cover flap because nylon offers little or no natural adhesion.

The traditional material used to sheath a fixed-blade knife is leather. While its appearance is strictly up to the artisan, leather sheath construction can be broken down into two basic designs. One design consists of a single piece of leather that is folded over and sewn. The other type of sheath is constructed by sewing and/or riveting together two separate pieces of leather. Nylon sheaths are also made to hold fixed-blade knives, but one of the latest innovations is to utilize a hard plastic such as polymer or kydex to improve stability and integrity.

Whereas a hard leather sheath will naturally display a rigid spine from the belt loop to the tip of the

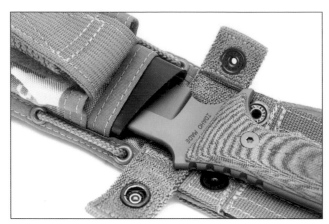

Nylon sheaths for fixed-blade knives can be beefed up with Kydex or polymer inserts. The benefits are a more stable mount and longer wear. The funnel-like opening at the mouth of this Spec Ops brand sheath also makes re-holstering much safer. Another innovation is the semi-elastic cross strap that resists shrinkage and gives rather than letting go in the course of leg movement or sudden impact. Photo courtesy of R. Eckstine.

« Nylon sheaths are almost always covered because nylon offers very little natural adhesion. Photo courtesy of Victorinox Swiss Army.

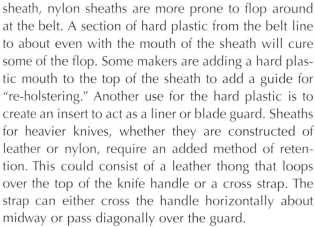

The Kershaw Sea Hunter comes with a polymer sheath that offers a positive lock to retain the knife. The sheath connects at the belt and around the thigh so it has less chance of being lost and won't flop around as the swimmer kicks his legs. Photo courtesy of Kershaw Knives.

sheath, nylon sheaths are more prone to flop around at the belt. A section of hard plastic from the belt line to about even with the mouth of the sheath will cure some of the flop. Some makers are adding a hard plastic mouth to the top of the sheath to add a guide for "re-holstering." Another use for the hard plastic is to create an insert to act as a liner or blade guard. Sheaths for heavier knives, whether they are constructed of leather or nylon, require an added method of retention. This could consist of a leather thong that loops over the top of the knife handle or a cross strap. The strap can either cross the handle horizontally about midway or pass diagonally over the guard.

Sheaths that are made entirely from hard plastic are becoming more popular. Many of these sheaths are for smaller knives that are designed to be carried vertically. This would include "key chain" knives, which can be dangled from a belt loop, and neck knives, which are worn concealed on a lanyard around the neck.

In this case a tight fit to a specific contour is necessary for retention. Hard plastic sheaths are also invaluable for the rescue swimmer or diver.

In this case the sheath generally is affixed at or below the belt line and tied down at the thigh with the knife itself retained by a locking system.

One of the newest methods of attaching the sheath is the MOLLE compatible system. MOLLE stands for Modular Lightweight Load-carrying Equipment. By

» MOLLE compatible is the latest terminology being applied to knife sheaths. That means the belt loop straps can also be connected to modern tactical gear known as Modular Lightweight Load-carrying Equipment. The surface of MOLLE gear is covered with a grid of small, snag-resistant loops. The back of the knife sheath may also have its own column of loops in place. This is a MOLLE compatible sheath with the belt loops threaded into the side of a MOLLE shoulder bag. Photo courtesy of R. Eckstine.

covering the surface of gear, backpacks, and ballistic vests with a grid of horizontal straps, load can be more evenly distributed over the soldier's body for better balance and convenience. The straps are sewn to the MOLLE surface at short intervals to create loops. The knife sheath is connected using straps that weave through the loops. This means that a knife can be carried just about anywhere on the person or as part of an assault pack.

Chris Reeve: A Modern Manufacturer

The story of Chris Reeve Knives spans decades over which technology has grown from bench and file to virtual conception and computer-run machine. Chris Reeve's journey has crossed continents as well as time. Now based in Boise, Idaho, Chris relocated from his native Republic of South Africa to escape political and social unrest and to have the opportunity to pursue his dreams in a country where the only limitation is your capacity for hard work.

Chris Reeve's knife-making career began in 1975 after returning to his hometown of Durban from his first tour of duty in the RSA military. Despite serving in a variety of rugged environments, issue of edged weapons was limited to a single bayonet. Determined not to return to the field without a good knife, but limited by his meager draw from working as an apprentice tool and die maker, Chris decided to make his own knife. The blade consisted of O1 High Carbon steel. Without a belt sander or other power tools, the blade was ground and sharpened using hand files. Chris's father worked in the electronics field, but his passion for woodworking and cabinetmaking meant there was plenty of South African hardwood in the garage from which to make a handle. The blade was attached using a narrow tang through the handle and glued into place. The top of the handle was checkered

for grip using a file. Chris's next tour of duty took him to the dry desert-like conditions around Angola and Namibia. Compared to the heat and humidity of Durban, the drastic change to dry heat caused the knife handle to crack. This lesson was not wasted by any means.

In the next few years Chris applied his machining talents to building a better knife and aspiring to Grand Prix motorcycle racing. But his talent for knife making won out. Driven to create a knife that was both strong and impervious to climate change, Chris developed a one-piece fixed-blade knife. The 7-inch blade MK II first became commercially available in 1983. It was constructed from a single bar of steel with a heavy blade and a hollow, round handle. The surface of the handle was checkered for grip and its interior served as a storage compartment. The end of the handle was threaded and the pommel screwed into place. The one-piece design was instrumental in allowing Chris to go into the knife-making business full time in 1984. All of this was accomplished while working by himself in his garage.

Over the next two years, Chris received his first orders from the United States and was able to display his knives personally at the New York Custom Knife Show. After returning to South Africa orders from the United States continued to grow. He formed an alliance with a fellow South African, who set up an import business in Los Angeles. Ultimately, the company was poorly managed and the partnership dissolved. But it did serve to increase the stateside demand for Chris Reeve knives.

By the end of the 1980s, the worldwide threat of sanctions and trade embargo against South Africa made regular export too risky, especially for small businesses. Not only was the cost of living spiraling out of control, but so was the cost of production. With political strife growing and social unrest looming, Chris and his wife Anne decided to immigrate to the United States and concentrate on making knives for the American buyers who had responded so positively to his designs.

In 1989 Chris and Anne settled in Boise, Idaho, but the next few years were spent traveling to as many knife shows as they could. By 1991 they were selling as many as twenty-one different models. A breakthrough

⌃ Chris Reeve is one of the most decorated and accomplished knife makers in the world. Inventor of the Integral Lock mechanism (now commonly referred to as the frame lock) and co-designer of the Yarborough Green Beret knife, he began his career as a machinist apprentice in his native South Africa. His ability to adapt and create new technology is just one key to his success.
Photo courtesy of Chris Reeve Knives.

⌃ Like so many knife makers, Chris Reeve's earliest products were designed out of necessity and made by hand. But at Chris Reeve Knives in Boise, Idaho, the plant is filled with modern high-tech machines. Perhaps Chris's greatest strength is his instinctive ability to adapt available means of production to generate new designs.
Photo courtesy of Chris Reeve Knives.

product was his Sabenza Integral Lock© folding knife. *Sabenza* is a verb in the Zuli language meaning "to work." Thus, the Sabenza was made to work, and in Chris's words, to work for a long time.

Chris Reeve fixed-blade knives had always been known for their strength. By introducing the Integral Lock© to the world, the Sabenza was designed to carry on this tradition with the added portability of a folding blade. Today, many people refer to this design as a frame lock, but the Integral Lock© utilizes the full girth of the handle rather than a thin slice of the liner to lock the blade in the open position. The result is not only greater strength but fewer moving parts and increased reliability. The Sabenza was fashioned from titanium, a metal that has always fascinated Chris for its strength, light weight, resistance to corrosion, and its ability to take on color by way of electrochemical process.

The success of the original Sabenza enabled Chris to expand his facility. By 2000, Chris Reeve Knives exhibited at the Blade Show and International Cutlery Fair in Atlanta, Georgia, as a full-fledged manufacturer.

He was awarded the Manufacturing Quality Award for 2000 and since then has dominated this award, winning it a total of eleven times. Chris Reeve Knives has also received the Best of the Best Award from *Gray's Sporting Journal* on two different occasions: once for the Sabenza and also for the Nyala knife.

If working from his own experience had resulted in the design of superior knives, then being awarded the 2003 Knife Collaboration of the Year for the Yarborough knife showcased his knowledge and insight into design and manufacture. The Yarborough knife was commissioned by the U.S. Army exclusively for use by American Special Forces. The knife was named after General William P. Yarborough. Under then-president John F. Kennedy, General Yarborough was tasked with developing the Green Beret program, and the Yarborough knife would be presented to the next class of graduates from Special Operations School. As many as one hundred different makers vied for the contract. Final judging was performed by a comprehensive panel of Special Operations soldiers.

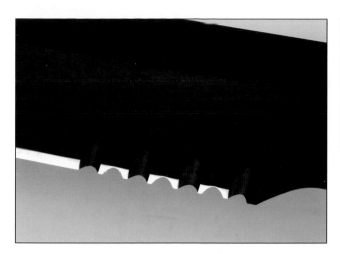

The Pacific knife is based on one of the most significant knives in American history, the Yarborough knife. Tasked by then-president John F. Kennedy, General William P. Yarborough was the architect and commanding officer of the Green Beret program. Chris collaborated with William Harsey to win a highly coveted contract for the production of "Green Beret" knives for graduates of the Special Operations School. The Pacific may not be an exact replica, but given Chris Reeve's thirst for innovation, the Pacific may in fact be a better all-around knife. Note the modern MOLLE sheath from Spec Ops Brand.
Photo courtesy of R. Eckstine.

Bill Harsey, custom knife maker and proprietor of Tactical and Survival, Inc., brought the Yarborough knife project to Chris, asking him to bring the knife from the drawing board to reality. One of Bill's patented ideas was his special "chisel-tooth" line of serrations. This design has proved extremely durable and effective.
Photo courtesy of R. Eckstine.

The Yarbrough project was brought to Chris Reeve by Bill Harsey, a custom knife maker and proprietor of Tactical and Survival, Inc., which offers logistical support for special operations.

Chris had met Harsey in 1987 at a knife show in California and the two became fast friends. The only criterion supplied by the military was that the knife be a full tang design with a 7-inch blade. With that much latitude left to the makers, Harsey and Reeve set about putting their experience to work. Together they strove to bring together as many known design solutions as they could in one single knife. Harsey had the essential design drawn up including his signature "chisel-tooth" pattern of serrations on the CPM S30V blade. Reeve focused on making the knife simpler to manufacture and added a few ideas of his own. One feature was the partially exposed tang. This gave the user more radial leverage and allowed for more tolerance in manufacture because the grip panels would not require a precise fit edge to edge along the 5.25-inch grip. The pommel offered a sharp striking surface and a lanyard hole. Micarta, commonly defined as a composite of cloth and phenolic resin formed under great pressure, was chosen over paracord because cord becomes mushy when wet. Other materials were avoided because they can become slippery. Chris Reeve Micarta is formed from canvas and phenolic plastic, one of the early and original plastics made from coal. Machining the Micarta to form a palm swell and finger grooves left the fibers partially exposed. This allowed the grip to actually pull in moisture and keep it away from sheeting upon the surface of the grip. The resulting swelling of the grip is normal and many feel this only serves to better fill the hand. There is also a double guard and a thumb ramp for blind indexing. This means in the dark the operator can tell whether the knife is edge down or warn them when the edge is facing up. The hand guard includes a swell to either side for additional safety and control. Overall the grip was designed to fit every hand. Today, a facsimile of the Yarborough, called the Green Beret knife, is available to civilians. In addition, the Pacific knife reflects the Yarborough design adapted for all-around use.

But this wasn't Chris Reeve's only award-winning collaboration. In 2010 Chris Reeve Knives garnered the 2010 Blade Magazine Overall Knife of the Year distinction. Designed by Grant Hawk, the Ti-Lock challenged the manufacturer to produce a unique design that put the locking mechanism outside the body of the knife. The result was as aesthetically pleasing as it was functional.

There are many craftsmen in the knife-making world that remain focused on maintaining high standards using only traditional methods and materials. But Chris Reeve sees no reason to be limited by the past. Always

Each one of Chris Reeve's knives is a composite of problem-solving designs. The Pacific grip was shaped to suit the widest variety of different-sized hands. Chris used one of the original formulas for Micarta to fashion the grip consisting of canvas and phenolic plastic made from coal. The shape presents a mild hand guard, both forward and to the rear. Machined like steel, the exposed fibers literally drink in moisture and expand. When the grip is wet the Pacific actually becomes easier to handle. The lined tang not only accommodates the thumb but tells the user when the sharpened edge is facing down without the need for visual confirmation. The practice of leaving space between the edges of the handle scales and the tang is referred to as an exposed tang. Not only does this make the knife simpler to manufacture, but it also gives the user more leverage should he need to twist or turn the knife.
Photo courtesy of R. Eckstine.

looking for new materials, Chris is one of the—if not the first—knife makers to work in titanium. Today the amount of time he spends hand tooling a new design is almost nil. CNC and CAD have become an extension of the hand. "Any good craftsman will use the latest technology," Chris said. "Why would the best cinematographers in the world use film when they can use digital? You can think in CAD design or pen and paper. It requires a change in thought process to work in the virtual. There shouldn't be a mental block. CNC is not magical. It's just a dumb machine."

Asked to compare Chris Reeve the hands-on craftsman with Chris Reeve the modern manufacturer, he said, "Back then I wanted to get to where I am now. I wanted to be in the future that I could see as a young man. I could see the possibilities. It was exciting stuff, like wanting to be an astronaut."

Folding Knives for Self Defense

This chapter is not a substitute for professional training. Do not practice with or utilize a knife for defensive purposes unless you have successfully completed a certified, defensive knife-safety training program.

Readers assume all liability for their own actions and practices. HOFFNERS LTD, Co., Roger Eckstine, Skyhorse Publishing, Inc., and all product providers assume no liability for any actions taken by readers of this publication.

Readers are responsible for knowing their local and state laws regarding firearms, knives, and the use of deadly force.

Use this information at your own risk!

The majority of people who carry a knife do so for reasons other than self defense. Some knives offer secondary components ranging from screwdrivers to corkscrews, but even a single-blade knife can be very useful. Legally, a knife can be carried just about anywhere. Exceptions would include an airport, court house, or sporting event. Whereas most people think of firearms as the standard tool of self defense, it is not always possible to have a gun in every situation. The knife, on the other hand, is a more versatile partner.

A jogger may not want a heavy gun flopping around but could easily carry a knife on her belt, along the wrist or clipped to a sports bra.

Extending the role of the knife to a means of self defense requires an effective method of deployment and an understanding of laws dealing with threat management and the use of deadly force. In this article we will review a set of knife handling techniques that anyone can master. The object of the techniques described herein was designed to stop an attack and preserve life.

There are some very good schools for learning to fight with edged weapons, but more often than not knife fighting techniques are the featured plan. We're not going to argue against having knife fighting skills per se, but there is another way of looking at how a knife can be used for self defense other than having a good offense. An alternative viewpoint is found in the introductory words of Tactical Knife One, taught by veteran police officer and training instructor Brian Hoffner: "We are not knife fighters. We are fighters with knives."

Tactical Folder One is part of the Hoffner System of Self Defense. The system is based on responsibility and self reliance. It begins with the preservation of life and an obligation to protect self and family. The Hoffner system calls for the practitioner to be able to use whatever tools are available to stop an attack. Given

the knife is easy to carry there is rarely any reason to go unarmed.

The Hoffner System favors the folding knife with locking blade over fixed-blade knives for several reasons. Fixed-blade knives are inherently stronger, but maximum strength is not necessarily an issue in stopping an attack. Fixed-blade knives also take up more space than a folder, and carry is limited to wherever a sheath can be attached to the user. In addition, the sheath must remain fixed in place for the knife to be drawn and safely stowed away. The presence of the sheath also makes the knife more difficult to conceal, inviting a knife takeaway. In the event of a fixed-blade knife being taken away, the rightful owner is going to have less time to react than might have been available during the time it takes for the thief to determine how to open a folded blade and bring it to an offensive position. Of course, a folding knife in a belt pouch or clipped to an outer pocket can also be snatched. But effective precautionary measures are easily applied. For example, before walking through a crowded area, a folded knife can be quickly and safely moved to deep inside a pocket. Bear in mind that for tactical purposes, a crowded area is defined as wherever you cannot keep people beyond your reactive gap distance. The danger is that once inside your reactive gap distance, anyone will be able to complete an offensive maneuver before you are able to mount a defense.

In choosing a folding knife, Brian Hoffner prefers a liner lock over other designs for its simplicity and ease of operation. In terms of dollars spent, money can be saved by not buying the fanciest-looking knife or the one that utilizes the most expensive materials, just so long as the lock is tough and fail safe. The lock should move into position quickly, preferably covering at least 50 percent of the blade. In relation to appearance, one concern is how the knife is styled or characterized in

≽ Pocket clip knives are favored because they provide instant access and a low profile. In the Hoffner System the knife is carried in the weak side pocket.

≽ When pocketing the knife, pushing outward against the top seam makes it easier for the clip to ride smoothly into place.

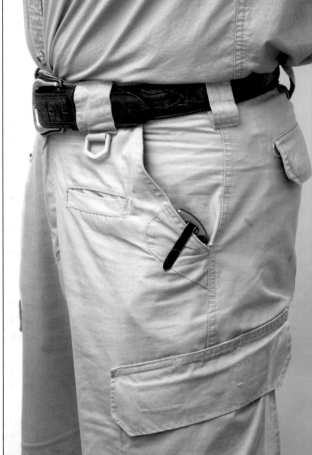

≽ Pocket ready (left-hand picture) is easily disguised. Despite a nonchalant stance the operator has complete control of the knife and is ready for the draw.

advertisements by the manufacturer. It is important to remember that should the knife be used as a weapon, even in the most justifiable manner, resulting legal actions can be costly. Brian warns that average cost could be as much as $100,000 or more. The point is that any good quality folding knife can serve as a defensive weapon. Despite the fact that combat-style knives drive sales, there is no need to buy an aggressive-looking knife, or a knife that goes by a name that sounds like trouble. It might also be a good idea to find out how a particular product is being portrayed on the Internet, inside social media, or in chat rooms. Intent as demonstrated by statements on the Internet is a growing source for legal problems. It would be wise to keep in mind that the preservation of one's life is not only a personal responsibility but begs a certain amount of discretion as well.

The preferred method of carry in the Hoffner System is by the pocket clip with the knife positioned on the weak side. That is, a right-handed person will have the knife inside the left side front pocket closer to the outer seam of the pant leg.

The clip should be connected to the knife in line with the hinge. Once inside the pocket, the back of the knife should be facing forward or towards the center line of the body. The proper way to insert a closed knife into the pocket is to insert the body of the knife pressing outward, stretching the mouth of the pocket.

The purpose of pressing outward on the pocket is to present a rigid line of cloth that even the tightest clip will be able to cross. Continue pressing down until the tension point of the clip rides

《 Spine Pick position affords a strong grip on the knife with several defensive options.
Photo courtesy of R. Eckstine.

over the top seam. Press the knife down into the pocket as far as it will go.

Standing with the thumb inside the pocket and the hand over the knife, it is very easy to appear nonchalant and relaxed. But this is actually a key position ready to respond, referred to as Pocket Ready.

In Pocket Ready the knife can be indexed for the draw while still inside the pocket. The knife is then drawn from the pocket and opened to the Spine Pick position.

Spine Pick position is holding the knife vertically with the blade tip down. The spine is in line with the arm, sharp edge facing outward. The thumb loops over the top of the handle. Because the knife is in effect held by a closed fist, the grip on the knife is very strong. To achieve spine pick position from the draw, the knife is grasped with fingers away from the open side of the handle as it is raised from the pocket hinge down, blade tip up. The hinge is resting over the lower crease in the palm. This is the load position.

In load position it is important that the back or hinged end of the knife is not buried inside the palm. The hinge must be free to rotate in order to release the blade.

The blade is released to the lock position by a wrist motion similar to cracking a whip or snapping a towel.

≫ In the load position it is important that the hinge overlaps the palm so the blade can rotate freely into the locked position.
Photo courtesy of R. Eckstine.

The skill of opening a folding knife to Spine Pick position is easily acquired.

Just about anyone can master it inside of ten minutes, says Brian. But it is important to note that you only get one chance to open the knife per wrist movement. Doubling up will only bounce the knife closed or in and out of the handle without locking. There is also the danger of cutting the fingers. If it happens on any one attempt that the operator does not feel or hear the blade lock into place, the instructions to bring the knife to full lock are as follows: continuing to hold the knife with fingers away from the open side of the handle, the edge of the blade is struck against the belt, a holster, or other impervious surface along the knife hand side of the operator.

This will force the blade into the lock position. It is important to strike directly against the surface and pull away. Dragging the knife across the striking surface may activate a cutting action.

From Spine Pick the operator has several defensive options. The first is the wedge block. The wedge block is also taught in the empty hands program of the Hoffner system and requires little or no skill to learn.

Setting a wedge block involves a number of simple movements performed simultaneously. Described from the perspective of the right-handed operator, the head drops down and moves toward the left shoulder as the left arm is raised. The left arm is bent from the elbow at about a 45-degree angle, forming a perimeter

⌄ If the blade does not lock open on the first attempt from load position, striking it on the belt is the best way to set the lock. Striking directly in and out, not sweeping forward or back, will prevent cutting into the belt.
Photo courtesy of R. Eckstine.

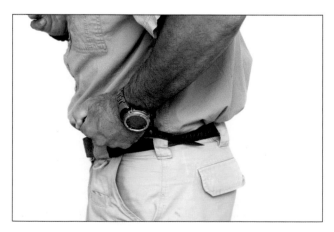

⌃ If the hinge does not overlap the palm, the blade will not be able to extend to the locked position.
Photo courtesy of R. Eckstine.

⌃ Versatile and strong, the Spine Pick position offers several defensive options.
Photo courtesy of R. Eckstine.

In the wedge block, the lower hand protects the throat, face, and eyes. The raised arm protects the temple as well as the brachial plexus. Located along the side of the neck, a blow to the brachial area can result in being rendered unconscious. Photos courtesy of R. Eckstine.

With the knife held in Spine Pick position, the wedge block becomes all the more hazardous for the attacker.

surrounding the head at approximately the scalp level. In this position an incoming blow would at its worst glance off the top the head. The right hand is raised to protect the face and possibly deliver a palm strike. With the left hand holding a knife in the Spine Pick position, the defensive properties of the wedge block are greatly enhanced.

The next defensive option is the sweep. The sweep requires little accuracy or timing. The object of the sweep is to set up a perimeter through which the attacker must advance in order to be cut. Therefore it is generally perceived as a less aggressive action in court. The sweep is a linear motion that leads with the edge of the blade. The sweep begins with moving the knife in front of you with palm down from the knife hand side to the support side. Once the arm is extended to cover the extremities, the grip is turned to palm up. Now the edge of the blade is once again leading as it crosses in front of the body in the opposite direction. Continuous motion back and forth will describe the

figure 8 with the blade side always facing the attacker. Actually, the figure 8 can be performed horizontally, vertically, or in any diagonal trail as necessary. Brian likes to refer to this zone as "The Blender."

The warning is obvious. Anything that gets inside the blender will be cut. The sweep can be used to hold off multiple attackers by working the knife further left and right to cover a larger area.

The next defensive option is the jab-thrust. Whereas the object is to stop the attack, a series of quick pokes thrusting the point of the blade towards the attacker may be enough to change your attacker's mindset. The jab does not require strength or power, just enough energy to penetrate at the level necessary. Speed and persistence are also helpful but keep in mind that this is an aimed technique. You must have a definitive target for each thrust. If the target moves, you move. If the thrusts are random and mechanical they can be timed and easily passed or blocked. Gripping the knife with the Spine Pick also allows for thrusts to the rear.

By sweeping the knife repeatedly in a figure 8 pattern you can create a safe perimeter through which the attacker must advance in order to be cut. By alternating the grip palm down/palm up, the sharp edge of the blade leads the way. Photos courtesy of R. Eckstine.

« The versatility of the Spine Pick position allows the operator to quickly jab or thrust in any direction, including to the rear. Photos courtesy of R. Eckstine.

⌃ Use of the thumb for one-handed opening of a blade that cannot be opened by any type of wrist movement or other source of inertia to the foil position may be the only alternative for those living in or traveling to a highly restrictive jurisdiction.

This is helpful because some folding knives are so resistant to opening that they cannot be opened by any other means. In addition, some jurisdictions forbid carrying a folding knife capable of being opened using any sort of wrist motion or inertia. With this in mind, the Hoffner system can also be taught beginning with opening the knife to foil position. In foil position the operator buries the end of the handle braced against the hollow of the palm.

The knife is held sideways so that thumb is locked down against the detent of the pocket clip and the fingers curl around the handle. The foil position is

« If a more powerful thrust becomes necessary to stop an attack, the palm of the off hand may be used to push the knife.

⌄ Holding the knife in the foil position in effect makes the knife longer and puts more distance between you and your attacker.

If quick jabs are not offering enough penetration, as might be the case if the attacker is wearing heavy clothing, then stopping the attack demands a greater deterrent. This might call for a two-handed thrust. To perform a two-handed thrust, the first step is to move the thumb from behind the knife handle. Then with the rear of the knife backed by the palm of the off hand, the power of the thrust is multiplied.

Bear in mind that both the jab and any manner of thrust may be construed as a stabbing motion in a court of law.

Holding the knife in the foil position is another defensive option. Foil position is important to learn because it naturally follows from opening the knife using the thumb stud or opening hole.

not as strong as the Spine Pick but it does put greater distance between you and your attacker. The ability to thrust or jab is secured by the backing of the palm. The foil position is also very effective when used to set up a defensive sweep. The knife can be easily swept back and forth leading with the edge in either direction with a simple turning over of the wrist.

The foil position may also be transitioned to from the Spine Pick position. Transitioning from Spine Pick to foil position begins with opening the grip slightly and placing the thumb on the near edge of the handle. The thumb pushes the edge of the handle, rotating it 90 degrees, so that the edge of the blade now faces away from the centerline of the body. Now the knife is hanging primarily between the thumb and forefinger. In a looping motion, the wrist is bent upward with the hand rotating into position beneath the knife handle. The blade has now been turned 180 degrees so that the edge is facing the center of the body. Finally, the handle is pulled into the hand to buttress against the well of the palm. The thumb presses down on the clip.

The folding knife is not always used as a standalone weapon. In the Hoffner System the knife can be integrated with the handgun to defend against multiple attackers. Not only can the handgun be fired with the support hand gripping a knife in the Spine Pick position but the Spine Pick also allows for slide manipulation should it become necessary.

In addition, the knife can be used to prevent a gun takeaway. We have all read reports wherein more police officers are killed with their own guns than by any other means. Private citizens with concealed weapons permits are also in danger, not to mention

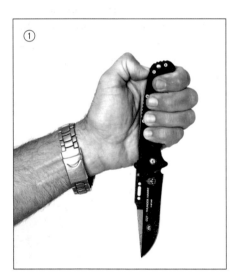
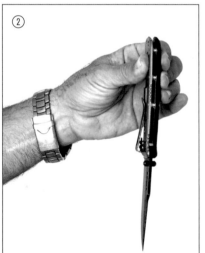
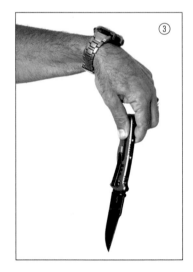
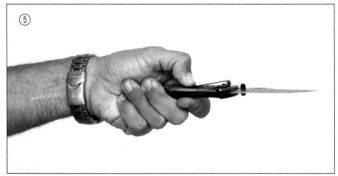
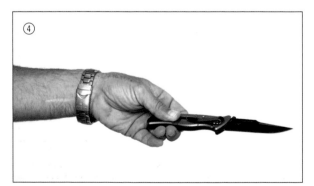

⌄ Transitioning from Spine Pick to foil position begins with rotating the knife with the thumb followed by a relaxed wrist motion. Note the final thumb position and how the back of the knife is braced against the hollow of the palm. Photos courtesy of R. Eckstine.

⭐ Integrating knife and pistol can add measurably to your ability to defend yourself. Held in Spine Pick position the knife should not interfere with common protocol such as manipulating the slide. Photo courtesy of R. Eckstine.

licensed individuals practicing in states where open carry is legal. For law enforcement and private citizens alike, being seen as the source of a free gun is a problem. With a knife in the pocket on the side opposite the handgun, the victim of a gun takeaway has more than a fighting chance.

If there is any disadvantage to carrying a knife on one side of the body or the other, it is that the knife is available from only one side. The professional operator or dedicated practitioner commonly chooses to conceal a secondary knife clipped to the top seam of the pants behind the belt buckle or at approximately the centerline of the body.

This knife should necessarily be lighter, thinner, and shorter than one's primary knife, according to the wearer. Available to both hands, this knife will more commonly be opened using the thumb.

Suffering through a violent confrontation can be terrorizing for the victim. But if you are prepared with a plan of action, you may be able to forestall the paralyzing sensations of fear and nervousness in favor of effective action until later. Just accepting the possibility of an attack on yourself

or loved ones can greatly improve your mindset. The mindset of the attacker, however, may be so clouded and singular in purpose that they may need to be reminded of what they're doing. An added recommendation is to challenge verbally, shouting, "Get back!" Or should they challenge defensive moves such as the sweep or the jab, words such as, "Get back, you're cut," might awaken a level of fear that the attacker would rather wish on their victims and cause them to retreat.

Brian Hoffner's philosophy regarding the knife is plain. He states that the folding knife is an incredibly effective defensive weapon that is easy to carry in almost all situations. With the Hoffners Training Academy system of defense, knife students can quickly master the skills to defend self and family in close-quarters violent attacks. Hoffner states, "With this newfound ability my students tend to enjoy a life filled with confidence, higher self esteem, and success, all because of a folding blade knife and a good training program."

⭐ When placed clipped along the top seam towards the center of the body, a smaller, secondary knife can be reached with either hand. When acquired by the strong side or pistol-side hand, the knife is opened by the thumb to foil position. Photo courtesy of R. Eckstine.

The Legal Edge:
What Every Knife Owner Should Know

*I*s it reasonable to believe that since there are fifty states, there are no more than fifty laws pertaining to the possession and application of knives? Unfortunately, that is not the case. If some states have a set of laws that rule from border to border, others have the further complication of local ordinances that can change from county to county and city to city. This makes it pretty tough on anyone who travels or, for that matter, for those abiding by the law in one's hometown. Some of the points at issue are not merely blade length but also means of carry, either open or concealed. Perhaps the most contentious issue is "bias towards closure." This means how much bias or mechanical force must be overcome to expose a hinged blade and bring it to its open position. The fear is that a folding knife with a lower level of bias can be opened while held in one hand, therefore promoting nefarious behavior. However, can the mechanical capability of an inanimate object be ruled as the cause of criminal action?

Laws prohibiting the freedom to implement and enjoy even the smallest aspect of knife ownership are sometimes viewed as "gateway" in nature. Erosion of rights generally starts with small prohibitions that pose only minor concessions. The cumulative effect often leads to attempts at larger, broader legislation. Apart from individual rights, the threat to industry—both manufacture and retail—is immense. If a feature is ruled illegal, factories must be retooled, or in the worst case scenario shut down or moved to a friendlier state. Retailers that stock a knife ruled "illegal" may have to liquidate inventory at a huge loss. In all cases, including litigation that is defeated, prices may rise due to remedial costs being passed on to the consumer.

For many Americans the realization that carrying a knife could leave them open to tremendous liability can foster a sense of being totally alone against a machine that is both complex and unpredictable. Most of us simply carry on in denial and keep our edged "partners" to ourselves. This is perhaps the same mindset gun owners experienced until the National Rifle Association brought pride of organization to the public. For the citizen knife owner there is an organization that, like the NRA, one should be a member of. The mission of the American Knife & Tool Institute (visit AKTI.org) is to educate, promote, and inform.

These three goals are aimed at public responsibility, industry growth regarding retail sales and manufacturing issues, and lobbying to ensure that Americans will always be able to buy, sell, own, carry, and use knives and edged tools.

The following is an interview with AKTI Executive Director, Jan Billeb.[1]

Roger Eckstine: What does a knife owner need to know about knife laws and the preservation of individual rights?

Jan Billeb: A knife owner needs to know about the law regarding knives in the location where he or she lives and where they may travel, as restrictions can vary greatly. In addition to state laws, many cities or counties have additional ordinances regarding knife possession. When traveling by commercial airlines, remember to put your knife in your checked baggage, not in your carryon or pocket! If traveling by bus or train, be sure to check out their specific prohibited items regulations.

A knife owner also needs to know enough about knife technology to understand knife laws based on design characteristics, mechanical functions, et cetera, and be able to discuss them intelligently. Unfortunately, many laws are based on a type of knife, blade length, and/or the mechanical movement of the blade instead of criminal intent.

As for preservation of individual rights, a knife owner needs to be proactive and also polite and dignified when using a knife in view of others. Avoid unnecessary flourishing movements or anything that might be misperceived as brandishing.

Additional American Knife & Tool suggestions available at http://www.akti.org/resources include the following:

If the Police Stop You with a Knife:
1. Remain calm and polite.
2. Do NOT resist a policeman physically.
3. Give your name and address information only.

---

1. *With thanks for assistance from Daniel C. Lawson, Esq., Legal Contributing Counsel to AKTI, Meyer Darragh Buckler Bebeneck & Eck PLLC.*

4. You do NOT have to answer any other questions.
5. You do NOT have to consent to a search without a warrant.
6. Do not refer to your knife as a weapon.

If the Police Arrest You with a Knife:
1. Ask for an attorney. Do not say anything else.
2. Expect that you will be handcuffed and searched.
3. Expect that you will be fingerprinted and photographed.
4. Do not talk to anyone else in the jail or any law enforcement officers about your case.

RE: How does one find out what the knife laws are as they pertain to a particular city or state?

JB: An internet search is a good starting point. Search terms such as "knife" or "knives," "crimes code," "prohibited weapons," "possessing dangerous weapons," and the name of the state or jurisdiction in question. Be sure to also look for published reports of cases construing or applying the statutes (written laws) to help in understanding the law's interpretation. Do not totally rely on websites that summarize the laws by state as this information may not be current or correctly stated.

AKTI has a page directing concerned citizens to several websites that help in the search, which you may find here: http://www.akti.org/legislation.

AKTI also has *A Guide to Understanding the Laws of America Regarding Knives* available at http://www.akti.org/legislation/finding-knife-laws.

RE: What knives, if any, are completely illegal to own?

JB: There probably is no knife that is completely illegal, compared to gun laws where a "sawed off shotgun" is illegal throughout the entire United States. Some people mistakenly believe that switchblades are completely illegal, but the Federal Switchblade Act deals with interstate knife commerce. In some states it is legal to own and carry a switchblade (for example Alabama, Arizona, and Oregon).

Even in states where a knife may be illegal, there are "curio" exceptions, which typically apply to items in a collection and not carried or possessed outside of one's home.

RE: How does carrying a knife relate to concealed weapon laws?

JB: Laws regarding concealed carry permits or licenses tend to focus on handguns. Typically these laws do not specifically reference knives, but possession of a license may be a defense to some weapons charges involving knives, depending upon the circumstances.

RE: What knives, if any, are illegal to conceal?

JB: The issue of open carry or concealment has an interesting historical background. Concealed weapons laws were developed in a time when many, or most, people openly carried weapons. Concealing a weapon was frowned upon as misleading others that a person was not armed. Now in our time, it is just the opposite. Many weapons laws require, for example, that a handgun be concealed and not visible.

In several states, knives that are legal to carry concealed may also be legal to carry openly, *but* there may be restrictions on the length of the blade, et cetera.

RE: What knives, if any, are illegal to carry openly?

JB: Folding knives are generally designed for pocket carry, which means concealed. But again, that does not mean that they are illegal to carry openly in your state. In some states, such as New York, a visible pocket clip may be enough to give rise to a police stop or search as being considered open carry.

A good rule of thumb regarding your knife is if concealment is not prohibited (and not inconsistent with the circumstances, such as harvesting, hiking, hunting), it is probably advisable to conceal.

The key, again, is to know the law and know your knife. Make intelligent decisions when purchasing a knife to avoid potential problems. Be sure you know what open carry means in your state. For example, is a knife in your car open or concealed?

RE: What are some of the landmark victories that have been won by AKTI or others?

JB: A major landmark victory for AKTI and other organizations was amending the 1958 Switchblade Act in 2009, using AKTI's bias toward closure language to clarify that assisted opening knives are not switchblades. Other victories have been won by AKTI on the state level in California, South Carolina, Florida, Arkansas, and Texas by introducing legislation that removed laws or clarified definitions. AKTI has worked behind the scenes on many other issues and supported individuals and other organizations in their efforts to change their state's laws. State Rep. Jenn Coffey was the force behind removing all New Hampshire knife restrictions and enacting a preemption law so that cities could not create restrictive knife laws. The Knife Rights, Inc. organization successfully campaigned for preemptive laws in Arizona and other states.

RE: What battles for the rights of knife owners are currently being fought?

JB: An ongoing battle for the rights of knife owners is educating legislators and law enforcement not only about the utility of knives and individuals' rights, but also about how knives work. As long as knife laws are based not on criminal intent but on factors such as blade length, mechanism of opening, archaic terminology, et cetera, AKTI will continue to work state by state to remove restrictions that infringe upon the knife owner's ability to buy, sell, own, and carry the knife or edged tool of their choice. The most recent efforts are updated at www.akti.org as information can be released.

RE: What can knife owners do to help maintain or regain their rights?

JB: Knife owners need to be aware of knife laws. Be proactive and make your views known to legislators—reasonably and politely. If you want to make changes in your state's knife laws, meet with your legislator's aide and begin a conversation about the restrictions and how individuals and businesses are affected by it. Address your concern that knife laws should be based on criminal activity, not the object or its features. Contact the American Knife & Tool Institute for guidance and help introducing changes.

Stay alert to any proposals that would further restrict a knife owner's ability to buy, sell, own, carry, or make knives. Pay attention to what is going on in your community and state regarding weapons laws because that is where restrictions will probably be written. AKTI monitors laws introduced in all fifty states and at the federal level, but we need eyes and ears on the ground to alert us as well. AKTI members have website access to all of the legislation we are tracking.

Introduce others (friends, coworkers, relatives, neighbors, etc.) to the wonderful world of knives. Let them know that knives are important objects and tools in everyday life that need to be protected because of restrictive laws and attitudes. Teach a youngster how to safely use a knife in the kitchen, carving a pumpkin, or around the campfire.

Support the AKTI with your membership or as a free Grassroots Supporter to receive email updates. Be ready to contact legislators or others when called to help keep knives in American lives.

NEW PRODUCTS

New Products

*I*f new products in the knife industry reflect the times in which we live, then these are very exciting times. It wasn't long ago that knives could be categorized by the types of chores associated with hunting and fishing, or farming and ranching. Military-style knives have always had appeal, but in terms of daily use they've seldom been center stage. But the war on terror and its potential for anarchy across the homeland is not only increasing the demand for but causing the design of such knives to evolve. Not only has this generated military and police contracts for major manufacturers, but a number of smaller specialty suppliers are now making themselves known. Knives for first responders, such as fire and rescue or emergency medical personnel, are not only reaching more and more professionals but the desire for private citizens to have such tools at their disposal is turning a niche market into a boom. At the same time, the popularity of concealed handgun licenses is fostering interest in additional forms of personal weaponry. First-time gun owners are rapidly becoming first-time knife owners, and style as well as function is becoming an important component of sales. To keep up with advancing trends, manufacturers are now more willing than ever to seek input from custom knife makers and to take direction from law enforcement and military experts. But traditional designs and practices are not in any danger of extinction, either. New buyers initially drawn by the tactical market are finding that the collection of knives, once started, is a difficult habit to break. The following is but a brief survey of new products that represents both the growth and affirmation of a vibrant industry.[1]

Benchmade Knives

Benchmade Knives was first established in California in 1988. Just two years later the company moved to Clackamas, Oregon. Considering this is a relatively short history, the total number of different model knives that Benchmade has produced is most impres-

sive. Key to their success is Benchmade's willingness to work with independent designers, including renowned custom knife makers and experts in field craft with experience and imagination. The current roster of designers include Mel Pardue, Eddie Killian, Warren Osborn, Seiichi Nakamura, Shane Sibert, Mike Snody, Ken Steigerwalt, Matthew Lerch, Bob Lum, Paul W. Poehlman, Charles Marlowe, and the team of Bill McHenry and Jason Williams. McHenry and Williams are the inventors of the Axis Lock, which is a hallmark achievement in folding knife design.

Benchmade's knives are categorized into four different classes. Gold Class knives are meant to be the best of the best. Designs found in the Gold Class may also appear in other classes—the difference being in the materials used, which may be more valuable or require greater skill and workmanship to produce. Limited production runs and annual premium models featuring high quality Damascus steel blades are common Gold Class fare. Blue Class knives are top of the line in their own right but function and design weigh in ahead of more expensive materials and ornamentation. Black Class knives aren't meant to be "third place" winners. Performance and durability are key because Black Class is where you will find extreme duty knives designed for in-service use by law enforcement, public safety, and elite military troops. Currently, knives listed as Red Class items are out of production. Conceived as budget priced versions of more expensive knives, Red Class products may still be available in the retail or wholesale pipeline.

Three of the newest products from Benchmade are found in the Black Class, which is rapidly becoming the most popular segment of the Benchmade catalog. The model number 176 SOCP Dagger is a thin dagger with a finger loop on the top. It comes with an injection-molded sheath in colors black or sand. The color of blade and sheath can be mixed and matched. A dulled-edge training version is available separately. This is important because there is no "safe" side to the two-edged blade and using the 176 SOCP for what it was designed to do requires practice. The letters SOCP stand for Special Operations Combative Programs. This knife/sheath combination was designed to work in the type of close quarter environment commonly experienced by today's military and law enforcement

---

1. All photographs are courtesy of their respective maker unless otherwise noted.

Benchmade Knives

www.benchmade.com

personnel. Traditionally, this type of engagement would be called hand-to-hand combat, meaning empty hands or in consort with a single weapon such as a knife. But today's soldier, police officer, or even concealed handgun licensee will more likely engage with an integration of hands, pistol, and edged weapon.

The 176 SOCP Dagger was designed by Greg Thompson. Thompson began teaching combatives in the 1990s, and it quickly became apparent that traditional combat knives didn't always offer the necessary speed of transition from hand to knife and/or knife to sidearm. Furthermore, such knives were difficult to conceal and would invite attack based on the assailant's knowledge of how or from where the knife would be deployed. Thompson designed the 176 knife/sheath combination to address these shortcomings.

The 176 SOCP can be easily concealed behind other gear such as a magazine pouch. Along with a belt loop clip, this sheath/knife combination will also fit securely within the woven channels of MOLLE gear. Since the sheath covers all but the finger ring, it would be very difficult for anyone but the wearer to draw the knife. Deployment in the event of being clinched or choked is fast and sure. Thanks to its slender profile and finger ring, a pistol cannot only be held simultaneously but even drawn without the necessity of switching the knife to the opposite hand. Tactical applications of the Benchmade 176 SOCP Dagger may be limited only by the amount of practice one puts in with the 176 Trainer in its place.

Shane Sibert's latest contributions are the 275 folder and the 375 fixed blade Adamas knives.

Both knives are sold with a portion of the proceeds going to the Ranger Assistance Foundation. The 275 Adamas folding knife utilizes the Axis Lock mechanism housed in a machined G10 handle and stainless steel liners. The drop point blade features a blood-let groove along the sides. A partially serrated combo edge is available. The handle color is sand, but a limited edition featuring black G10 handles and a black plain-edge blade is also available. The sheath is a MOLLE pouch (black or sand in color), and the knife features a fully reversible pocket clip.

The 375 fixed blade Adamas offers a longer blade, and the spine is fully serrated. The handle is skeletonized. There does not appear to be any accommodation for wrapping it with paracord or attaching handle scales, but the grip is ridged fore and aft, top and bottom. There is also a definite finger groove and handguard on the lower edge. The injection-molded sheaths (black or sand) primarily cover the blade without a handle backing, but a security strap does reach over the handguard and snap into place. An adjustable tension screw is provided.

Not everyone is concerned with martial combat or with carrying a knife for personal protection. But the needs of first responders and concerned citizens continue to drive the sales of rescue knives. Indeed, with the experience of 9/11 and the possibility of more terrorist attacks or civil unrest, a lot of thought is going into their design. Benchmade's 916 Opposing Bevel knives are their latest offering.

The blade offers a blunt pry tip. To support the levels of stress that using the 916 as a pry bar might incur, the center of the blade offers maximum thickness. This is achieved by beveling from the spine on one side and towards the edge on the other side. The bevels are in fact diagonally opposed, thus the name. Viewing the 916 from the tip produces a sort of optical illusion leading you to believe that the blade is twisted. Of course this is not the case. Among the eight different configurations, the satin stainless blade with orange color G10 handle scales is likely the most visible. This would make it easier to find in dim or smoke-diffused light. The seat belt/cloth "hook" cutter is longer than most we've seen and is deployed by a thumb stud. The carbide glass cutter is effective but not oversized. It is also placed off center to make room for a thumb-over grip, which might be necessary in order to apply more power to a thrusting motion or when chopping with the blunt tip. Corrosion resistance has been enhanced by the use of N680 steel.

176 SOCP DAGGER BKSN COMBO

Blade Length: 3.22 in.
Blade Material: 440C
Length: 7.25 in.
Handle: 440C
Weight: 2.2 oz.
Features: Skeletonized dagger w/finger loop; injection molded sheath w/clip and lanyard; dagger and sheath, $90; trainer only, $50
Options: Black or sand color
MSRP: **$130**

275/375 ADAMAS FOLDING AND FIXED BLADE KNIVES

Blade Length: 3.82 in./4.2 in.
Blade Material: D2
Length (Open/Closed): 8.7 in./4.88 in.
Overall Length (375): 9.03 in.
Handle: G10
Lock: Axis
Weight: 7.7 oz./5.6 oz.
Features: Stainless steel liners; dual thumb studs; tip up reversible belt clip; MOLLE pouch; 375 uses injection molded sheath; Mike Siebert design; portion of sale benefits Ranger Assistance Foundation
Options: Black or sand color handle and MOLLE pouch; 375: black or sand color knife and sheath
MSRP: . . . . **$130/$140**

916 OPPOSING BEVEL TRIAGE

Blade Length: 3.5 in.
Blade Material: N680 Primary blade/440C Hook Cutter
Length (Open/Closed): 8.2 in./4.7 in.
Handle: G10
Lock: Axis
Weight: 5.1 oz.
Features: Stainless steel liners; reversible tip up pocket clip; seatbelt cutter; carbide glass break; dual thumb stud opening
Options: Black or orange handle; plain or partially serrated edge; satin- or black-coated finish blade
MSRP: . . . . **$165–$180**

BENCHMADE 275/375 ADAMAS FOLDING AND FIXED BLADE KNIVES

BENCHMADE 176 SOCP DAGGER BKSN COMBO

BENCHMADE 916 OPPOSING BEVEL TRIAGE

NEW PRODUCTS

Blackhawk! Knives

Based in Norfolk, Virginia, Blackhawk! not only offers a wide range of tactical supplies such as packs, holsters, and apparel, but also provides corporate security. Additionally, Blackhawk! offers custom manufacturing capability, making it one of the world's foremost outfitters of tactical gear. If you need weapon- or gear-specific packs for a platoon or security detail, Blackhawk! has OEM manufacturing and design capability including injection molded composites, cut and sew nylon, in-house machining and tooling on an ISO 9001 level, field testing, and design. Knife making may be a small part of their business, but judging by the product line and input from specialists like combatives instructor and anti-terrorist expert Kelly McCann, we suspect it is one of their favorites.

The Night Edge Serrated Edge is an Allen Elishewitz design fixed-blade knife that features a serrate spine or back edge. The extra serration makes it suitable for heavy cutting as well as increasing its offensive capability in terms of back cutting and draw cuts. Despite the extra machining, the central strength of the blade is maintained. The tip is reinforced for added strength and penetration.

The Tatang was designed by edged weapons expert Michael Janich. It was intended as a variation on the Philipino Barong. The barong is a leaf-shaped bolo knife capable of being used as a chopping tool as well as a weapon. Michael's design not only adapts the barong to the modern practitioner but also modifies the grip to enhance both its practical use and maneuverability as a weapon. Making full use of the forward grip gives it greater balance for more controlled cutting, trapping, and back cutting. Sliding the hand fully rearward to the pistol grip handle brings forth a forward bias that not only extends its reach but also adds chopping power.

The United Kingdom Special Forces knife photographs larger than it really is. If it seems to have the appearance of a sword from the days of King Arthur, we're sure the British special operatives appreciate it all the more. Overall length is actually less than 11 inches, and there is a mighty cross guard dividing the 6.2-inch blade from the handle. The cross guard plays a role in keeping it in its injection-molded nylon sheath by snapping into place below an integral catch, which is deactivated by pressing inward against the body of the sheath.

Kelly McCann's Crucible knives reflect his interpretation of what is needed for modern in-fighting. The recipe is simple: The Crucible features a moderate length blade with sharp central point for balance and maximum strength upon thrust, and a grip that affords a secure hold and radial leverage. To these last two characteristics the grip is flat. In addition, the handle offers finger grooves plus a handguard-like drop both fore and aft. This protects the hand both on thrust and draw (retraction). Once opened the folding knife is remarkably close in handling to the fixed-blade model. Take away the thumb studs and the folder could at first glance be mistaken for the full tang fixed-blade knife. The fixed-blade Crucible FX2 comes with an injection molded sheath that can be carried as a neck knife or connected to MOLLE gear.

There is also a belt loop plate and a paddle for quickly adding the Crucible knife to your attire.

The Small Pry may not be a knife per se. We might choose to define it as a battle ax in a pouch. Battle axes were not specifically meant for fighting but could be used if a sword was not available. Mostly, they were used for breeching and the same could be said for the Small Pry. Secure carry is provided by the Pack Kit by integrating it with a bug out bag or other equipment. The S.T.R.I.K.E. system (Blackhawk!'s Soldier Tactical Retro Integrated Kit Enhanced) hardware adapts the injection molded nylon sheath to MOLLE gear.

CRUCIBLE 2 FOLDER SERRATED

Blade Length: 3.25 in.
Blade Material: AUS8A
Length (Open/Closed): 8 in./4.75 in.
Handle: G10
Lock: Liner lock
Weight: 6.25 oz.
Features: PVD coat finish; left or right side, tip up or tip down pocket clip; Kelly McCann design
Options: Plain edge or partially serrated blade
MSRP: **$90**

BLACKHAWK! CRUCIBLE
2 FOLDER SERRATED

BLACKHAWK! CRUCIBLE
FX2 FIXED BLADE

CRUCIBLE FX2 FIXED BLADE SIGNED

Blade Length: 3.2 in.
Blade Material: AUS 8 Stainless steel
Length: 7.9 in.
Handle: G10
Weight: 6.2 oz.
Features: Kelly McCann signature on blade; PVD Coat finish blade; injection molded nylon sheath; accessories include neck sheath and chain, molle connect, adjustable cant belt loop, and paddle; hardware
Options: Plain edge or partially serrated blade; unsigned, $129
MSRP: **$129**

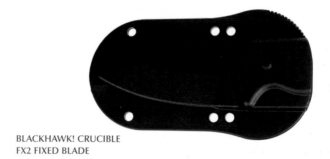

BLACKHAWK! CRUCIBLE
ACCESSORIES

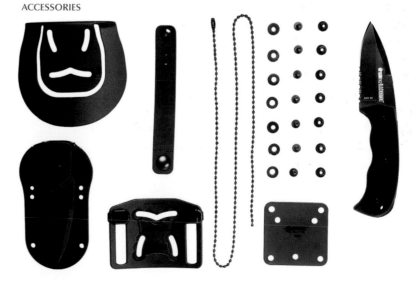

Blackhawk! Knives

www.blackhawk.com

BLACKHAWK! DYNAMIC
ENTRY SMALL PRY

BLACKHAWK!
DYNAMIC ENTRY
SMALL PRY STRICK
KIT

DYNAMIC ENTRY
SMALL PRY

Blade Length: 4.4 in.
Blade Material: D2 Tool steel
Length: 14.5 in.
Handle: Overmolded Thermoplastic
Rubber
Weight: 1.5 lbs.
Features: Epoxy Powder coat blade;
injection molded nylon sheath
Options: S.T.R.I.K.E. or MOLLE com-
patible hardware; tactical back pack
hardware
MSRP: **$200**

BLACKHAWK! DYNAMIC
ENTRY SMALL PRY PACK
KIT

BLACKHAWK! TATANG

BLACKHAWK! NIGHT EDGE
SERRATED COYOTE TAN

NIGHT EDGE SERRATED
COYOTE TAN

Blade Length: 5.9 in.
Blade Material: 1085C High Carbon
tool steel
Length: 10.9 in.
Handle: Thermoplatic Rubber
Weight: 9 oz.
Features: Epoxy coat finish; injection
molded sheath; S.T.R.I.K.E. (MOLLE)
vest or drop leg connect
Options: Black knife and sheath
MSRP: **$150**

TATANG

Blade Length: 8.6 in.
Blade Material: 1085C High Carbon
tool steel
Length: 13.5 in.
Handle: Thermoplastic Rubber
Weight: 15.4 oz.
Features: Epoxy coat finish; reinforced
Ballistic Nylon sheath; Michael Janich
design
Options: Plain edge or partially serrat-
ed blade
MSRP: **$100**

UNITED KINGDOM SPECIAL FORCES

Blade Length: 6.2 in.
Blade Material: D2 Tool steel
Length: 11.4 in.
Handle: G10
Weight: 9.4 oz.
Features: Brushed satin finish; enjection molded sheath; S.T.R.I.K.E. (MOLLE) vest or drop leg connect
Options: Epoxy coat finish
MSRP: $200

BLACKHAWK! UNITED KINGDOM SPECIAL FORCES

Black Label Tactical by Browning

Tactical knives are designed and built to address critical moments and to get the job done. They are rarely elegant, yet that is precisely the word being used to introduce Browning's Black Label Tactical knives. Designed by master hunter Russ Kommer and internationally recognized peace officer Jared Wihongi, the tag line for the Black Label is "Tactical Elegance." Kommer and Wihongi have successfully combined their individual expertise to produce some very appealing hardware. Perhaps the two most "elegant" offerings in the Black Label catalog are the Deterrent and the Volatile push dagger. The Deterrent is reminiscent of a delicate skinner. The push dagger is a little more ominous.

Either one might fit in with old-time gentlemen's apparel as they stepped into a horse and carriage on the way to the opera. A more modern, seemingly upscale knife would be the Turning Point Carbon Fiber gripped folder. The laser etched pattern on the blade is unique and serves as an effective complement to the carbon fiber scales.

Traditionalists in search of a fixed-blade knife in the USMC tradition will want to take a look the Point Blank knives. These are 4.6-inch clip-blade knives with either a leather ringed handle or black G10 grip machined to display a wood-like grain. Smaller fixed-blade knives, such as the Stone Cold and First Priority, use wrapped paracord to enhance the grip. But the paracord spools around an inner portion of the tang. This expands the width of the grip frame but leaves the edges exposed for greater radial leverage. The Stone Cold is also available with flat profile G10 scales bolted into place.

Both models feature a glass break on the butt.

The Stone Cold Tanto liner lock folder is one of the least expensive knives we've found offered with G10 scales and a glass break. It also has a flipper and dual thumb studs. The Pandemonium fixed-blade and folding-blade models offer a large modified tanto profile, adding a secondary cutting surface and beefing up the tip. The rear of the grip drops dramatically to assist in draw cutting or retracting the knife when stuck. The Shadow Fax fixed-blade knife also offers a handguard on the butt end of the grip. There is a full handguard dividing the blade from the handle as well. The Perfect Storm offers a 3.9-inch tanto point blade that is ground to provide maximum blade width directly behind its point. All folders offer a left- or right-side pocket clip attachment, tip up or tip down.

NEW PRODUCTS

Black Label Tactical by Browning

www.browning.com

BLACK LABEL TACTICAL
DETERRENT

BLACK LABEL TACTICAL FIRST
PRIORITY STONE COLD FIXED
SPEAR CORD

BLACK LABEL TACTICAL
PANDEMONIUM FIXED BLADE

BLACK LABEL TACTICAL
PERFECT STORM FOLDER

BLACK LABEL TACTICAL
PANDEMONIUM FOLDER

NEW PRODUCTS

DETERRENT 12320101
Blade Length: 2.75 in.
Blade Material: 154CM
Length: 6.5 in.
Handle: G10
Weight: 7 oz.
Features: Satin finish blade; hawksbill/wharncliffe blade shape; Blade Tech polymer belt sheath
Options: None
MSRP: $150

FIRST PRIORITY STONE COLD FIXED SPEAR CORD 12320130
Blade Length: 2.9 in.
Blade Material: 440
Length: 6.5 in.
Handle: Paracord
Weight: 6 oz.
Features: Black Oxide finish blade; index finger grooves/guard; Blade Tech polymer belt sheath

Options: None
MSRP: $50

PANDEMONIUM FIXED BLADE 12320126
Blade Length: 4.25 in.
Blade Material: 440
Length: 8.6 in.
Handle: G10
Weight: 10.6 oz.
Features: Bead blast finish blade; Blade Tech polymer belt sheath
Options: Folding blade Pandemonium, $30
MSRP: $50

PANDEMONIUM FOLDER 12320124
Blade Length: 3.25 in.
Blade Material: 440
Length (Open/Closed): 7.75 in./4.5 in.
Handle: G10
Lock: Liner lock

Weight: 4.7 oz.
Features: Black Oxide finish blade; left or right side, tip up or tip down pocket clip; dual thumb studs
Options: Full tang fixed-blade model offers 4.25 in. bead blast finish blade, $50
MSRP: $30

PERFECT STORM FOLDER 12320105
Blade Length: 3.9 in.
Blade Material: 154CM
Length (Open/Closed): 9.95 in./6.05 in.
Handle: G10
Lock: Liner lock
Weight: 6.2 oz.
Features: Black Oxide coat blade; left or right side, tip up or tip down pocket clip
Options: None
MSRP: $180

Black Label Tactical by Browning

POINT BLANK G10 12320112

Blade Length: 4.6 in.
Blade Material: 440
Length: 9 in.
Handle: G10
Weight: 11.2 oz.
Features: Black Oxide finish blade; hand guard; hidden tang; Blade Tech polymer belt sheath
Options: Leather handle; bead blast finish blade
MSRP: $60

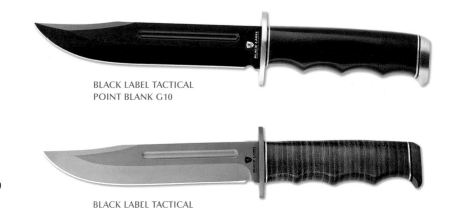

BLACK LABEL TACTICAL
POINT BLANK G10

BLACK LABEL TACTICAL
POINT BLANK G10 LEATHER

BLACK LABEL TACTICAL
SHADOW FAX

BLACK LABEL TACTICAL STONE
COLD FIXED BLADE TANTO G10

SHADOW FAX 12320104

Blade Length: 4.6 in.
Blade Material: 154CM
Length: 9 in.
Handle: G10
Weight: NA
Features: Satin finish blade; Blade Tech polymer belt sheath; handguard; full finger grooves
Options: None
MSRP: $250

STONE COLD FIXED BLADE TANTO G10 12320115

Blade Length: 5.6 in.
Blade Material: 440
Length: 10.75 in.
Handle: G10
Weight: 15.2 oz.
Features: Black Oxide finish blade; partially serrated edge blade; deep finger grooves; glass break pommel; Blade Tech polymer belt sheath

BLACK LABEL TACTICAL STONE
COLD FIXED SPEAR CORD

Options: Paracord grip
MSRP: $60

STONE COLD FIXED SPEAR CORD 12320118

Blade Length: 5.6 in.
Blade Material: 440
Length: 10.75 in.

Handle: Paracord
Weight: 12.4 oz.
Features: Black Oxide finish blade; partially serrated edge blade; deep finger grooves; glass break pommel; Blade Tech polymer belt sheath
Options: Tanto point blade
MSRP: $60

NEW PRODUCTS

Black Label Tactical by Browning

www.browning.com

BLACK LABEL TACTICAL STONE
COLD TANTO FOLDER

BLACK LABEL TACTICAL TURNING
POINT CARBON FIBER FOLDER

BLACK LABEL TACTICAL
VOLATILE PUSH
DAGGER

STONE COLD TANTO FOLDER 12320113

Blade Length: 3.75 in.
Blade Material: 440
Length (Open/Closed): 8.6 in./4.85 in.
Handle: G10
Lock: Liner lock
Weight: 5 oz.
Features: Black Oxide coat blade; rough checkered grip; deep finger grooves; flipper or dual thumb stud opening; glass break; left or right side, tip up or tip down pocket clip; partially serrated edge blade
Options: Spear point; partially serrated edge blade
MSRP: $35

TURNING POINT CARBON FIBER FOLDER 12320133

Blade Length: 3 in.
Blade Material: 154CM
Length (Open/Closed): 7.4 in./6.05 in.
Handle: Carbon fiber
Lock: Liner lock
Weight: 3.8 oz.
Features: Laser etched finish blade; tip up or tip down pocket clip; dual thumb studs
Options: None
MSRP: $100

VOLATILE PUSH DAGGER 12320108

Blade Length: 4 in.
Blade Material: 154CM
Length: 5.55 in.
Handle: G10
Weight: 6 oz.
Features: Satin finish blade; double edge blade; Blade Tech polymer belt sheath
Options: None
MSRP: $150

Blade Tech Knives

Blade Tech Industries began life as a small, one-man holster company in the early 1990s when Kydex®, a high performance thermoplastic, was new on the scene. Whereas many synthetic holster makers were popping up, Blade Tech's founder, Tim Wegner, had the winning designs and progressive manufacturing techniques to become a leader in the industry. Success in the competitive shooting community led to manufacturers' making components for law enforcement and military. Wegner, an avid outdoorsman, also designed folding knives for the hunter, which translated easily to tactical use. And thanks to their presence in the gun world, Blade Tech knives are among the few choice edged weapons available from Brownells, an online megastore with a traditional catalog format as well.

Today, design and manufacture has expanded to include tactical knives designed in Blade Tech's Puyallup, Washington, location but manufactured by Fox Knives in Maniago, Italy—a company that specializes in contract production. One such knife is the Profili, designed by Mike Vellekamp and Laurie DeMars. The name was taken in honor of Laurie's grandfather, Eugene Profili. The literal translation of profili is "profile." With this in mind, the Profili was designed not as a heavy pry bar but rather as a scalpel-like instrument.

Its flowing lines are visually quite artistic. The blade can be described as leaf-shaped or perhaps an elongated droplet. The finger grooves offer a visual dynamic as well as a natural grip. The first finger groove is actually a part of the blade. Directly above there is a contour for the thumb at the rear of the spine. The Profili is available in both folding and fixed-blade configurations. Once opened, the folder appears to be nearly identical to the fixed-blade model. The liners mirror the full tang of the fixed-blade knife. They extend like fins at the butt end and are strong enough to be used for striking. This liner lock knife offers a locking lever to keep the blade open for added strength and security.

The pocket clip can be placed at either end and on either side of the scales. A Kydex® sheath with Tek-Lok (another Tim Wegner invention) is available for the Profili fixed-blade knife as well as a military style MOLLE connect option. But many buyers will prefer to see the Blade Tech Profili offered as a refined tactical knife for the gentleman.

Photo courtesy of R. Eckstine.

BLADE TECH PROFILI

Photo courtesy of R. Eckstine.

PROFILI
Blade Length: 3.95 in.
Blade Material: N690CO
Length (Open/Closed): 9 in./5.05 in.
Handle: G10
Lock: Liner plus safety
Weight: 5.2 oz.
Features: Kydex sheath; bright red safety lever; butt, suitable for striking
Options: Tek Lok or MOLLE locking sheath
MSRP: $160

BLADE TECH
PROFILI LOCK

Böker Knives

Böker, with an umlaut over the "o," should probably be pronounced Becker. The original spelling was actually Boeker, belonging to the Boeker family, which operated a small tool factory in Remscheid, Germany, in the seventeenth century. But it was during the 1820s, a dangerous time of political unrest, that the company began turning out sabers. By 1830, international demand became an essential part of the business. By 1860, Heinrich Boeker had moved the factory to Solingen, Germany, while his brothers Hermann and Robert chose to immigrate to North America. Hermann set up H. Boeker & Sons in New York. Robert began enterprises in Canada and later in Mexico. All four ventures were successful, including the establishment of Casa Boeker, which remains a market leader, and of course the factory in Solingen, a city whose name is synonymous with steel. By the turn of the twentieth century, America was Böker's primary market. But during World War II, sale and resale of the company interrupted the narrative. Nevertheless, happy-ever-after was still in reach when Böker USA was founded by Dan Weidner in 1986, with the relationship to the Solingen plant still intact.

One of the benefits from being an international firm with a long history is worldwide resources. That's why there is such a wide variety of natural as well as synthetic materials found across the Böker spectrum of products. For example, Böker has long been famous for their Damascus steel, consisting of up to 320 layers. The Classic Mokume lock back folding knife has a 300-layer Damascus blade and bolsters that show an unusual pattern. This pattern is the result of a layering process similar to that of Damascus, bringing together non-ferrous and precious metals.

Some of the more unusual Böker knives are found in the Illumination series. The glow coating makes the Bud Nealy Illumination fixed-blade knife glow in the dark. In dim light the G10 scales appear to be floating on the tang. So do the black color inlays on the handle of the Illumination Top Lock II folder.

Three knives that are the brainchild of famous designers are the Davis Classic Hunter, the Anso67, and the Blackwood Pipsqueak. The Classic Hunter by W. C. Davis of Missouri is refreshingly elegant. This is a slim line back-lock knife ideal for pocket carry. It has an N690BO steel blade manufactured in Solingen, Germany. The blade is highly polished and includes a fine cut nail nick for opening. The stainless steel bolsters and tang have a brushed finished. The grip scales are green canvas Micarta accented by layers of red fiber, giving this knife a completely unique appearance.

Neil Blackwood's Pipsqueak is a tactical folder that otherwise defies classification. Blackwood designed the Pipsqueak to be either the "smallest big knife or biggest small knife," depending on one's point of view. Collector value may be enhanced as the Pipsqueak is Blackwood's first folding blade design. This is a frame-lock knife featuring titanium construction, but the left side is covered by Micarta. The rear spacer is also Micarta. The pocket clip is right side only and matches the contour of the grip. The short 2.6-inch long blade was fashioned from S30VN high performance steel.

Jens Anso contributes the Anso 67 pocket knife. This is a titanium frame-lock knife with the left side of the frame consisting of a heavy G10 scale. The right side is exposed bead-blasted titanium and features a pocket clip that can be reversed for tip up or tip down carry. The thumb stud can also be moved to the opposite side of the wharncliffe blade.

To commemorate its twenty-fifth anniversary, Böker USA is releasing a limited edition series of knives. All Twenty-fifth Anniversary editions feature white Micarta handle scales and Twenty-fifth Anniversary etching on the blade. Collector value is enhanced by individualized serial numbers limited to 150 pieces to be sold in Europe, with 150 additional pieces reserved for sale in the United States. Commemorative knives include a Trapper-style knife with nickel silver bolsters. The Anniversary Edition Trapper houses a clip point and a spey point blade. The folding Anniversary Hunter is a lock back knife with 3.1-inch clip-point blade. Each of these knives utilizes 440C carbon steel blades. The Gentleman's folding knife offers a single forward nickel silver bolster, lock back operation, and a 2-inch-long blade. The Camp Knife Anniversary edition has two blades, can opener, bottle opener, corkscrew, screwdriver, marlin spike, and lanyard ring. Both the Gentleman and the Camp Knife utilize 4034 blade steel. Perhaps the most impressive of the Twenty-fifth

BÖKER ANSO 67

BÖLER BUD NEALY ILLUMINATION

BÖKER BLACKWOOD PIPSQUEAK

BÖKER CLASSIC MOKUME

Anniversary commemoratives is the Minx, designed by Neil Blackwood. The Minx is a 6.25-inch-long, full tang fixed-blade knife made from S30VN steel. The white Micarta scales are accented by blue color liners exposed along the edges of the tang.

ANSO 67 110620
Blade Length: 3 in.
Blade Material: N690BO steel
Length (Open/Closed): 7 in./4 in.
Handle: G10
Lock: Frame lock
Weight: 5 oz.
Features: Titanium construction; removable thumb stud; left or right side, tip up or tip down pocket clip
Options: None
MSRP: $250

BLACKWOOD PIPSQUEAK 110623
Blade Length: 2.6 in.
Blade Material: S35VN
Length (Open/Closed): 6.25 in./3.65 in.
Handle: Micarta/Titanium
Lock: Frame lock
Weight: 4.7 oz.
Features: Titanium construction; left side capped with Micarta; right side pocket clip
Options: None
MSRP: $300

BUD NEALY ILLUMINATION 102567
Blade Length: 3.1 in.
Blade Material: 440C
Length: 7 in.
Handle: G10
Weight: 2.9 oz.

Features: Glow coated blade; Polymer sheath; TekLok belt attachment
Options: None
MSRP: $220

CLASSIC MOKUME 112101DAM
Blade Length: 3.1 in.
Blade Material: Damascus Composite
Length (Open/Closed): 7 in./3.9 in.
Handle: Micarta
Lock: Lockback
Weight: 4.3 oz.
Features: 300 layer Damascus blade; brown canvas Micarta scales accented with red fiber; nickel silver tang capped with Mokume bolsters; mokume is the result of a Damascus-like process of non-ferrous and precious metals
Options: None
MSRP: $600

NEW PRODUCTS

Böker Knives

www.boker.de/us/

BÖKER DAVIS CLASSIC HUNTER

BÖKER CAMP KNIFE ANNIVERSARY EDITION

BÖKER TOP LOCK II

BÖKER FOLDING HUNTER ANNIVERSARY EDITION

DAVIS CLASSIC HUNTER 110624

Blade Length: 3.5 in.
Blade Material: N690BO
Length (Open/Closed): 8.5 in./5 in.
Handle: Canvas Micarta
Lock: Lockback
Weight: 5.3 oz.
Features: Nail nick open; Stainless steel bolsters
Options: None
MSRP: $260

TOP LOCK II 110117

Blade Length: 2.75 in.
Blade Material: 4034 Stainless
Length (Open/Closed): 6.75 in./4 in.
Handle: Glow coat aluminum
Lock: Frame lock
Weight: 2.9 oz.
Features: Handle glows in the dark; Cordura nylon belt carry sheath; handmade, Solingen, Germany
Options: None
MSRP: $130

BÖKER TWENTY-FIFTH ANNIVERSARY EDITIONS

CAMP KNIFE ANNIVERSARY EDITION 110182M

Blade Length (Max): 2.5 in.
Blade Material: 4034 Stainless
Length (Open/Closed): 7.6 in./3.5 in.
Handle: Micarta
Lock: None
Weight: 3.3 oz.
Features: 1.75 in. secondary clip point blade; can opener, flat head screwdriver, cork screw; cap opener, marlin spike/leather punch; nickel bolsters
Options: None
MSRP: $200

FOLDING HUNTER ANNIVERSARY EDITION 112002M

Blade Length: 3.1 in.
Blade Material: 440C
Length (Open/Closed): 7.25 in./4.15 in.
Handle: Micarta
Lock: Lockback
Weight: 5.6 oz.
Features: Nickel silver bolsters
Options: None
MSRP: $160

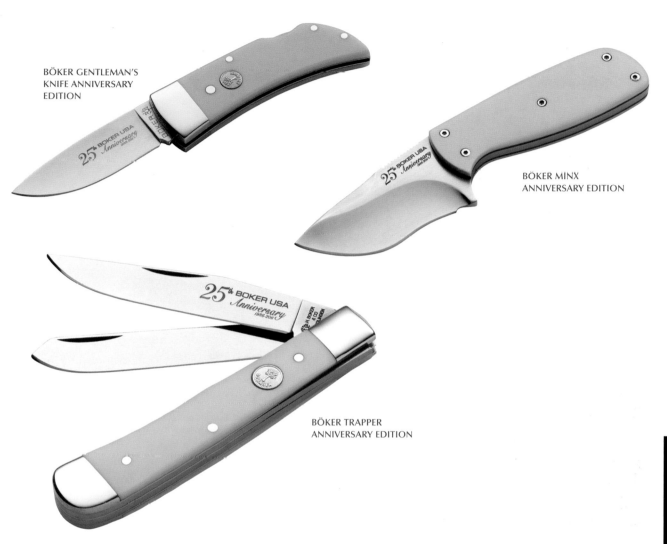

BÖKER GENTLEMAN'S
KNIFE ANNIVERSARY
EDITION

BÖKER MINX
ANNIVERSARY EDITION

BÖKER TRAPPER
ANNIVERSARY EDITION

GENTLEMAN'S KNIFE ANNIVERSARY EDITION 111004M

Blade Length: 2 in.
Blade Material: 4034
Length (Open/Closed): 4.5 in./5 in.
Handle: Micarta
Lock: Lockback
Weight: 1.3 oz.
Features: Nickel silver bolsters
Options: None
MSRP: $100

MINX ANNIVERSARY EDITION 120617

Blade Length: 2.6 in.
Blade Material: S35VN
Length: 6.25 in.
Handle: Micarta
Weight: 3.5 oz.
Features: Blue liner; leather sheath w/ handle shield and handguard style cross strap
Options: None
MSRP: $265

TRAPPER ANNIVERSARY EDITION 112525M

Blade Length (Max): 3 in.
Blade Material: 440C
Length (Open/Closed): 7 in./4.25 in.
Handle: Micarta
Lock: None
Weight: 5.6 oz.
Features: Nickel silver bolsters; clip and spey point blades
Options: None
MSRP: $95

Buck Knives

Buck Knives is one of the oldest continuously run, family-owned companies in the industry. Hoyt Buck, a young Kansas blacksmith, started the company in 1902. Since then the company has been passed down to Al Buck and now to CJ (Chuck Buck). The Buck Knives philosophy is perhaps rooted in the words of CJ Buck: "defining the best way to deliver our products so you can rely on them like a trusted friend."

Once opened, the Chuck Buck–signed Chairman Leather lockback knife measures 8.25 inches long. Buck's signature appears in the cherry dymondwood scales between polished nickel bolsters. A leather belt pouch is supplied. The Ranger Skinner is a fixed-blade knife with polished brass bolsters and Macassar Ebony dymondwood scales over a full tang. The black leather sheath matches the handle. The PakLite Large is a skeletonized knife made from 440C carbon steel. Without handle scales in place, the tang becomes the grip frame. The lower edge offers two finger grooves and a guard. Top and bottom, the profile swells to fill the palm. The edges are cut with ridges to enhance grip. Cutouts in the knife not only reduce weight but offer additional hold points for directing a fine cut. The PakLite is also available with a satin finish, but the Black Traction coat makes the knife less slippery when wet and lends a stunning contrast to the ground surfaces of the blade.

The Buck CSAR knives are sturdy tactical and rescue knives produced in conjunction with TOPS Knives. TOPS is an Idaho-based manufacturer that refers to its products as tools, first; knives, second. The vast majority of the TOPS catalog is devoted to military and law enforcement design and application. Whereas TOPS offers few folding knives, working in conjunction with Buck is a natural fit. Buck's folding system is strong and smooth. Buck Knives are warranted forever and they are wholly made in America. The CSAR series includes one fixed-blade knife and three liner lock folders including CSAR-T, CSAR-T Avid, and the CSAR-T Responder. The new CSAR-T Avid is lighter and less bulky than its CSAR teammates. The 3.5 tanto blade is still in place but overall length is reduced by about one-quarter inch and carry weight is some 1.5 ounces less. Some of this is attributable to the use of Santoprene scales applied to the stainless steel liners, rather than using heavily carved G10. Blade material is 420HC instead of 154CM stainless. All CSAR knives include a hex adaptor for aid in working various tools, including a hex tool set with driver and fifteen bits sold separately. There are also utility slots in the blade that can be used to bend wire or other material. Pocket clip is tip up and movable to right or left side. The supplied black nylon sheath is built for hard use and is MOLLE compatible.

BUCK CHAIRMAN LEATHER

CHAIRMAN LEATHER 0110CWSNK-B
Blade Length (Max): 3.75 in.
Blade Material: 420HC
Length (Open/Closed): 8.65 in./4.9 in.
Handle: Cherry dymondwood
Lock: Lockback
Weight: 7.2 oz.
Features: Nickel bolsters; Chuck Buck signature; leather sheath
Options: With Nylon sheath, $89
MSRP: **$100**

BUCK CASR-T
AVID 090

BUCK PAKLITE
SKINNER LARGE

BUCK RANGER
SKINNER

CSAR-T AVID 090

Blade Length (Max): 3.5 in.
Blade Material: 420HC
Length (Open/Closed): 8.25 in./4.75 in.
Handle: Stainless steel/Santoprene rubber
Lock: Liner lock
Weight: 7.1 oz.
Features: MOLLE compatible nylon sheath; tip up reversible pocket clip; hex tool adaptable, driver, and bits sold separately
Options: CSAR-T Responder adds full coverage G10 scales; seatbelt cutter; glass break; ATS 34 steel blade, $140
MSRP: $110

PAKLITE SKINNER LARGE 141BK

Blade Length: 3.5 in.
Blade Material: 420HC
Length: 8 in.
Handle: 420HC
Weight: 4.1 oz.
Features: Black nylon sheath; black traction coat finish
Options: Satin finish, $30
MSRP: $35

RANGER SKINNER 0113BRS-B

Blade Length: 3.1 in.
Blade Material: 420HC
Length: 7.25 in.
Handle: Macassar Ebony dymondwood
Weight: 5.2 oz.
Features: Black leather sheath
Options: None
MSRP: $80

NEW PRODUCTS

Case Knives

Based in Bradford, Pennsylvania, W. R. Case and Sons Cutlery is an American success story. As stated on the company website: "The company's rich history began in 1889 when four brothers—William Russell (W. R.), Jean, John, and Andrew Case (a.k.a. "The Case Brothers")—began fashioning knives and selling them along a wagon trail in upstate New York." W. R.'s son John is the one that formally opened the company at the turn of the century. Today the company is owned by Zippo Manufacturing, but this was far from a hostile takeover. Evidence of their friendly alliance is the Zippo/Case museum, also located in Bradford. There visitors can learn how World War II played a part in making Case knives and Zippo Lighters famous around the world. From 1943 until the end of the war, Zippo's entire production run was sent to U.S. troops. More importantly, it was the Case V-42 Stiletto that was used by the First Special Service Force known as "The Devil's Brigade." According to the Army Historical Foundation, the official designation of this 12-inch long knife with 7- and 5/16-inch blade in Ordnance Department documents reads, "Knife-Fighting-Commando Type V42."

Today Case knives are primarily sold through authorized dealers. In fact, they are more likely to be found in hardware stores than gun shops or sporting good stores. As would follow, the Case catalog lists many knives for the hunter and the working man. This may change in the next twelve months as Case introduces its Tec-X line of tactical folding knives. As it stands now, a substantial portion of Case customer sales is collector driven. In fact, the Case Collector's Club boasts the largest active membership of any collector's club in the world, numbering around 19,000. A recent offering is in the Select double-X category. The Select Winter Bottom Copperlock is a mid-lock knife with a single clip point blade measuring about 3.16 inches in length. Thumbnail openings are enhanced by supplying a long rectangular "French" nail nick. The upper edge of the lock spring, or spline, is worked with a series of scalloped-style cuts. So is the spine of the blade. The nickel silver bolsters are highly polished. Case XX is inscribed on the badge, the rear bolster, and on the flat just forward of the blade—sometimes referred to as the ricasso. The scales are bone culled from Zebu cattle found in Brazil. The scales are jigged in the Case Winter Bottom pattern. The Winter Bottom pattern might be described as giving the appearance of lines or ridges cut into a snow drift by gusting winds.

SELECT XX WINTER BOTTOM COPPERLOCK
05382

Blade Length (Max): 3.16 in.
Blade Material: Stainless steel
Length (Open/Closed): 7.5 in./4.25 in.
Handle: Winterbottom Jigged Bone
Lock: Mid lock
Weight: 2.8 oz.
Features: Nickel silver bolsters; rectangular "French" nail nick opening; worked blade and spline (scalloped decorations on locking spring and blade spine)
Options: None
MSRP: $92

CASE SELECT XX
WINTER BOTTOM
COPPERLOCK

Grayman Knives

Grayman Knives is a different sort of knife company. It's a mom-and-pop operation but that's not really unusual. It began with a dedicated maker that had a vision of what a knife should be able to do. Again, that's not so different either. Here are some of the details that set Grayman Knives apart. Grayman started out making knives for soldier friends of Mike, the company president. It should be noted that we're referring to contemporary soldiers. Not even as early as Desert Storm. We're talking about post-9/11 front liners serving in Iraq and Afghanistan for both the U.S. military and private contractors. These were soldiers fighting a new kind of war, and to meet their needs traditional military design was off the table. Nevertheless, Mike hit upon a combination that worked—one that has proven as brutally effective as it has durable. Fixed-blade knives make up the bulk of the Grayman catalog—primarily full tang knives made from a single piece of quarter-inch-thick 1095 high carbon steel. The metal is covered end to end with GunKote. GunKote is a military grade anticorrosive coating that will not attract or carry dust or dirt, which is advantageous considering the current theatre of war, which has been nicknamed the "sandbox." Micarta or G10 scales are applied to form the handle. Most Grayman knives are sharpened using a chisel grind for maximum strength. It also makes cutting a straight line a little more difficult. Hence, a wound dealt by one of these knives can be difficult to fix. Safe carry is supplied by a heavy Kydex guard that fills out a nylon MOLLE style sheath.

For the first four years Mike only made knives for his closer associates. Grayman knives are now, thanks to the website talents of his wife Sue, available to the general public. But they are still handmade by Mike, one at a time. Maybe that's why shopping on the Grayman Knives website can sometimes be confusing. When you see a knife you like it might read "SOLD." But that's okay. They'll make another one just for you and engraving (up to 15 words) is free.

Not counting special run knives, Grayman lists twelve different models—two folders and ten fixed-blade models. Within these design categories are variations in blade length. It is also not unusual for each model to have a "middle" name, such as the Grayman Darfur Defender or the West Nile Warrior. Such is the focus and bond with the war on terror.

The Merdeka (the Malay/Indonesian word for "free" or "independent") was designed to offer the most possible chopping power in a compact 8-inch blade knife. It also features a point that is directly in line with the axis of the tang to deliver a massive wound channel from its 3-inch tall blade. Variation from the use of 1095 high carbon steel includes the use of 9AL/4V titanium blades with a layer of carbide applied to the edges. The addition of carbide offers greater edge retention to the titanium and also a measure of fine natural serration. Knives that are available with carbide-coated titanium blades are the Dinka, Rav 3, Suenami, Warrior, and Sub-Saharan.

Titanium is also used in the making of Grayman's folding knives. Both the Dua and Satu folders are frame-lock knives of titanium construction. This includes the frame and the pocket clip. The blades are ground from CPM S30V steel. Both sides of the Dua folders are bare titanium. The Satu Folder covers the non-locking side with G10 but limited runs featuring carbon fiber scales come and go on demand.

Grayman Knives

www.graymanknives.com

GRAYMAN DARFUR DEFENDER

DARFUR DEFENDER

Blade Length: 7.5 in.
Blade Material: 1095HC
Length: 13.25 in.
Handle: G10
Weight: 19 oz.
Features: Heavy gauge Kydex inner sheath in Cordura nylon MOLLE compatible outer sheath; vertical or small of the back carry; ¼-inch-thick blade; single bevel (chisel) grind for maximum strength
Options: Black or green G10 handle; free engraving up to 15 letters
MSRP: $235

DINKA/MINI DINKA

Blade Length: 4 in./3 in.
Blade Material: 1095HC
Length: 8.25 in./6.25 in.
Handle: G10
Weight: 10.25 oz./6.5 oz.
Features: Heavy gauge Kydex inner sheath in Cordura nylon MOLLE compatible outer sheath; GunKote finish
Options: Black or green G10 handle; Dinka available with titanium blade, $265; free engraving up to 15 letters
MSRP: . . . . $185/$150

MERDEKA

Blade Length: 8 in.
Blade Material: 1095HC
Length: 13.5 in.
Handle: G10
Weight: 24 oz.
Features: Heavy gauge Kydex inner sheath in Cordura nylon MOLLE compatible outer sheath; vertical or small of the back carry; ¼-inch-thick blade; single bevel (chisel) grind for maximum strength
Options: Black or green G10 handle; free engraving up to 15 letters
MSRP: $285

GRAYMAN DINKA/MINI DINKA

GRAYMAN MERDEKA

GRAYMAN SATU FOLDER

⟨⟨ Viewing the left and right side profiles of the Grayman Satu Folder can be misleading. The right side of the knife consists of a massive titanium plate nearly .02 inches in width. This means the locking strut is super strong. The left side of the knife is just as wide but consists of a thinner titanium plate covered by G10 to enhance grip. We weighed the Satu to be about 10.4 ounces, but it's difficult to portray the sheer presence of the Satu in a mere photograph. The circumference of the middle finger groove is about 3.9 inches and edge to spine we measured the CPM S30L blade to be about 1.65 inches tall.

SATU FOLDER
Blade Length (Max): 4 in.
Blade Material: CPM S30V
Length (Open/Closed): 9.9 in./5.9 in.
Handle: Titanium/G10
Lock: Frame lock
Weight: 10.4 oz.
Features: Titanium frame and pocket clip; handle scale covers non-locking, left side, only; heat treated blade; oversize (³⁄₈ in.) pivot pin
Options: Black G10, green G10 handle; carbon fiber handle, $445
MSRP: $375

SINGLE BEVEL WEST NILE WARRIOR 7.5/5.5
Blade Length: 7.5 in./5.5 in.
Blade Material: 1095HC
Length: 13.5 in./11.25 in.
Handle: G10
Weight: 21.9 oz./18 oz.
Features: GunKote coated blade; heavy gauge Kydex inner sheath; Cordura nylon MOLLE compatible outer sheath; vertical or small of the back carry; ¼-inch-thick blade; single bevel (chisel) grind for maximum strength
Options: Black or green G10 handle; free engraving up to 15 letters
MSRP: . . . . $215/$195

Photo courtesy of R. Eckstine.

GRAYMAN
SINGLE BEVEL
WEST NILE
WARRIOR

GRAYMAN SINGLE
BEVEL WEST NILE
WARRIOR CHISEL
GRIND

Photo courtesy of R. Eckstine.

GRAYMAN SINGLE BEVEL WEST NILE WARRIOR SHEATH

Photo courtesy of R. Eckstine.

NEW PRODUCTS

Havalon Knives

Cincinnati, Ohio's Havalon Knives offers a unique approach to producing an effective skinning knife for hunters. A division of Havel's Incorporated, and long known as a supplier of surgical blades, Havalon adapts the scalpel to the needs of the hunter. Whereas it is not unusual for hunters to carry a pack of scalpels or replaceable blade knives more suitable to crafts than for skinning, few such tools offer the ergonomics or appeal of a hunting knife. The problem is it's not unusual for a skinning knife to need sharpening after only one or two dressings. In the case of accidental contact with bone, stopping to sharpen the blade may become necessary before a single dressing is complete. Havalon's "Quik-Change" knives are designed to eliminate sharpening and offer the handling and convenience of a field-worthy folding blade knife.

Each Havalon knife is a locking blade folder with a stem that rotates out from the handle body. The stem is fit with a connecting clip, or "fitment," that is very similar to the one found on surgical scalpels. The fitment, as well as the other mechanical parts of the Havalon knives, is made from stainless steel; so are the blades that are tempered to resist bending and provide rigid spring-like tension. The manufacturer recommends that loading a blade on to the fitment can be achieved using a small pair of pliers such as those found in a multi-tool set. The first step is to make sure the blade stem is locked fully open. The fitment has a slot opening from the tip. The rear of the fitment is slightly raised. Using pliers to hold the blade from the dull side—ninety degrees to the cutting edge—the blade is then slipped over the fitment so that the inner forward edge of the locking notch works into the slot inside the fitment. Continue sliding the blade towards the knife handle until the rear edge of the notch snaps over the top of the fitment. A tug with the pliers should be all that is required to make sure the blade is locked into place.

Removing the blade also begins with verifying that the blade stem is locked in the open position. The manufacturer recommends holding the knife with the sharp edge facing away from the user. The blade should be held using pliers approaching from the dull side of the blade. The index finger of the left hand is used to push the rearward lower edge, or "heel," of the blade sideways so that it can pass over the fitment. As many as twelve extra blades are shipped with each knife.

The Piranta Pro Skinning knife features a Stainless steel handle with finger grooves for better control and G10 inlaid on the left side. Unlike the Havalon's other knives, the Piranta Pro is a frame-lock knife. All others utilize a liner lock with Stainless steel liners. Thumb studs for opening are of the paddle style and machined as one piece with the rotating blade stem. Blade length for each of the Piranta series knives is 2.75 inches.

The Piranta Edge and the Piranta Z knives each utilize high grade plastic handles with rubber inserts on the left side only. The Edge features a high visibility bright orange handle made from ABS plastic. The Piranta Z comes with a black military grade Zytel handle. The right-side-only pocket clip is removable. The Piranta Predator knives feature ornate scrimshaw-style laser engravings on their ABS plastic handles.

The Baracuta series liner lock knives feature Havalon's Zytel grip with rubber inlaid on the left-hand side. The Blaze is a skinning knife with bright orange handle and a blade measuring 4.4 inches in length. The Baracuta Edge and Z models pack a thin 5-inch-long blade intended primarily for filet cuts. One of the more versatile Havalon knives is the Tracer22. The Tracer22 can be fitted with several different size and style blades that range from a drop point profile to the number 25 triangular-shaped spearpoint razor-edged blade. With its helpful finger grooves on the bottom side of the grip, this knife shares a profile similar to the Havalon's Pro skinning knife. But this is a liner lock knife with black Zytel handle scales and blue rubber insert over Stainless steel liners. Blade length is 2.75 inches. Havalon knives may also be carried in a belt pouch with snap closure and a separate compartment for spare blades. Available materials are nylon or leather.

BARACUTA EDGE/ BARACUTA Z XT127 EDGE/ XT127Z

Blade Length: 5 in.
Blade Material: 127XT Stainless steel
Length (Open/Closed): 11 in./6 in.
Handle: Zytel plastic/rubber inserts
Lock: Liner lock
Weight: 3 oz.
Features: Replaceable blades; five-pack replacement blades included; dual thumb studs; open back design for easy cleaning; removable pocket clip; Stainless steel action
Options: Orange or gray rubber grip inserts; snap over belt pouch
MSRP: **$60**

PIRANTA ORIGINAL STAINLESS STEEL SKINNING KNIFE XT-60KNP

Blade Length: 2.75 in.
Blade Material: 60XT Stainless steel
Length (Open/Closed): 6.75 in./3.75 in.
Handle: Stainless steel/G10
Lock: Frame lock
Weight: 2.3 oz.
Features: Replaceable blades; 12-pack replacement blades included; dual thumb studs; removable pocket clip; finger groove handle; bead blast finish
Options: None
MSRP: **$50**

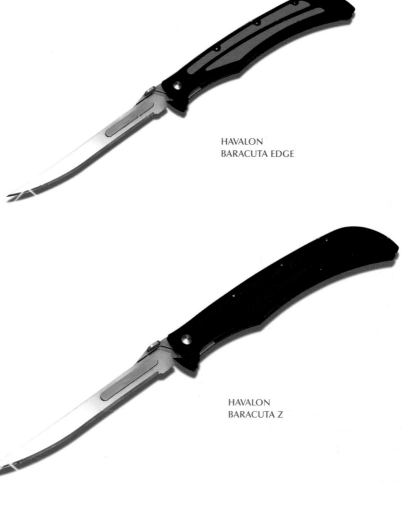

HAVALON
BARACUTA EDGE

HAVALON
BARACUTA Z

HAVALON PIRANTA ORIGINAL
STAINLESS STEEL SKINNING KNIFE

NEW PRODUCTS

Havalon Knives

www.havalon.com

PIRANTA EDGE

Blade Length: 2.75 in.
Blade Material: 60XT Stainless steel
Length (Open/Closed): 7.25 in./
4.25 in.
Handle: ABS plastic/rubber inserts
Lock: Liner lock
Weight: 2 oz.
Features: Replaceable blades; 12-pack replacement blades included; dual thumb studs; removable pocket clip; high visibility orange handle; Stainless steel action
Options: None
MSRP: **$36**

PIRANTA Z XT-60Z

Blade Length: 2.75 in.
Blade Material: 60XT Stainless steel
Length (Open/Closed): 7.25 in./
4.75 in.
Handle: Zytel plastic/rubber inserts
Lock: Liner lock
Weight: 2 oz.
Features: Replaceable blades; 12-pack replacement blades included; dual thumb studs; removable pocket clip; Stainless steel action
Options: None
MSRP: **$36**

PIRANTA TRACER 22 XT-22TR

Blade Length: 2.25 in.
Blade Material: 22XT Stainless steel
Length (Open/Closed): 6 in./3.75 in.
Handle: Aluminum/rubber inserts
Lock: Liner lock
Weight: 1.4 oz.
Features: Replaceable blades; 12-pack replacement blades included; dual thumb studs; removeable pocket clip; open back design for easy cleaning
Options: Can accommodate numbers 20 thru 25 size blades
MSRP: **$42**

PIRANTA PREDATOR TIMBER WOLF XT-60-PRW

Blade Length: 2.75 in.
Blade Material: 60XT Stainless steel
Length (Open/Closed): 7 in./4.25 in.
Handle: ABS plastic
Lock: Liner lock
Weight: 2 oz.
Features: Replaceable blades; 12-pack replacement blades included; dual thumb studs; removeable pocket clip; scrimshaw style laser engraved handle scales; Stainless steel action
Options: Cougar or Grizzly Bear engraved handle
MSRP: **$40**

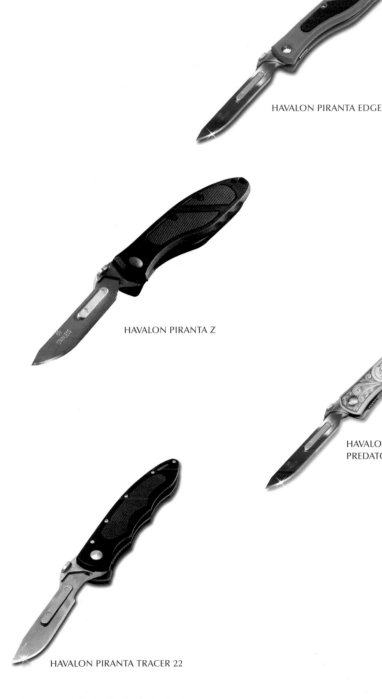

HAVALON PIRANTA EDGE

HAVALON PIRANTA Z

HAVALON PIRANTA PREDATOR TIMBER WOLF

HAVALON PIRANTA TRACER 22

Hogue Elishewitz Extreme Knives

When Guy Hogue retired from his post as armorer and shooting instructor for the Los Angeles Police Department, he had an idea for an improvement to handgun grips, specifically for the revolver. The traditional revolver grip consisted of two opposing pieces that screwed together over the butt frame. The inner surface of the two halves was usually cut to match the framework to one degree or another, but unless the retaining screw was secure, the two halves were in danger of shifting about. This could be a real problem if you were dealing with bad guys. But even if you were merely taking in a day at the range, accommodation for the cross-mounted locking screw was prone to rubbing a blister into the shooter's palm or being just plain annoying. So, Guy Hogue invented the Monogrip®. As you might have guessed Hogue's invention was a one-piece design. Made from wood or rubber, the Monogrip® was slipped on from the bottom of the frame and secured by a single screw that locked tightly into a yoke-like attachment that was included with the grip.

Whereas making grips for all sorts of handguns has been very good to the Hogue family, the manner in which the company has grown is nothing short of astounding. Hogue HandALL Tool Grip®, Hogue Tool and Machine, Hogue OEM molding, woodworking, and packaging are just some of the interests that began with a simple idea. The production of Hogue Fine Sporting Cutlery began in 2010 when the company entered into collaboration with Allen Elishewitz. Elishewitz's designs have in the past shown up in the catalogs of several major manufacturers, but in this case the latest Hogue EX01 knives share a similar profile with Allen's most current custom designs. In terms of technology the EX01 knives utilize the Elishewitz button lock. The button lock acts as an automatically locking cross bolt. Many experts considered the Elishewitz button lock to be the strongest available design for a portable folding knife. In addition, the Hogue FX01 knives have a left side mounted safety that can be slid forward to prevent the button lock from releasing the blade.

HOGUE EXTREME KNIFE

Photo courtesy of R. Eckstine.

HOGUE EXTREME KNIFE BUTTON LOCK

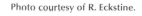
Photo courtesy of R. Eckstine.

HOGUE EXTREME KNIFE CLIPSIDE

EXTREME KNIFE #1 EX01
Blade Length (Max): 3.5 in.
Blade Material: 154CM
Length (Open/Closed): 8 in./4.5 in.
Handle: 6061T-6 aluminum
Lock: Button lock
Weight: 4.5 oz.
Features: Blade double tempered cryogenically heat treated; right side pocket clip, tip or tip down; left side mounted blade lock; dual thumb studs
Options: Tanto or drop point blade; 4-inch blade, $198; G-10 fiber G-Mascus© textured handle, $198–$216
MSRP: **$180**

Photo courtesy of Hogue Extreme Knives.

Kershaw Knives, KAI USA Ltd., and Zero Tolerance

Kershaw knives opened for business in the United States in 1974 with its main office located in Lake Oswego, Oregon. Kershaw traces its roots to the formation of the Endo Manufacturing Company in 1908. This begins a timeline that includes such names as Sanwa Precision Works and KAI Razor, both of which are widely respected giants of marketing and manufacturing in Japan and elsewhere in Southeast Asia. But Kershaw and its sister companies Zero Tolerance and Shun Cutlery—which together make up KAI USA Ltd—display the imagination and creativity of American design. Milestones in development include collaboration with designer Ken Onion and their patented SpeedSafe® assisted opening technology.

The Kershaw 1880 Echelon is literally a showpiece for the SpeedSafe® mechanism. The handle is semi-translucent. Therefore, the mechanism is visible in silhouette, including operation of the Inset Liner Lock, which results in an unusually streamlined body. The thumb stud is set inside a bold relief in the blade that designers liked to refer to as "floating." The idea was to produce a discreet pocket knife that was almost ghostly, light in weight, but imminently effective.

Zero Tolerance knives are the result of KAI USA Ltd.'s desire to service the rigorous demands of the military and law enforcement. A portion of the proceeds from the sale of Zero Tolerance knives goes to the Paralyzed Veterans of America Heritage fund (pvaheritagefund. org). A new offering is the Hinderer Folder 0560, featuring an ELMAX® powdered steel blade. ELMAX® is a through-hardening, corrosion-resistant mold steel created by powder metallurgy processing techniques. Primary components are chromium, vanadium, and molybdenum. ELMAX® is also renowned for being highly wear resistant with very good dimensional stability and high compressive strength. Hardness as per the Rockwell scale can vary from 48 HRC to 62 HRC. But for knife blade applications a rating of about 58 HRC is the norm. The designer of the 0560 is Rick Hinderer. Hinderer is a first responder specializing in fire and EMT. His earliest custom knives were decidedly artful in nature. But since joining his response unit's dive team, the emphasis of his designs has shifted to hard-use tactical applications.

The Hinderer Folder 0560 is a frame-lock knife. The locking side is made from titanium. The non-locking side utilizes a heavy slab of machined G10. The stonewashed finish blade can be opened by flipper or with thumb studs that are located on both sides of the blade. The locking tab rides on a ball bearing action. Other details that make the Hinderer Folder 0560 easier to use are thumb studs that tuck out of the way after the blade is opened and a deep finger groove formed by the contour of the handle and the flipper that also becomes a guard once the blade is opened.

KERSHAW ECHELON 1880

ZERO TOLERANCE HINDERER

ECHELON 1880
Blade Length (Max): 3.25 in.
Blade Material: Sandvik 14C28N
Length (Open/Closed): 7.25 in./4 in.
Handle: G10
Lock: Liner lock (inset)
Weight: 2.6 oz.
Features: Speed assist opening; thumb stud mounted slightly forward; semi-translucent handle; reversible pocket clip; liner lock is inset for slimmer profile

Options: None
MSRP: $90

ZERO TOLERANCE

HINDERER FOLDER 0560
Blade Length (Max): 3.75 in.
Blade Material: ELMAX® powdered steel
Length (Open/Closed): 8.8 in./5 in.

Handle: G10 and Titanium
Lock: Frame lock
Weight: 5.8 oz.
Features: Stonewash finish blade; snag resistant dual thumb studs; thumb stud or flipper opening; ball bearing action; integral hand guard; locking side is titanium; right or left side tip up or tip down pocket clip
Options: None
MSRP: $325

Knives of Alaska

Charles Allen, President of Knives of Alaska, is one of the most widely respected guides and outfitters working in southeast Alaska. Experience has told him that gear plays a major role in determining the success, comfort, and enjoyment of the hunt. Developing a lineup of lifetime-guaranteed knives was Allen's way of ensuring that his customers had the best possible knives to rely upon. For the production and distribution of his knives, Allen chose to set up shop in his native state of Texas in the town of Denison, about 75 miles north of Dallas. Knives of Alaska are perhaps best known for their multiple knife sets that include as many as two or three knives, plus a sharpening stone, in the same belt sheath. Among the sixteen different varieties of combination sets are roll-up packs that include portable wood or bone saws and hatchets as well as skinning knives.

One of the most versatile and useful new offerings from Knives of Alaska is the Magnum ULU. The ULU is based on a centuries-old native Alaskan design. Its slightly oval profile offers a wide grip area above a broad heavy blade, presenting about 160 degrees of finely ground edge. Its design not only offers tre-mendous downward leverage for chopping, but the fine-edge blade can also be used for skinning. As with many blades from Knives of Alaska, the steel has been draw tempered and cryogenically treated. The ULU's compact shape allows it to be carried easily on the belt. A leather sheath with snap-over keep is supplied.

The KOA Blue/Black Assisted opening folder is an example of their new line of folders that can be used for tactical applications as well as a general service knife. Assisted opening has been added to help out when hands are full or cold weather makes removing one's gloves inconvenient or just downright inadvisable. D2 tool steel is used for the blades with an Emralon anticorrosive coating. The spine features a lined surface about midway between the handle and point of the blade. This is an alternate thumb position enabling the user to safely maneuver the tip while performing such chores as removing a hook from the mouth of a fish. Assisted opening is powered by a torsion bar. A heavy liner lock assures that the knife will stay open. There is also a cross bolt lock to keep the blade closed. This makes carrying the knife loose inside a pack or pocket all the more safe. The pocket clip is right side only and the handle material is G10 or optional Suregrip synthetic composite. Combination or plain-edged blades are available.

KNIVES OF ALASKA BLAZE
BLUE/BLACK ASSISTED OPENER

KNIVES OF ALASKA ULU

KNIVES OF ALASKA ULU POUCH

BLAZE BLUE/BLACK ASSISTED OPENER
Blade Length (Max): 3.5 in.
Blade Material: D2 Tool steel
Length (Open/Closed): 8.75 in./5.1 in.
Handle: G10
Lock: Liner lock
Weight: 4.8 oz.
Features: Torsion bar assist spring; Emralon anti-rust and corrosion coat; single side pocket clip
Options: Plain edge or partially serrated blade; black G10 handle
MSRP: $200

ULU
Blade Length: 3.4 in.
Blade Material: D2 Tool steel
Length: 3.25 in.
Handle: Suregrip rubber composite
Weight: 4.1 oz.
Features: Based on Alaskan native design; used for skinning, fleshing, and slicing; leather belt sheath
Options: None
MSRP: $65

Ontario Knife Company

Not to be confused with the province of Ontario, the Ontario Knife Company was named after its county of origin, which is located in the scenic southern tier of upstate New York. The origin of the Ontario Knife Company can be traced as far back as 1889, when production was driven by a waterpower-run grind stone located in or near the city of Naples, New York. In 1902 the company was moved to larger quarters located in Cadiz, which is now part of Franklinville, New York—its current location.

Servotronics purchased the Ontario Knife Company in 1967, but the new owners preferred to keep the well-respected OKC name. Two years later Servotronics also purchased Queen Cutlery. Queen Cutlery became OKC's "sister" company, originally specializing in the manufacture of pocket knives mostly for collectors, while OKC focused primarily on fixed-blade knives. Today, the two businesses complement each other, with Queen continuing to offer high grade traditional designs and OKC-branded knives designed for hard use by outdoorsman, military, and law enforcement.

The Ontario Knife Company Blackbird is a straightforward full-tang fixed-blade knife of simple design. The full profile blade is handled by rounded Micarta scales that include a guard profile up front and a guard before the butt to secure the grip in retraction or draw cut. The nylon MOLLE compatible sheath is lined with a Kydex guard that is ventilated for drainage and to promote drying.

Two other hard use knives are the Ranger Silver Skeleton and Neck Knife. Ranger knives are designed by Justin Gingrich, former Army Ranger. Designed for carry in pack or inside a Kydex neck sheath (supplied), these are "crossover" products that should appeal to hunters as well as special operators. Both the Ranger Silver Skeleton and Neck Knife are lightweight, durable, and very sharp.

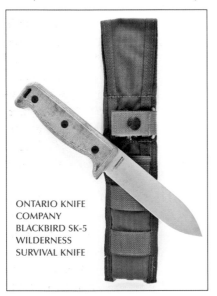

ONTARIO KNIFE COMPANY BLACKBIRD SK-5 WILDERNESS SURVIVAL KNIFE

ONTARIO KNIFE COMPANY NECK KNIFE

ONTARIO KNIFE COMPANY RANGER SILVER SKELETON

BLACKBIRD SK-5 WILDERNESS SURVIVAL KNIFE

Blade Length: 5 in.
Blade Material: 154CM
Length: 10 in.
Handle: Micarta
Weight: 8.4 oz.
Features: MOLLE/belt loop sheath; sheath has rigid protective liner with drain hole

Options: None
MSRP: $117

NECK KNIFE

Blade Length: 2.75 in.
Blade Material: 440 Stainless
Length: 7 in.
Handle: 440 Stainless
Weight: NA
Features: Kydex sheath for neck or pack
Options: None
MSRP: $80

RANGER SILVER SKELETON

Blade Length: 2.7 in.
Blade Material: 440 Stainless
Length: 6 in.
Handle: 440 Stainless
Weight: NA
Features: Kydex sheath for neck or pack
Options: None
MSRP: $80

Puma® Knife Company USA

The PUMA® trademark harkens back to the eighteenth century. That it was first registered with the Knifemakers Guild in Solingen, Germany, in 1769 tells us how long the creation of edged weapons has been a part of life in the Northern Rhine-Westphal area. More specifically, it is interesting to note that by the mid-1700s there was already a recognized guild in place. The original location of PUMA® was northeast of Solingen, along the Wupper River, but the factory was moved to the big city, which is sometimes referred to as the "City of Blades." Swordsmen of medieval times are said to have coined its crest (two swords crossed behind a ship's anchor against royal blue topped with a crown). It is estimated that some 90 percent of German knives are made in Solingen.

From the time the company was moved to Solingen in 1855 to the 1920s, PUMA® managed to establish itself on the international market. However, the company was put under the authority of the War Production board during WWII. In the years that followed, emphasis was put on the production of hunting, fishing, and outdoor knives. By 1953 staple designs, such as the Waidmesser and Jagdnicker, had been added to the catalog. In 1956, the White Hunter knife was developed in conjunction with the East African Professional Hunter's Association. The White Hunter remains one of the most versatile and popular knives available today.

In 1957, stateside distribution was established out of New York. In 2009, PUMA® Knife Company USA was established in Lenexa, Kansas. Since then the PUMA® brand has had a rebirth with reliance on the SGB™ German Blade line of knives.

One of the more interesting knives made available to the American public is PUMA® USA's Falknersheil 2, or Falcon's Shield. This may sound like the name of a Special Forces knife but it was actually designed to fill a much more utilitarian role. If you have ever been hunting with a falcon as your primary weapon then you know that falcons are as stubborn as they are proud. Once they've caught their prey, they like to hold on to it for a while. Retrieval of prey often calls for you to cut the bird's catch out of its claws. A very special knife, such as the Falknersheil 2, is called for

so this can be done without harming (or dare we say upsetting) the bird. The knife must be long enough to offer proper leverage and somewhat lithe so it can be worked in tight spaces. It actually must include two grip areas: a traditional grip area so the knife can be handled administratively (such as in and out of its sheath), and a safe grip area closer to the tip. If you will notice the Falknersheil 2 has a notch in the blade edge about halfway along its 3.8-inch length. From this point forward the edge is finely sharpened. This serves to limit the amount of cutting surface that can actually be introduced between the claws. Rearward from this notch the blade is dull. This affords a safe area of grip so the knife can be worked in shorter strokes with greater strength and more control. The sides of the blade have a bloodletting channel to help draw blood away from the tip. This helps prevent the target area from being obscured by blood. It is certainly easy to imagine other hunting applications for this knife aside from falconry. But its visual appeal alone is enough reason to make it part of one's collection.

The German Expedition Knife is a one-piece knife with skeletonized handle billed as the ultimate remote country knife. Made entirely of 1.4116 steel, a full 6.7 inches of its 11.4-inch length is devoted to a bowie-style blade. This is a handmade knife and part of PUMA® USA's gold class. It comes with a leather sheath and hardwood presentation case, but the Expedition knife is also capable of roughing it. One of PUMA® USA's most sought-after designs is the White Hunter knife.

Like other PUMA® products, the new standard offering of the White Hunter features handle scales made from true naturally dropped antler stag. The handle has a brass-lined lanyard eyelet and includes a large rounded handguard. A leather bowie-style sheath with cross guard leather keep, thigh strap, and lanyard are supplied. The 9-inch blade is designed with a thumb rest and a 1.2-inch-long row of serrations. The curved blade is suitable for cutting, slicing, and skinning. Its contours are the product of four separate grinds that produce a flat surface above the heaviest part of the blade that can be used for hammering or striking. A new offering with similar profile but in a more compact size is the Wildcat SGB™ Stag. It features natu-

Puma® Knife Company USA

www.pumaknifecompany.com

rally dropped antler Stag, polished brass hand guard, and 4.6-inch blade. The Elk Hunter Stag also offers a stag handle with guard but a slightly shorter, more stout, 4.2-inch drop point blade.

Identification of model and maker are found on the left side of all PUMA® SGB blades. On the right side can be found a tiny dot that looks like someone has touched a layer of clear coat with a fine sewing needle. This has been the cause of some buyers calling the factory to ask what is wrong with the finish. This is actually a Rockwell hardness proofmark. Whereas most makers simply claim an HRC number for a series of knives, PUMA® actually tests each knife blade individually. In 1965, PUMA® began date stamping all of their knives on the enclosed owner's information sheet. To reassure buyers that their knives are in no way defective, the company is considering the addition of an explanation of the proofmark, if not the actual reading.

Several new SGB folders—ranging from traditional to modern—are available from PUMA® USA. The most traditional is the Stockman Stag. Not only does it feature antler stag scales and polished nickel bolsters but a worked French-style nail nick on its 3-inch clip-point blade. Spey and sheepfoot blades are also included. The Boss Bone features bone scales between brass bolsters, affording this lock back workingman's knife something extra to be proud of.

The Warden Saw Wood and Trapper Stag are two lockback knives with multiple blades. The Trapper has stag scales with equal length clip and spey point blades. The secondary blade on the Warden is a wood saw with teeth that are actually quite functional. An added feature is that there are separate back locks for each blade or blade and saw. The Ranger series of lockback knives are budget priced but still offer SGB steel blades with proofmarks. The handle scales are ABS plastic for hard use, and the blades are treated to a black titanium coating.

PUMA® BOSS SGB BONE

PUMA® FALKNERSHEIL 2

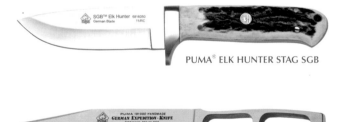

PUMA® ELK HUNTER STAG SGB

PUMA® GERMAN EXPEDITION KNIFE

BOSS SGB BONE 6169640
Blade Length (Max): 4.1 in.
Blade Material: 440A Stainless
Length (Open/Closed): 9.5 in./5.5 in.
Handle: Bone
Lock: Back lock
Weight: 5.6 oz.
Features: Rectangular "French" nail nick
Options: Jacaranda wood handle scale, $80
MSRP: $70

ELK HUNTER STAG SGB 6816050
Blade Length: 4.2 in.
Blade Material: 440A Stainless
Length: 8.5 in.

Handle: Natural dropped Stag Antler
Weight: 7 oz.
Features: Rockwell proofmark; nylon sheath
Options: None
MSRP: $100

FALKNERSHEIL 2 123515
Blade Length: 3.8 in.
Blade Material: 440A Stainless
Length: 7.8 in.
Handle: Jacaranda wood
Weight: 3.8 oz.
Features: Handmade; leather sheath

Options: None
MSRP: $500

GERMAN EXPEDITION KNIFE 181000
Blade Length: 6.7 in.
Blade Material: 1.4116 steel
Length: 11.4 in.
Handle: 1.4116 steel
Weight: 9.5 oz.
Features: Leather sheath; black hardwood presentation case
Options: None
MSRP: $448

NEW PRODUCTS

Puma® Knife Company USA

www.pumaknifecompany.com

PUMA® RANGER 20 SGB FINE EDGE

PUMA® SGB TRAPPER STAG

PUMA® DOUBLE BACK LOCK

PUMA® WARDEN W/SAW SGB WOOD

Photo courtesy by R. Eckstine.

PUMA® WILDCAT SGB STAG

PUMA® SAW TEETH

PUMA® STOCKMAN STAG HORN

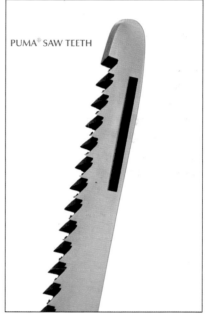

Photo courtesy by R. Eckstine.

RANGER 20 SGB FINE EDGE 623055A

Blade Length: 2.3 in.
Blade Material: 440A Stainless
Length (Open/Closed): 5.2 in./2.9 in.
Handle: ABS plastic
Lock: Back lock
Weight: 2 oz.
Features: Black titanium coated blade; rectangular "French" nail nick
Options: 2.8-inch blade, $35; 3.2-inch blade, $40
MSRP: $25

SGB TRAPPER STAG 6410631S

Blade Length (Max): 2.8 in.
Blade Material: 440A Stainless
Length (Open/Closed): 6.3 in./3.5 in.
Handle: Stag
Lock: None
Weight: 3 oz.
Features: Equal length clip and spey point blades; clip point has worked

French nail nick; Rockwell proofmark; nylon sheath
Options: 3.3-inch blades Grand Trapper, $70
MSRP: $50

STOCKMAN STAG HORN 6410675S

Blade Length (Max): 3 in.
Blade Material: 440A Stainless
Length (Open/Closed): 6.5 in./3.5 in.
Handle: Stag
Lock: None
Weight: 1.7 oz.
Features: Sheepfoor and spey point blades; clip point has worked French nail nick
Options: Brown bone scales, $40; wood, $30
MSRP: $65

WARDEN W/SAW SGB WOOD 6169623W

Blade Length: 3.7 in.

Blade Material: 440A Stainless
Length (Open/Closed): 8.5 in./2.9 in.
Handle: Jacaranda wood
Lock: Back lock
Weight: 7.2 oz.
Features: 3.7-inch saw blade; separate back lock for saw and clip point blade; rectangular "French" nail nick
Options: 4.1-inch clip point blade only, $60
MSRP: $80

WILDCAT SGB STAG 6816300

Blade Length: 4.6 in.
Blade Material: 440C Stainless
Length: 9.2 in.
Handle: Natural dropped Stag Antler
Weight: 7.6 oz.
Features: Rockwell proofmark; nylon sheath
Options: None
MSRP: $96

Remington Knives

Remington is, of course, best known for ammunition and firearms. But in 2009 they instituted the Remington Cutlery Collector's Club with admittedly little fanfare. Having recognizable brand support is a good way to build a customer base, but the latest trend is to actively compete in the hunting and law enforcement market with knives that are not just collectible but viable tools that complement one's personal battery of weapons. Nevertheless, the collector's side continues to be energized by products like the Double Lockback Trapper Bullet Knife. The Bullet Knife series is distinguished by the insignia rifle cartridge plate on the handle scale. This traditional style folder is special not only because it locks the blade open with release at the rear of the handle, but also that the premium version utilizes a Damascus steel blade. The scales are a distinctive Mahogany Gun Stock Jigged bone, and both the clip and spey point blades are approximately the same length. This knife is also available with 440HC blades.

The use of Green Bone scales accentuates another new Remington family of traditional pattern folding knives, dubbed the Heritage series. Each knife will have the Remington Arms Co. crest on its bolster. Possibly the most interesting version is the Upland Green Bone. The term "upland" refers to the type of bird hunting that takes place away from the marshes in search of ground-dwelling fowl, such as grouse and pheasant. This is a shotgunner's game, so the Upland includes a fold-out choke tube wrench that can be used for both twelve- and twenty-gauge tubes. There is also a bird hook that can be used to gut the birds.

The Elite Skinner series is a highly functional group. They can be sheathed locked open or closed. The Remington Insignia knives are available in traditional patterns, both fixed and folding, with the "R" insignia on each side of the handles. Available with black laminate scales, optional burlwood handles makes these knives look much more expensive and more enjoyable to collect.

Tactical knives can be found under the names Zulu and Tango series I and II, (fixed and folding blades respectively). Available configurations are drop, clip, or tanto-style blades.

Blade material varies according to target demographic, such as civilian, law enforcement, and military. But there are no actual limitations regarding who can buy which combination of materials. The civilian formula is a 440C stainless blade in a nylon sheath, but the buyer is just as welcome to purchase the military combination of a Mil-C 13924 blade with MOLLE sheath and leg extension (consisting of a drop-style thigh strap). The law enforcement formula also comes with a MOLLE compatible sheath but without the leg extension. The LE blade is comprised of DLC-coated N690 stainless steel. Both the Tango II and Zulu II folding blade knives are manually operated and utilize a liner locking system.

The Zulu series knives have an anodized aluminum handle with 3M non-skid inserts. The spine of the fixed-blade knives are ground with a serrated edge. The Zulu Series II folding knives are available with a plain-edged blade only.

The Tango series knives have G10 covered handles and each one offers a partially serrated combination-edged blade. The serrations are located towards the rear of the blade in an arc-like pattern that increases surface area without adding length to the blade.

Remington also offers two new folding knives for concerned citizens and first responders. Both models, the Premier Rescue Single and the Premier Rescue Double, offer a glass break punch and a 3.5-inch partially serrated sheepfoot blade. The sheepfoot configuration was chosen for its blunt point. This prevents the responder from having to worry about accidentally cutting or stabbing the victim or one's partner while cutting away clothing or a seatbelt, for example. The Rescue Double adds a hooked cutter specifically designed for these chores, so the primary blade can be saved for heavier tasks. Forprene synthetic grips with self-illuminating handles make these knives easier to locate in the dim light of a closed pack or if they are misplaced during a nighttime operation.

REMINGTON DOUBLE LOCKBACK
TRAPPER BULLET KNIFE DAMASCUS

REMINGTON ELITE
SKINNER SERIES II 19854

REMINGTON ELITE
SKINNER SERIES II 19856

REMINGTON HERITAGE
UPLAND GREEN JIGGED BONE

REMINGTON INSIGNIA BLACK LAMINATE
WOOD LARGE STOCKMAN

REMINGTON INSIGNIA
BURLWOOD CANOE

DOUBLE LOCKBACK TRAPPER BULLET KNIFE DAMASCUS 18964

Blade Length (Max): 3.5 in.
Blade Material: Damascus
Length (Open/Closed): 8 in./4.5 in.
Handle: Mahogany Gun Stock Jigged Bone
Lock: None
Weight: NA
Features: Equal length clip and spey blades
Options: 440HC blades, $122
MSRP: $266

ELITE SKINNER SERIES II 19854

Blade Length: 3 in.
Blade Material: 440C
Length (Open/Closed): 7 in./4 in.
Handle: 6061 aluminum/olive wood
Lock: Axis lock
Weight: NA
Features: Leather sheath with cross strap and pocket clip; sheath carry with blade open or closed; lanyard loop in handle
Options: Olive wood; G10 insets; black or brown sheath
MSRP: $143

ELITE SKINNER SERIES II 19856

Blade Length: 3 in.
Blade Material: 440C
Length (Open/Closed): 7 in./4 in.
Handle: 6061 aluminum/G10
Lock: Axis lock
Weight: NA
Features: Gut hook blade; leather sheath with cross strap and pocket clip; sheath carry with blade open or closed; lanyard loop in handle
Options: Olive wood; G10 insets; black or brown sheath
MSRP: $154

HERITAGE UPLAND GREEN JIGGED BONE 19833

Blade Length (Max): 3 in.
Blade Material: 440 High Carbon Stainless
Length (Open/Closed): 6.9 in./3.9 in.
Handle: Green Jigged Bone
Lock: None
Weight: NA
Features: Remington crest on bolster dating back to the 1800s; birdhook; screwdriver; choke tube wrench; 20ga, and 12ga

Options: Laminated wood scales no. 19841, $65
MSRP: $79

INSIGNIA BLACK LAMINATE WOOD LARGE STOCKMAN 19320

Blade Length (Max): 3.9 in.
Blade Material: 440 Stainless
Length (Open/Closed): 8.1 in./4.25 in.
Handle: Black laminate wood
Lock: None
Weight: NA
Features: Clip; spey; sheepfoot blade
Options: Burlwood
MSRP: $15

INSIGNIA BURLWOOD CANOE 19329

Blade Length (Max): 3.4 in.
Blade Material: 440 Stainless
Length (Open/Closed): 7 in./3.6 in.
Handle: Burlwood
Lock: None
Weight: NA
Features: Spear point and pen blade
Options: Black laminate
MSRP: $14

NEW PRODUCTS

Remington Knives

www.remington.com

REMINGTON INSIGNIA EDITION
LARGE BURLWOOD

REMINGTON PREMIER
RESCUE DOUBLE

REMINGTON PREMIER
RESCUE SINGLE

REMINGTON SPORTSMAN SERIES
INSIGNIA EDITION FIXED BLADE

REMINGTON TANGO SERIES I
CIVILIAN DROP POINT FIXED BLADE

INSIGNIA EDITION LARGE BURLWOOD 19317

Blade Length: 3.75 in.
Blade Material: 440
Length (Open/Closed): 7.75 in./4 in.
Handle: Burlwood
Lock: Liner lock
Weight: NA
Features: Thumb stud opening; leather belt sheath
Options: Black laminate wood
MSRP: $21

PREMIER RESCUE DOUBLE 19848 4

Blade Length (Max): 3.5 in.
Blade Material: 440C
Length (Open/Closed): 8.9 in./5.4 in.
Handle: Forprene (Thermoplastic)
Lock: Axis lock/Button lock
Weight: NA
Features: Teflon coat blades; glow handle insert; partially serrated sheep-foot blade; thumb stud open; auto open seatbelt cutter w/button lock; glass break stud; right side pocket clip; MOLLE compatible Cordura sheath
Options: Black or olive green handle
MSRP: $194

PREMIER RESCUE SINGLE 19847 7

Blade Length (Max): 3.5 in.
Blade Material: 440C
Length (Open/Closed): 8.9 in./5.4 in.
Handle: Forprene (Thermoplastic)
Lock: Liner lock
Weight: NA
Features: Teflon coat blades; glow handle insert; partially serrated sheep-foot blade; thumb stud open; glass break stud; reversible pocket clip; MOLLE compatible Cordura sheath
Options: Black or olive green handle
MSRP: $152

SPORTSMAN SERIES INSIGNIA EDITION FIXED BLADE 19311-2

Blade Length: 3.5 in.
Blade Material: 440 Stainless
Length: 8 in.
Handle: Black laminate
Weight: NA
Features: Black leather sheath
Options: Burlwood handle; gut hook blade
MSRP: $36

TANGO SERIES I CIVILIAN DROP POINT FIXED BLADE 19698

Blade Length: 5.25 in.
Blade Material: 440C Civilian/LE; N690 Military
Length: 10.5 in.
Handle: G10
Weight: NA
Features: Black Cordura nylon sheath
Options: Black coated blade; Teflon coat for civilian version; Mil C-13924 for law enforcement version, $205; N690 Stainless w/DLC for military, $273; Tanto, clip, or drop point blade; MOLLE compatible sheath with or w/o leg extension
MSRP: $138

REMINGTON TANGO
SERIES II

REMINGTON ZULU SERIES
II FOLDER

REMINGTON ZULU SERIES I
CIVILIAN CLIP POINT FIXED BLADE

NEW PRODUCTS

TANGO SERIES II 19706
Blade Length: 3.6 in.
Blade Material: 440C Civilian/LE; N690 Military
Length (Open/Closed): 8.4 in./4.75 in.
Handle: G10
Lock: Liner lock
Weight: NA
Features: Equal length clip and spey blades
Options: Drop, clip, or Tanto point; Teflon coat for civilian version; Mil C-13924 for law enforcement version; N690 Stainless w/DLC for military; reversible pocket clip
MSRP: **$115**

ZULU SERIES I CIVILIAN CLIP POINT FIXED BLADE
Blade Length: 4.75 in.
Blade Material: 440C Civilian/LE; N690 Military
Length: 10.5 in.
Handle: Aluminum w/3M inserts
Weight: NA

Features: Black Cordura nylon sheath
Options: Black coated blade; Teflon coat for civilian version; Mil C-13924 for law enforcement version, $205; N690 Stainless w/DLC for military, $273; Tanto, clip, or drop point blade; MOLLE compatible sheath with or w/o leg extension
MSRP: **$133**

ZULU SERIES II FOLDER
Blade Length: 3.6 in.
Blade Material: 440C Civilian/LE; N690 Military
Length (Open/Closed): 8.35 in./4.75 in.
Handle: Aluminum w/3M inserts
Lock: Liner lock
Weight: NA
Features: Equal length clip and spey blades
Options: Drop, clip, or Tanto point; Teflon coat for civilian version; Mil C-13924 for law enforcement version; N690 Stainless w/DLC for military; reversible pocket clip
MSRP: **$122**

Schrade Cutlery

Schrade Cutlery is a proud name with a very interesting history. Its roots lay with George Schrade, an inventor from Sheffield, England. The cutlery company began with the formation of the New York Press Button Knife Company in 1892. The name of the company refers to Schrade's invention and patent of a switch-controlled automatic-opening knife. About ten years later Schrade sold a partial interest in the company to the Walden Knife Company in upstate New York. By 1907 Schrade had patented an improved Safety Press Button "switch-blade" knife and opened his own company—Schrade Cutlery—in the town of Walden. For many years hence, the Schrade name dominated the automatic opening market with many twists and turns regarding sale and consolidation of the company and use of the Schrade name. Today, Schrade Cutlery is a part of Taylor Brands, LLC. That a small if not seminal maker of a landmark design is now owned by a large corporation is interesting but not necessarily remarkable. What might be looked upon with even greater interest is that one of Schrade's latest offerings is indeed an automatic/assisted opening knife. Call it irony or a distant salute to the vision of George Schrade, the Schrade Viper is an aluminum-framed knife that opens under spring-assisted pressure, folding outward from the side. In the closed position the blade is surrounded by the frame. However, the frame has an opening in its center, exposing the side of the blade. The operator pushes on the exposed surface of the blade and the assist spring does the rest. Upon reaching its fully open position, the blade automatically locks into place. In order to fold the blade, the button on the side of the frame is pushed to release the blade. Blade material is 4034 stainless steel. Blade configurations include tanto, drop, and spear point blades.

SCHRADE VIPER SIDE ASSIST
AUTO BLACK TANTO

VIPER SIDE ASSIST AUTO BLACK TANTO
Blade Length (Max): 3.2 in.
Blade Material: 4034 Stainless steel
Length (Open/Closed): 7.7 in./4.5 in.
Handle: Aluminum
Lock: Button lock open and closed
Weight: 3.4 oz.
Features: Assisted opening
Options: Spear, drop, and tanto point blade
MSRP: **$64**

SureFire

SureFire is probably better known for its blinding white light tactical flashlights than any other product. This includes handheld as well as weapon-mounted lights. But they also make super high capacity magazines, fore ends, suppressors, muzzle breaks, and rapid acquisition auxiliary sights for the AR-15 platform. Knives are listed under edged weapons on the company website, and indeed they are weapons. However, the new Charlie knife is referred to as a Folding Utility Knife. Perhaps the term "weapon"—or for that matter "tactical"—is becoming old hat. More and more operators are beginning to favor the classification "hard use" for such tools. Certainly the SureFire Charlie Folding Utility Knife EW-11, with modified spear-point blade, is up to the task of many different types of hard use. The 154CM blade is housed in a frame of aluminum and titanium. The aluminum side is black, and the titanium side is silver. The titanium side is on the right and supports the integral frame-style lock. The pocket clip is also located on the right side. The clip is mounted on the tip up end of the handle when the knife is in the folded position. There is no accommodation for the clip to be moved to any other position. The blade can be opened with either one of the dual thumb studs or by using the flipper. Once in the open position, the flipper acts as a guard, increasing the radius of the finger groove at the front of the grip.

SUREFIRE CHARLIE FOLDING
UTILITY KNIFE EW-11

SUREFIRE DART COMPACT
FOLDING UTILITY KNIFE

CHARLIE FOLDING UTILITY KNIFE EW-11
Blade Length (Max): 4.1 in.
Blade Material: 154CM
Length (Open/Closed): 8.5 in./5 in.
Handle: Titanium and 7075 aluminum
Lock: Frame lock
Weight: 5.4 oz.
Features: Dual thumb studs; thumb stud or flipper opening; integral hand guard; locking side is titanium, silver colored; aluminum side is black; right side tip up only pocket clip
Options: None
MSRP: $295

DART COMPACT FOLDING UTILITY KNIFE EW-13
Blade Length (Max): 3 in.
Blade Material: 154CM
Length (Open/Closed): 6.2 in./3.7 in.
Handle: Titanium and 7075 aluminum
Lock: Bar lock
Weight: 2.8 oz.
Features: Dual Thumb studs; enhanced access to flipper opening; bottle opener; right side tip up only pocket clip
Options: None
MSRP: $180

FIXED BLADE KNIVES

Fixed Blade Knives

Fixed blade knives have come a long way since man first recognized that a sharp object could be an asset. Just how much time has elapsed since then may one day be answered by an anthropologist, a geologist, or an amateur digger. For now we'll just marvel and celebrate the designs we can choose from today.

If you are a collector, you're going to want one of each across a broad spectrum or within a specific category, such as blade type. It might be interesting to start a collection devoted strictly to the Bowie-style knife. Subcategories could be blade length or overall length, handle material, and the different shapes and materials used for the guard, and the pommel. The variety of blade steel used might be an interesting study in itself.

Compared to folding knives, fixed blade knives are not creatures of mechanism. So many times we find that we prefer one folder over another based on how it opens and closes. There is no such distraction with a fixed blade knife. The buyer can concentrate on the grind and finish of the blade. From this perspective buyers find the fixed blade knife more essential, pure, or even more primal.

We can have a good time arguing over hand grinding versus computer-controlled production. But we have to agree that one of the truly valuable improvements modern technology has provided is the availability of better, more stable adhesives and handle materials. Sure, a full tang knife will always be stronger than a through tang or half tang design. But space-age adhesives make bondings last longer, and they are far less impervious to changes in climate than the glue that was used not that long ago. The best great aspect of today's knife market is that the most traditional methods and materials haven't gone away. Imagine you wanted to buy a brand new '55 Chevy with its big chrome bumpers or a vintage Cadillac with huge fins. You can't do that in 2012. But you can still buy a brand new skinner with leather or wood grip and stag pommel. In fact, you can bring it home in the same shopping bag as a CNC machined titanium blade knife that features carbide coating, two types of serration, and a handle covered with carbon fiber. What we're trying to say is that as ancient as the fixed blade knife might be, it may never be obsolete.

A. G. Russell™

www.agrussell.com

A. G. RUSSELL™ HOLLOW GROUND STING 3

A. G. RUSSELL™ SHOPMADE 1917 CAMP KNIFE

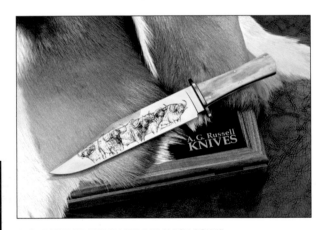

A. G. RUSSELL™ SHOPMADE BANOVICH BOWIE

A. G. RUSSELL™ SHOPMADE CALIFORNIA BOWIE

FIXED BLADE KNIVES

HOLLOW GROUND STING 3

Blade Length: 3.5 in.
Blade Material: 440C
Length: 7.25 in.
Handle: Black Linen Rucarta™
Weight: 3.9 oz.
Features: Double edged blade; leather sheath with metal boot/belt clip
Options: None
MSRP: **$100**

SHOPMADE 1917 CAMP KNIFE RU-SM8LCB-3

Blade Length: 8 in.
Blade Material: A-2
Length: 12.9 in. (approx.)
Handle: Leather/Stag

Weight: NA
Features: Bill Scagel signature Crown Stag pommel; heat treated; handmade
Options: Clip or modified clip point blade
MSRP: **$525**

SHOPMADE BANOVICH BOWIE B-1A

Blade Length: 10 in.
Blade Material: 154CM
Length: 15.4 in.
Handle: Giraffe bone
Weight: 17.4 oz.
Features: Presentation box; John Banovich signed painting, "The Defensive Line" etched on blade; stabilized bone handle; heat treated;

handmade; limited to 100 pieces
Options: None
MSRP: **$1,495**

SHOPMADE CALIFORNIA BOWIE SMR-773DI

Blade Length: 8.5 in.
Blade Material: 154CM
Length: 13.25 in.
Handle: Desert Ironwood
Weight: 12 oz.
Features: Leather sheath; Ed Henry tribute design; Henry-style stainless hand guard
Options: India stag or Leopardwood scales
MSRP: **$395**

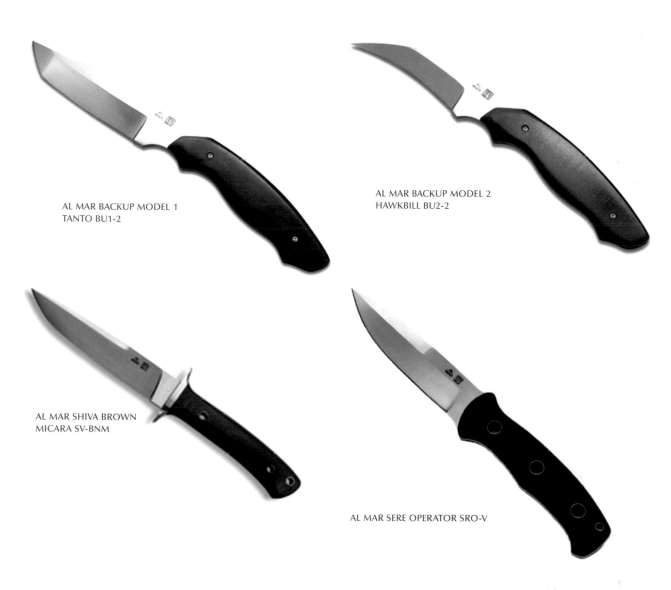

AL MAR BACKUP MODEL 1
TANTO BU1-2

AL MAR BACKUP MODEL 2
HAWKBILL BU2-2

AL MAR SHIVA BROWN
MICARA SV-BNM

AL MAR SERE OPERATOR SRO-V

BACKUP MODEL 1 TANTO BU1-2
Blade Length: 4 in.
Blade Material: AUS-8
Overall Length: 8.5 in.
Handle: Linen Micarta
Lock: Al Mar front lock
Weight: 4 oz.
Features: Leather sheath
Options: None
MSRP: $219

BACKUP MODEL 2 HAWKBILL BU2-2
Blade Length: 3 in.
Blade Material: AUS-8
Overall Length: 7.75 in.
Handle: Linen Micarta
Lock: Al Mar front lock
Weight: 3 oz.
Features: Leather sheath
Options: None
MSRP: $219

SERE OPERATOR SRO-V
Blade Length: 5 in.
Blade Material: S30V steel
Overall Length: 10.25 in.
Handle: Prylon
Weight: 6 oz.
Features: Full length tang; ambidextrous Prylon sheath; adjustable for angle
Options: Mini with 4-inch blade;

MSRO-V, $319
MSRP: $395

SHIVA BROWN MICARTA SV-BNM
Blade Length: 5.25 in.
Blade Material: Laminated VG10 Cobalt Stainless steel
Overall Length: 10 in.
Handle: Brown canvas Micarta
Weight: 5 oz.
Features: VG-10 blade laminated between two layers of 400 series Stainless steel; nickel hilt; black leather sheath
Options: Black canvas Micarta grip
MSRP: $595

Benchmade

www.benchmade.com

BENCHMADE 110H20 FIXED

BENCHMADE 201 ACTIVATOR+

BENCHMADE 141 NIMRAVUS

BENCHMADE 147 NIM CUB II

BENCHMADE 150BK MARK LEE GLORY

FIXED BLADE KNIVES

110H20 FIXED
Blade Length: 3.43 in.
Blade Material: N680 steel
Overall Length: 7.56 in.
Handle: Santoprene
Weight: 3.1 oz.
Features: Corrosive resistant; blunt tip; locking sheath
Options: Yellow grip
MSRP: $100

201 ACTIVATOR+
Blade Length: 3.63 in.
Blade Material: D2 Tool steel
Overall Length: 8.13 in.
Handle: Winewood
Weight: 2.2 oz.
Features: Full tang; leather sheath
Options: 2.1-inch blade; Model 211, $110

MSRP: $130

141 NIMRAVUS
Blade Length: 4.5 in.
Blade Material: 154CM steel
Overall Length: 4.5 in.
Handle: 6061 T-6 aluminum
Weight: 5 oz.
Features: Full tang, large finger groove
Options: Belt/MOLLE fit nylon sheath w/ color options; plain or combo edge; drop point model 140, trainer model 140T, $130
MSRP: . . . . $175–$190

147 NIM CUB II
Blade Length: 3.50 in.
Blade Material: 154CM steel

Overall Length: 7.87 in.
Handle: Noryl GTX
Weight: 1.1 oz.
Features: Full tang; belt/Molle sheath; tanto point model 148BK
Options: None
MSRP: $140

150BK MARK LEE GLORY
Blade Length: 7.3 in.
Blade Material: 154 CM steel
Overall Length: 12.5 in.
Handle: G10
Weight: 4.8 oz.
Features: Honors 1st Navy Seal killed in Iraq war; sheath included
Options: None
MSRP: $350

Benchmade

www.benchmade.com

BENCHMADE 174CBK

BENCHMADE 512 RANT

174CBK

Blade Length: 2.5 in.
Blade Material: 440C Stainless steel
Overall Length: 5.47 in.
Handle: Vinyl coated
Weight: 1.7 oz.
Features: Push dagger with double edge spear point; Kydex sheath
Options: None
MSRP: $90

512 RANT

Blade Length: 4.48 in.
Blade Material: 440C Stainless steel
Overall Length: 9.11 in.
Handle: Black Santoprene
Weight: 2.7 oz.
Feature: MOLLE fit sheath
Options: Bowie, drop, or tanto blade; plain or combo edge SS or coated; sheath colors, black or coyote
MSRP: . . . . $85–$100

Blackhawk!

www.blackhawk.com

BLACKHAWK!
CRUCIBLE FX2

BLACKHAWK! KALISTA II
15K200BK

BLACKHAWK! RAZORBACK
TROCAR

CRUCIBLE FX2 15C200BK

Blade Length: 3.2 in.
Blade Material: AUS8A Stainless steel
Length: 7.9 in.
Handle: Textured G10
Weight: 6.2 oz.
Features: Coated blade; molded nylon sheath
Options: Combo edge (15C210BK)
MSRP: $130

KALISTA II 15K200BK

Blade Length: 3.3 in
Blade Material: AUS8A Stainless steel
Length: 8.4 in.
Handle: Textured G10
Weight: 3.6 oz.
Features: Coated blade; molded nylon sheath
Options: Combo edge blade (5K210BK)
MSRP: $100

RAZORBACK TROCAR 15RT10BK

Blade Length: 3.875 in
Blade Material: AUS8A Stainless steel
Length: 7 in.
Handle: Fiberglass/nylon
Weight: 3 oz.
Features: Coated blade; molded nylon sheath
Options: Plain edge blade (15RT00BK)
MSRP: $75

FIXED BLADE KNIVES

Blade Tech

www.blade-tech.com

N'YATI
Blade Length: 5 in.
Blade Material: S30V steel
Length: 8.5 in.
Handle: G-10 Nylon
Weight: 8 oz.
Features: Indent in handle for reverse grip; Kydex sheath w/ Tek Lok belt keep
Options: Clip point blade
MSRP: **$180**

BLADE TECH N'YATI

PROFILI
Blade Length: 4.4 in.
Blade Material: N690CO steel
Length: 9 in.
Handle: Coarse G-10 Nylon
Weight: 6.4 oz.
Features: Tungsten DLC coated blade; Polypryopolene, TekLok, or MOLLE
Options: Black, earth, or sage green handle
MSRP: **$160**

BLADE TECH PROFILI

Böker USA

www.boker.de/us/

BENDER 120622
Blade Length: 2.75 in
Blade Material: 440C Stainless steel
Length: 7 in.
Handle: Micarta and Paracord
Weight: 3.5 oz.
Features: Stonewash finished blade; Kydex sheath
Options: Interchangeable handle scales (green or orange), sold separately
MSRP: **$190**

BÖKER BENDER

ORCA OUTDOOR GEN 2 120595
Blade Length: 5.25 in.
Blade Material: N690BO Stainless steel
Length: 7 in.
Handle: Micarta and Paracord
Weight: 3.5 oz.
Features: Detachable scales; Kydex sheath
Options: None
MSRP: **$350**

BÖKER ORCA OUTDOOR GEN 2

BÖKER PLUS CK1 RESCUE

BÖKER PLUS CLB MICROCOM

BÖKER PLUS KWAITO

BÖKER PLUS KAL
10 FIXED BLADE

BÖKER MAGNUM
CERAMIC BACK PACK

PLUS CK1 RESCUE 02BO284

Blade Length: 3.5 in.
Blade Material: 440C Stainless steel
Length: 7.75 in.
Handle: Zytel
Weight: 3.5 oz.
Features: Detachable handle scales; titanium coated blade; sheepsfoot tip; forward serrations; Kydex sheath; Tek-Lok belt carry
Options: None
MSRP: $50

PLUS CLB MICROCOM 02BO021

Blade Length: 2 in.
Blade Material: 440C Stainless steel
Length: 4 in.
Handle: G10

Weight: 1.5 oz.
Features: Kydex sheath; ball chain
Options: None
MSRP: $35

PLUS KAL 10 FIXED BLADE 02KAL10

Blade Length: 5.9 in.
Blade Material: 440C Stainless steel
Length: 11.25 in.
Handle: Aluminum
Weight: 12.5 oz.
Features: Notched thumb ramp; cordura sheath
Options: None
MSRP: $70

PLUS KWAITO 02BO290

Blade Length: 4.1 in.

Blade Material: Swedish Sandvik12C27
Length: 8.25 in.
Handle: G10
Weight: 3.8 oz.
Features: Kydex sheath; ball chain
Options: Belt or neck carry
MSRP: $90

MAGNUM CERAMIC BACK PACK 02LL701

Blade Length: 3.1 in.
Blade Material: Ceramic
Length: 7.5 in.
Handle: Synthetic
Weight: 1.2 oz.
Features: Socket style sheath
Options: None
MSRP: $22

Böker USA

www.boker.de/us/

BÖKER MAGNUM
COMBAT DAGGER

BÖKER MAGNUM
TANTO NECK

BÖKER MAGNUM
ELK SKINNER

BÖKER MAGNUM
YOUTH ELK HUNTER

BÖKER PLUS
GNOME STAG

MAGNUM COMBAT DAGGER 02GL033
Blade Length: 7 in.
Blade Material: 420 Stainless steel
Length: 11.75 in.
Handle: Wood
Weight: 8.5 oz.
Features: Lanyard; leather sheath
Options: None
MSRP: $50

MAGNUM ELK SKINNER 02RY688
Blade Length: 3.25 in.
Blade Material: 440C Stainless steel
Length: 7.5 in.
Handle: Rosewood and walnut
Weight: 3.7 oz.

Features: Leather sheath
Options: None
MSRP: $33

MAGNUM TANTO NECK 02MB1026
Blade Length: 3 in.
Blade Material: 440C Stainless steel
Length: 6.75 in.
Handle: G10
Weight: 2.2 oz.
Features: Kydex sheath/ball chain
Options: None
MSRP: $30

MAGNUM YOUTH ELK HUNTER 02MB362
Blade Length: 3.25 in.

Blade Material: 440C Stainless steel
Length: 6.25 in.
Handle: Rosewood and walnut
Weight: 2.2 oz.
Features: Dulled tip; leather sheath
Options: None
MSRP: $30

PLUS GNOME STAG 02BO268
Blade Length: 2.1 in.
Blade Material: 12C27 steel
Length: 4 in.
Handle: Stag
Weight: 2 oz.
Features: Neck knife; leather sheath
Options: None
MSRP: $70

Böker USA

www.boker.de/us/

PLUS RHINO STAG
02BO269
Blade Length: 3 in.
Blade Material: 12C27 steel
Length: 6.1 in.
Handle: Stag
Weight: 3.8 oz.
Features: Lanyard; leather sheath
Options: None
MSRP: $90

TERRA AFRICA II 120623
Blade Length: 4.25 in
Blade Material: N690BO steel
Length: 8.6 in.
Handle: Palmira wood
Weight: 6.5 oz.
Features: Two tone blade; leather sheath
Options: None
MSRP: $300

BÖKER PLUS RHINO STAG

BÖKER TERRA AFRICA II

Buck Knives

www.buckknives.com

060 HOOD HOODLUM
Blade Length: 10 in.
Blade Material: 5160 steel
Length: 15.5 in.
Handle: Linen Micarta
Weight: 14.6 oz.
Features: MOLLE compatible nylon sheath w/ leg strap and pouch; oxygen wrench/utility notches; removable handle scales
Options: None
MSRP: $230

113 RANGER SKINNER
Blade Length: 3.1 in.
Blade Material: 420HC
Length: 7.25 in.
Handle: Macassar Ebony dymondwood
Weight: 5.2 oz.
Features: Leather pouch
Options: None
MSRP: $80

BUCK 060 HOOD HOODLUM

BUCK 113 RANGER SKINNER

FIXED BLADE KNIVES

Buck Knives

www.buckknives.com

BUCK 119BR
SPECIAL

BUCK 141 PAKLITE
LARGE SKINNER

BUCK 391CM OMNI
HUNTER 10PT.

BUCK 499 EGO
HUNTER PRO

BUCK 498 EGO
HUNTER PRO

119BR SPECIAL
Blade Length: 6 in.
Blade Material: 420HC
Length: 10.5 in.
Handle: Cocobola dymondwood
Weight: 10.5 oz.
Features: Leather sheath
Options: Phenolic handle; aluminum butt and guard
MSRP: $119

141 PAKLITE LARGE SKINNER
Blade Length: 3.5 in.
Blade Material: 420HC
Length: 8 in.
Handle: 420HC steel
Weight: 10 oz.

Features: Nylon sheath; black traction coat handle
Options: Stainless steel color handle; 2.9-inch Skinner (140); 2.5-inch Caper (135)
MSRP: $30

391CM OMNI HUNTER 10PT.
Blade Length: 3.25 in.
Blade Material: 12C27 Mod Sandvik
Length: 7.75 in.
Handle: Alcry rubber
Weight: 4.3 oz.
Features: RealTree hardwoods; green HD camo; nylon sheath

Options: Optional camo styles
MSRP: $60

498/499 EGO HUNTER PRO
Blade Length: 4.75 in.
Blade Material: S30V
Length: 9.75 in.
Handle: Aleryn rubber/rosewood dymondwood
Weight: 7.7 oz.
Features: Includes PakLite gut hook leather combo sheath
Options: None
MSRP: $210

650 TOPS NIGHTHAWK

Blade Length: 6.5 in.
Blade Material: 420HC
Length: 11.25 in.
Handle: Nylon/rubber
Weight: 10 oz.
Features: Black oxide coated blade; MOLLE compatible nylon sheath with pouch, oxygen wrench/utility notches
Options: 4.9-inch blade (655), $95
MSRP: $110

690 TOPS C-SAR T

Blade Length: 4.5 in.
Blade Material: 420HC
Length: 10 in.
Handle: G10
Weight: 8.8 oz.
Features: MOLLE compatible nylon sheath with outer pouch; hex bit compatible handle cut-out; oxygen wrench; removable scales for spear lashing
Options: None
MSRP: $150

ALPHA HUNTER 193

Blade Length: 3.75 in.
Blade Material: 12C27 Mod Sandvik
Length: 8.5 in.
Handle: Rosewood dymondwood
Weight: 7.2 oz.
Features: Leather sheath; gut hook
Options: Standard tip blade
MSRP: $154

BUCK TOPS 650
NIGHTHAWK

BUCK 690 TOPS
C-SAR T

BUCK ALPHA
HUNTER 193

Busse Combat Knives

www.bussecombat.com

BOSS JACK LIMITED EDITION

Blade Length: 6.25 in.
Blade Material: Busse INFI
Length: 11.25 in.
Handle: Black paper Micarta
Weight: 9.6 oz.
Features: Choil; proprietary steel blade; flat sabre grind
Options: Black paper; black or tan canvas handle; black G10, add $25; two-tone G10, add $35
MSRP (as shown): $397

BUSSE BOSS
JACK LIMITED
EDITION

Busse Combat Knives

www.bussecombat.com

COMBAT BOSS JACK

Blade Length: 6.25 in.
Blade Material: Busse INFI
Length: 11.25 in.
Handle: Black paper Micarta
Weight: 11.3 oz.
Features: Choil; proprietary steel blade
Options: Convex grind; blade colors, sage, green, gray, muddy; Camo, Desert, Jungle, Urban Shadow, add $30; double cut blade, add $60; black or tan canvas handle; black or two-tone G10 add $35; with or without choil
MSRP (as shown): $267

BUSSE COMBAT BOSS JACK

Camillus Knives

www.camillusknives.com

7.75" FIXED 18509

Blade Length: 3.75 in.
Blade Material: AUS8
Length: 7.75 in.
Handle: Micarta
Weight: 7.9 oz.
Features: Carbonitride Titanium coated blade; nylon sheath
Options: None
MSRP: $50

CAMILLUS 7.75" FIXED

8" FIXED 18506

Blade Length: 3.5 in.
Blade Material: AUS8
Length: 8 in.
Handle: Bamboo
Weight: 7.5 oz.
Features: Carbonitride Titanium coated blade; nylon sheath
Options: None
MSRP: $50

CAMIILLUS 8" FIXED

8" TIGER SHARP 18568

Blade Length: 3 in.
Blade Material: AUS8
Length: 8 in.
Handle: Zytel
Weight: 7.4 oz.
Features: Replaceable blade; ships with two Titanium coated plain edge blades; nylon sheath
Options: None
MSRP: $49

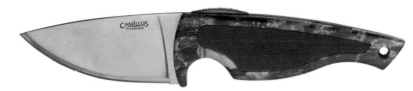

CAMILLUS 8" TIGER SHARP

Camillus Knives

8.25" FIXED 18510
Blade Length: 4 in.
Blade Material: AUS8
Length: 8.25 in.
Handle: Aluminum and nylon
Weight: 10.4 oz.
Features: Carbonitride Titanium coated blade; nylon sheath
Options: None
MSRP: $52

CAMILLUS 8.25" FIXED

8.25" TIGER SHARP 18560
Blade Length: 3.75 in.
Blade Material: AUS8
Length: 8.25 in.
Handle: Zytel
Weight: 6.6 oz.
Features: Replaceable blade; ships with two Titanium coated plain edge blades; nylon sheath
Options: None
MSRP: $49

CAMILLUS 8.25" TIGER SHARP

9" OVB LIMITED EDITION 19048
Blade Length: 4 in.
Blade Material: AUS8
Length: 9 in.
Handle: Curly maple
Weight: 12.6 oz.
Features: Carbonitride Titanium coated blade; leather sheath
Options: None
MSRP: $190

CAMILLUS 9" OVB LIMITED EDITION

9.25" FIXED 18537
Blade Length: 4.5 in.
Blade Material: AUS8
Length: 9.25 in.
Handle: Bamboo
Weight: 7.9 oz.
Features: Carbonitride Titanium coated blade; nylon sheath
Options: None
MSRP: $77

CAMILLUS 9.25" FIXED

9.75" FIXED 18538
Blade Length: 4.5 in.
Blade Material: AUS8
Length: 9.75 in.
Handle: Bamboo
Weight: 7.5 oz.
Features: Carbonitride Titanium coated blade; nylon sheath
Options: None
MSRP: $77

CAMILLUS 9.75" FIXED

FIXED BLADE KNIVES

Camillus Knives

www.camillusknives.com

10" FIXED 18508

Blade Length: 4.75 in.
Blade Material: AUS8
Length: 10 in.
Handle: Bamboo
Weight: 10.4 oz.
Features: Carbonitride Titanium coated blade; nylon sheath
Options: None
MSRP: **$65**

CAMILLUS 10" FIXED

Case Knives

www.wrcase.com

DEER HUNTER 5557

Blade Length: 3.2 in.
Blade Material: Stainless steel
Length: 7 in.
Handle: Stag
Weight: 2.7 oz.
Features: Deer design on blade; leather sheath
Options: Buffalo horn handle
MSRP: **$133**

CASE DEER HUNTER

DESK KNIFE 20104

Blade Length: 2.86 in.
Blade Material: Stainless steel
Length: 6.1 in.
Handle: Stag
Weight: 2.7 oz.
Features: Wharncliffe blade
Options: Jigged red bone, natural bone, embellished bone, dogwood, cocobolo wood, or abalone handle; palomino leather sheath
MSRP: **$166**

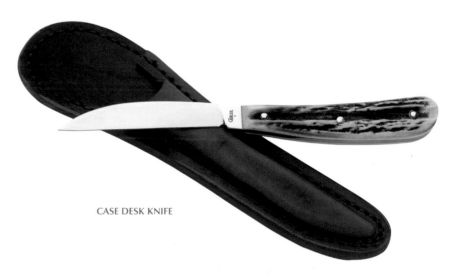

CASE DESK KNIFE

LEATHER HUNTER GUT HOOK 517

Blade Length: 4.45 in.
Blade Material: Stainless steel
Length: 8.5 in.
Handle: Polished leather
Weight: 2.7 oz.
Features: Leather sheath
Options: None
MSRP: **$93**

CASE LEATHER HUNTER GUT HOOK

CASE LIGHTWEIGHT HUNTER

CASE OUTDOOR AND HUNTING PHEASANT

CASE OUTDOOR AND HUNTING UTILITY KNIFE

CASE PRESENTATION BOWIE

CASE PRESENTATION USMC

CASE PRESENTATION KODIAK

LIGHTWEIGHT HUNTER 533

Blade Length: 4.45 in.
Blade Material: Stainless steel
Length: 8.5 in.
Handle: Polished leather
Weight: 4.2 oz.
Features: Nylon ballistic sheath
Options: Guthook blade (532)
MSRP: **$53**

OUTDOOR AND HUNTING PHEASANT 341

Blade Length: 3.25 in.
Blade Material: Stainless steel
Length: 7 in.
Handle: Stag
Weight: 2.7 oz.
Features: Pheasant image on blade; leather sheath
Options: Buffalo horn handle (397)
MSRP: **$133**

OUTDOOR AND HUNTING UTILITY KNIFE 3775

Blade Length: 5.9 in.
Blade Material: Stainless steel
Length: 10.25 in.
Handle: G10
Weight: 10.5 oz.
Features: Concave ground blade; leather sheath
Options: 9.25-inch, 10.5-inch blades; bone or orange G10 handle
MSRP: **$134**

PRESENTATION BOWIE

Blade Length: 9.5 in.
Blade Material: Stainless steel
Length: 14.25 in.
Handle: White synthetic
Weight: 20 oz.
Features: Mirror polished blade; brass guard; leather sheath
Options: None
MSRP: **$193**

PRESENTATION BOWIE USMC 334

Blade Length: 7.1 in.
Blade Material: 1095 Carbon steel
Length: 12 in.
Handle: Polished leather

Weight: 10.2 oz.
Features: Authentic reproduction
Options: None
MSRP: **$76**

PRESENTATION KODIAK 356

Blade Length: 6 in.
Blade Material: Stainless steel
Length: 10.6 in.
Handle: Stag
Weight: 11 oz.
Features: Mirror polished blade with Kodiak image; brass guard; brass butt cap; leather sheath
Options: None
MSRP: **$218**

FIXED BLADE KNIVES

Case Knives

www.wrcase.com

RIDGEBACK™ WOOD CAPER 1401
Blade Length: 3.6 in.
Blade Material: Stainless steel
Length: 8 in.
Handle: Rosewood
Weight: 4.1 oz.
Features: Leather sheath
Options: Zytel handle; drop point blade
MSRP: **$67**

CASE RIDGEBACK™ WOOD CAPER

TWIN FINN LEATHER HUNTER 2-KNIFE SET 372
Blade Length: 3.2 in./4.75 in.
Blade Material: Stainless steel
Length: 6.5 in./9.5 in.
Handle: Polished leather
Weight: 2.5 oz./5.4 oz.
Features: Single leather sheath holds both knives
Options: $62/$81 purchased separately
MSRP: **$143**

CASE TWIN FINN LEATHER HUNTER 2-KNIFE SET

Chris Reeve Knives

www.chrisreeve.com

PACIFIC
Blade Length: 6 in.
Blade Material: S35VN SS
Length: 11.5 in.
Handle: Black Micarta
Weight: 11.6 oz.
Features: Nylon and polymer combat sheath; lanyard; glass break
Options: Black leather sheath
MSRP: **$309**

CHRIS REEVE PACIFIC

Cold Steel Knives

www.coldsteel.com

DOUBLE AGENT II 39FN
Blade Length: 3 in.
Blade Material: AUS 8A
Length: 7.9 in.
Handle: Grivory
Weight: 2.4 oz.
Features: Secure-Ex neck sheath

Options: Karambit or clip point blades; plain edge or serrated
MSRP: **$45**

COLD STEEL DOUBLE AGENT II

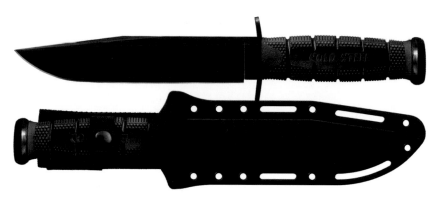

COLD STEEL LEATHERNECK SF

LEATHERNECK SF 39LSF
Blade Length: 6.75 in.
Blade Material: SK 5 High Carbon
Length: 11.75 in.
Handle: Propylene and Kraton (reg)
Weight: 10.4 oz.
Features: Secure-Ex sheath
Options: None
MSRP: $90

MIN TAC TANTO 49HT
Blade Length: 3.75 in.
Blade Material: AUS 8A
Length: 6.75 in.
Handle: G10
Weight: 2.9 oz.
Features: Secure-Ex neck sheath
Options: Beavertail, Kiridashi, or
Skinner point blades
MSRP: $65

COLD STEEL MIN TAC TANTO

COLD STEEL NATCHEZ BOWIE IN SK5

NATCHEZ BOWIE IN SK5
Blade Length: 11.75 in.
Blade Material: SK 5 High Carbon
Length: 17.1 in.
Handle: Composite wood
Weight: 24 oz.
Features: Secure-Ex sheath; brass
pommel
Options: None
MSRP: $290

FIXED BLADE KNIVES

PENDLETON CUSTOM CLASSIC 60SPH
Blade Length: 3.5 in.
Blade Material: 4116 Krupps SS
Length: 8.25 in.
Handle: Micarta
Weight: 7.1 oz.
Features: Leather sheath
Options: None
MSRP: $35

COLD STEEL PENDLETON CUSTOM CLASSIC

Cold Steel Knives

www.coldsteel.com

TANTO LITE 20T

Blade Length: 6 in.
Blade Material: 4116 Krupp Stainless
Length: 11.4 in.
Handle: Propylene and Kraton (reg)
Weight: 5.7 oz.
Features: Cordura sheath
Options: 6-inch drop point (20PH)
MSRP: $35

URBAN DART STAG HANDLE 53JDS

Blade Length: 5.75 in.
Blade Material: AUS 8A
Length: 8 in.
Handle: Sanbar stag
Weight: 3.3 oz.
Features: Secure-Ex neck sheath
Options: Kraton handle (53JD)
MSRP: $135

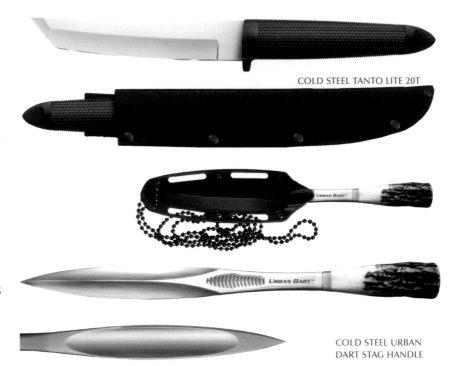

COLD STEEL TANTO LITE 20T

COLD STEEL URBAN DART STAG HANDLE

Columbia River Knife and Tool

www.ckrt.com

CRAWFORD N.E.C.K. 2030CW NO-NONSENSE EMERGENCY COMPACT KNIFE

Blade Length: 2.75 in.
Blade Material: 2CR13
Length: 6.5 in.
Handle: Paracord
Weight: 2.8 oz.
Features: Black EDP coating; recurved tanto blade; Kydex neck or belt sheath with quick attach/release loop; vertical or horizontal carry
Options: Satin finish; bare handle (2030)
MSRP: $50

F.T.W.S. FOR THOSE WHO SERVE 2060

Blade Length: 6.3 in.
Blade Material: SK 5 Carbon steel
Length: 11.6 in.
Handle: Textured Zytel
Weight: 10.8 oz.

CRKT CRAWFORD N.E.C.K. 2030 CW NO-NONSENSE EMERGENCY COMPACT KNIFE

CRKT F.T.W.S. FOR THOSE WHO SERVE

Features: Black powder coat blade; Cordura/Zytel sheath; leg or MOLLE straps
Options: None
MSRP: $160

Columbia River Knife and Tool

www.ckrt.com

CRKT GRANDPA'S FAVORITE

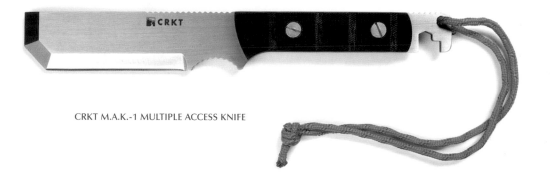

CRKT M.A.K.-1 MULTIPLE ACCESS KNIFE

CRKT SHAKAULU K900KKP

CRKT SHAKAULU SHEATH

GRANDPA'S FAVORITE 2824
Blade Length: 3.15 in.
Blade Material: Sandvik 12C27
Length: 7.3 in.
Handle: Stag
Weight: 3.8 oz.
Features: Stainless steel bolster; leather sheath
Options: None
MSRP: $175

M.A.K.-1 MULTIPLE ACCESS KNIFE 2050
Blade Length: 3 in.
Blade Material: 2CR13
Length: 10 in.
Handle: G10
Weight: 10 oz.

Features: Blunt chisel pri-bar tip blade; twist break groove; carbide glass break; 8-mm wrench; Cordura multi-pocket sheath
Options: Black Teflon finish; combo packages with belt cutter and Kydex sheath (2052)
MSRP: $90

SHAKAULU K900KKP
Blade Length: 5.5 in.
Blade Material: 65 MN Carbon steel
Length: 9.5 in.

Handle: Twin Fused PP/PTE
Weight: 15.3 oz.
Features: Pin locking Kydex sheath for inverted, right, or left side carry
Options: None
MSRP: $90

Columbia River Knife and Tool

www.ckrt.com

SHINBU 2915
Blade Length: 9.25 in.
Blade Material: YK-30 Carbon steel
Length: 14.75 in.
Handle: Cord wrap over Stingray
Weight: 13.3 oz.
Features: Kydex sheath with wide entry lips; vertical or angle mount; wood presentation box
Options: None
MSRP: $325

CRKT SHINBU

STING 2020
Blade Length: 3.2 in.
Blade Material: 1050 Carbon steel
Length: 6.85 in.
Handle: 1050 Carbon steel
Weight: 3.9 oz.
Features: Double-edged spear point; powder coat finish; Cordura/Zytel sheath
Options: None
MSRP: $60

CRKT STING 2020

ULTIMA 2125KV
Blade Length: 4.95 in.
Blade Material: 1.4116 Stainless steel
Length: 10 in.
Handle: Injection-molded Zytel
Weight: 8.4 oz.
Features: Zeff serrations; multiposition Cordura/Zytel sheath
Options: None
MSRP: $130

CRKT ULTIMA 2125KV

Dark Ops Knives

www.darkopsknives.com

INTERCEPTOR E&E DOH126
Blade Length: 8.25 in.
Blade Material: CTV2 Stainless steel
Length: 13.5 in.
Handle: Aramid composite
Weight: 10.5 oz.
Features: Back saw; splitter hilt; ballistic nylon sheath
Options: TiCarbon Nitride finish (DOH113), $229
MSRP: $249

DARK OPS INTERCEPTOR E&E

FIXED BLADE KNIVES

PAUL BASAL SHADOW DOH114

Blade Length: 8.75 in.
Blade Material: CTV2 Stainless steel
Length: 14 in.
Handle: Aramid composite
Weight: 15 oz.
Features: Back saw; finger choil; quartz impregnated grip; wire cutting notch
Options: Digital camo finish (DOH127), $249
MSRP: **$219**

RAVEN URBAN SHARK FINISH DOH188

Blade Length: 7.05 in.
Blade Material: CTV2 Stainless steel
Length: 12.2 in.
Handle: Aramid composite
Weight: 10.5 oz.
Features: Nylon sheath; glass break stud; nylon sheath for calf, thigh, belt, or vest carry
Options: TiCarbon Nitride finish, $199; hard anodized IR invisible finish, $199
MSRP: **$249**

VENDETTA NECK KNIFE DOH 110

Blade Length: 3.64 in.
Blade Material: CTV2 Stainless steel
Length: 6.8 in.
Handle: CTV2 Stainless steel
Weight: 3.8 oz.
Features: Sheath configuration for neck, ankle, or forearm carry
Options: None
MSRP: **$129**

VINDICATOR COVERT ATTACK KNIFE DOH111

Blade Length: 5.15 in.
Blade Material: CTV2 Stainless steel
Length: 10.25 in.
Handle: Synthetic composite
Weight: 7.8 oz.
Features: Nylon sheath; glass break stud; nylon sheath w/ Kydex insert; calf, thigh, shoulder, or MOLLE vest carry; Paracord grooves in handle
Options: Special finishes available
MSRP: **$219**

DARK OPS PAUL BASAL SHADOW

DARK OPS RAVEN URBAN SHARK FINISH

DARK OPS VENDETTA NECK KNIFE

DARK OPS VINDICATOR COVERT ATTACK KNIFE

FIXED BLADE KNIVES

Emerson Knives

www.emersonknives.com

EMERSON KARAMBIT FIXED BLADE

EMERSON LAGRIFFE BT

KARAMBIT FIXED BLADE
Blade Length: 3.2 in.
Blade Material: 154CM
Length: 7.6 in.
Handle: G10
Weight: 6.4 oz.
Features: Kydex belt sheath
Options: Black or silver finish
MSRP: **$258**

EMERSON POLICE UTILITY KNIFE

LAGRIFFE BT
Blade Length: 1.75 in.
Blade Material: 154CM
Length: 4.9 in.
Handle: Skeletonized 154CM
Weight: 1.5 oz.
Features: Kydex neck sheath

Options: Plain or partially serrated; black or satin finish
MSRP: **$108**

POLICE UTILITY KNIFE SF
Blade Length: 3.6 in.
Blade Material: 154CM

Length: 8.5 in.
Handle: G10
Weight: 5.5 oz.
Features: Kydex belt sheath
Options: Plain or partially serrated; black or stonewash finish
MSRP: **$248**

Gerber Knives

www.gerbergear.com

BEAR GRYLLS 31-000751
Blade Length: 4.8 in.
Blade Material: 420HC
Length: 10 in.
Handle: Rubber
Weight: 11.2 oz.
Features: Stainless steel pommel; whistle in lanyard; nylon sheath carries fire starter and sharpener
Options: None
MSRP: **$80**

GERBER BEAR GRYLLS

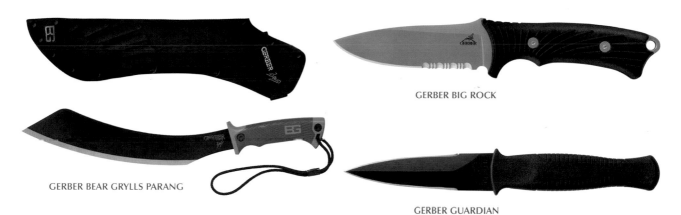

GERBER BIG ROCK

GERBER BEAR GRYLLS PARANG

GERBER GUARDIAN

GERBER LHR

GERBER METOLIUS GUT HOOK

GERBER SILVER TRIDENT

BEAR GRYLLS PARANG 31-000698
Blade Length: 13.5 in.
Blade Material: 420HC
Length: 19.5 in.
Handle: Rubber
Weight: 19.4 oz.
Features: Lanyard; nylon sheath
Options: None
MSRP: $43

BIG ROCK 22-41588
Blade Length: 4.5 in.
Blade Material: 440A
Length: 9.4 in.
Handle: Glass-filled nylon/rubber overmold
Weight: 6.3 oz.
Features: Operator only safety on sheath
Options: Plain edge blade (22-41589), $37
MSRP: $37

GUARDIAN 45803
Blade Length: 3.4 in.
Blade Material: 420HC
Length: 7.3 in.
Handle: Santoprene-covered, glass-filled nylon
Weight: 3 oz.
Features: Double-edge blade; adjustable tension sheath; SoftGrip inserts on handle
Options: None
MSRP: $60

LHR 30-000183
Blade Length: 6.9 in.
Blade Material: 420HC
Length: 12.5 in.
Handle: TacHide

Weight: 11.2 oz.
Features: Operator only safety on sheath
Options: None
MSRP: $154

METOLIUS GUT HOOK 30-000008
Blade Length: 3.75 in.
Blade Material: 9Cr19MoV
Length: 8.5 in.
Handle: Glass-filled nylon/rubber overmold
Weight: 7.7 oz.
Features: Nylon sheath

Options: Plain edge drop point blade; fixed or folding
MSRP: $37

SILVER TRIDENT 06995
Blade Length: 6.2 in.
Blade Material: 154CM
Length: 11.2 in.
Handle: Hytrel
Weight: 17.4 oz.
Features: Double edge serrated blade; nylon sheath; SoftGrip inserts on handle
Options: None
MSRP: $269

Gerber Knives

www.gerbergear.com

WARRANT TANTO
31000560

Blade Length: 4.5 in.
Blade Material: 420HC
Length: 9.5 in.
Handle: Aluminum
Weight: 54 oz.
Features: Digital camo nylon sheath
Options: None
MSRP: $43

GERBER WARRANT TANTO

Grayman Knives

graymanknives.com

GRAYMAN KNIVES DINKA

GRAYMAN KNIVES SUENAMI 5

DINKA

Blade Length: 4 in.
Blade Material: 1095 HC
Length: 8.25 in.
Handle: G10
Weight: 10.25 oz.
Features: GunKote coated blade; cordura sheath
Options: Black or green handle; free engraving up to fifteen letters
MSRP: $185

SUENAMI 5

Blade Length: 5 in.
Blade Material: 1095 HC
Length: 10.5 in.
Handle: G10
Weight: 11 oz.
Features: GunKote coated blade; cordura sheath
Options: Black or green handle; free engraving up to fifteen letters; 3.75-inch blade Suenami 4, $215; 7-inch blade Suenami 7, $255
MSRP: $235

FIXED BLADE KNIVES

Hogue Elishewitz Extreme Knives

www.elishewitzknives.com

HOGUE DAMASCUS FX-01 LIMITED EDITION

HOGUE 7-INCH FX-01 BLACK

HOGUE 5.5-INCH FX-01 TAN

5.5-INCH FX-01 TAN
Blade Length: 5.5 in.
Blade Material: A2 Tool steel
Length: 10.5 in.
Handle: G-Mascus
Weight: 10.5 oz.
Features: G10/Damascus pattern handle; nylon belt/MOLLE sheath; cryogenically heat treated; KG Gun Kote blade; wrench stored beneath handle
Options: Plain or partially serrated blade; black or stonewash finish; OD green or black handle
MSRP: $240

7-INCH FX-01 BLACK
Blade Length: 7 in.
Blade Material: A2 Tool steel

Length: 12 in.
Handle: G10
Weight: 12.5 oz.
Features: G10/Damascus pattern handle; nylon belt/MOLLE sheath; cryogenically heat treated KG Gun Kote blade; wrench stored beneath handle
Options: Plain or partially serrated; tan, OD green handle
MSRP: $250

DAMASCUS FX-01 LIMITED EDITION
Blade Length: 5.5 in.
Blade Material: Damascus Stainless
Length: 10.5 in.
Handle: Cocobolo
Weight: 11 oz.
Features: Annual limited edition; exotic hardwood handles; nylon belt/MOLLE sheath
Options: None
MSRP: $750

KA-BAR Knives

www.kabar.com

KA-BAR 9164 911 NEVER FORGET

KA-BAR BECKER ESKABAR

9164 911 NEVER FORGET
Blade Length: 7 in.
Blade Material: 1095 Cor-Van
Length: 11.9 in.

Handle: Polished leather
Weight: 11.2 oz.
Features: Leather sheath

Options: None
MSRP: $97

BECKER ESKABAR BK14
Blade Length: 3.25 in.
Blade Material: 1095 Cro-Van
Length: 7 in.
Handle: 1095 Cro-Van
Weight: 2.4 oz.
Features: Glass-filled nylon sheath
Options: None
MSRP: $56

KA-BAR Knives

www.kabar.com

KA-BAR DOG'S HEAD
TRAILING POINT HUNTER

KA-BAR BESH BOGA

KA-BAR JOHNSON ADVENTURE
BACON MAKER

KA-BAR KUKRI MACHETE

KA-BAR LARGE TDI LAW
ENFORCEMENT KNIFE

KA-BAR LARGE TDI LAW
ENFORCEMENT KINIFE TRAINER

BESH BOGA 3030BP
Blade Length: 2.2 in.
Blade Material: 3Cr13
Length: 5.5 in.
Handle: 3Cr13
Weight: 1.6 oz.
Features: Glass-filled nylon sheath
Options: None
MSRP: $23

DOG'S HEAD TRAILING
POINT HUNTER 8576
Blade Length: 3.5 in.
Blade Material: 440C
Length: 7.75 in.
Handle: Ram's Horn
Weight: 4.8 oz.
Features: Leather sheath
Options: None
MSRP: $202

JOHNSON ADVENTURE
BACON MAKER 5601
Blade Length: 7.1 in.
Blade Material: 1095 Cro-Van
Length: 12.75 in.
Handle: GFN-PA66
Weight: 13.6 oz.
Features: Cordura nylon sheath
Options: Heavy chopping blade
(Johnson Adventure Potbelly, 5600)
MSRP: $134

KUKRI MACHETE 1249
Blade Length: 11.5 in.
Blade Material: 1085 Carbon steel
Length: 17 in.
Handle: Kraton G

Weight: 27.2 oz.
Features: Leather/cordura sheath
Options: None
MSRP: $76

LARGE TDI LAW
ENFORCEMENT KNIFE 1482
Blade Length: 3.7 in.
Blade Material: AUS 8A
Length: 7.6 in.
Handle: Zytel
Weight: 9.6 oz.
Features: Glass-filled nylon sheath
Options: Tanto point blade, plain or
serrated; black, coyote brown, foliage
green handles; trainer (1489)
MSRP: $68

KA-BAR LEATHER
HANDLED GAME HOOK

KA-BAR LEATHER HANDLED LARGE SKINNER

KA-BAR TDI LAW ENFORCEMENT
KNIFE BLAZE ORANGE

KA-BAR TDI LDK
LAST DITCH KNIFE

KA-BAR TDI LAW ENFORCEMENT
MOLLE SHEATH

KA-BAR TDI LAW
ENFORCEMENT KNIFE
ANGKLE RIG

LEATHER HANDLED GAME HOOK 1234

Blade Length: 3.25 in.
Blade Material: DIN 1.4116 Stainless steel
Length: 7.25 in.
Handle: Polished leather
Weight: 3.2 oz.
Features: Leather sheath
Options: None
MSRP: $49

LEATHER HANDLED LARGE SKINNER 1237

Blade Length: 5.25 in.
Blade Material: AUS 8A
Length: 9.6 in.

Handle: Polished leather
Weight: 4.8 oz.
Features: Leather sheath
Options: None
MSRP: $51

TDI LAW ENFORCEMENT KNIFE BLAZE ORANGE 1480BO

Blade Length: 2.3 in.
Blade Material: AUS 8A
Length: 5.6 in.
Handle: Zytel
Weight: 5.6 oz.
Features: Glass-filled nylon sheath; metal belt clip

Options: Black, coyote brown, foliage green handles; plain or serrated blade; ankle rig; MOLLE sheath; trainer (1479)
MSRP: $57

TDI LDK LAST DITCH KNIFE 1478BP

Blade Length: 1.6 in.
Blade Material: 9Cr18 Stainless steel
Length: 3.60 in.
Handle: 9Cr18 Stainless steel
Weight: 2.4 oz.
Features: Glass-filled nylon sheath
Options: None
MSRP: $21

Kershaw Knives

www.kershawknives.com

KERSHAW AMPHIBIAN

KERSHAW FIELD KNIFE

KERSHAW MILITARY KNIFE

AMPHIBIAN 1006K
Blade Length: 3.75 in.
Blade Material: 420J2 Stainless steel
Length: 7.75 in.
Handle: Polymer insert
Weight: 3.2 oz.
Features: Kydex diver's sheath; press and pull release; depth/pressure compensating leg straps; double-edged, plain and serrated
Options: None
MSRP: $55

KERSHAW OUTCAST

FIELD KNIFE 1082
Blade Length: 3.25 in.
Blade Material: Sandvik 14C28N Stainless steel
Length: 7.25 in.
Handle: G10
Weight: 2.6 oz.
Features: Leather sheath
Options: Black or orange handle
MSRP: $60

KERSHAW ROCKY MTN. ELK
FOUNDATION SKINNING KNIFE

MILITARY KNIFE 4351
Blade Length: 4.5 in.
Blade Material: 1.4116 High Carbon
Length: 9 in.
Handle: POM scales
Weight: 4.4 oz.
Features: German steel; bead blast finish; polymer sheath; leg strap
Options: None
MSRP: $65

OUTCAST 1079
Blade Length: 10 in.
Blade Material: D2 Tool steel
Length: 16 in.
Handle: Santoprene

Weight: 22 oz.
Features: Teflon coat blade; Kydex sheath
Options: None
MSRP: $130

ROCKY MTN. ELK FOUNDATION SKINNING KNIFE 1080ORRMEF
Blade Length: 2.4 in.
Blade Material: Sandvik 14C28N

Stainless steel
Length: 6 in.
Handle: G10
Weight: 2.2 oz.
Features: Leather sheath; price includes logo on blade and donation to RMEF
Options: Black or orange handle without RMEF logo
MSRP: $55

KERSHAW ROUGHNECK

ROUGHNECK 1010

Blade Length: 6.25 in.
Blade Material: AUS 6A Stainless steel
Length: 11.1 in.
Handle: Co-Polymer
Weight: 6.3 oz.
Features: Leather sheath
Options: None
MSRP: **$60**

KERSHAW SEA HUNTER

SEA HUNTER 1008

Blade Length: 3.75 in.
Blade Material: 420J2 Stainless steel
Length: 7.75 in.
Handle: Polymer insert
Weight: 3.2 oz.
Features: Polymer/neon plastic diver's
sheath; press and pull release; depth/
pressure compensating leg straps;
B-belt notch; double-edged, plain and
serrated
Options: Blunt point, 1008BL-P, $50
MSRP: **$50**

KERSHAW SEA HUNTER
WITH SHEATH

Knives of Alaska

www.knivesofalaska.com

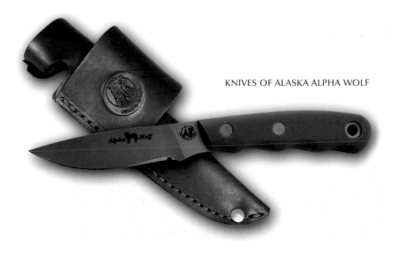

KNIVES OF ALASKA ALPHA WOLF

ALPHA WOLF D2 G10 OD

Blade Length: 3.75 in.
Blade Material: D2 Tool steel
Length: 7.9 in.
Handle: G10
Weight: 2.9 oz.
Features: Double drawn heat tem-
pered; vegetable tanned oil leather
sheath
Options: Stag handle, $155; Suregrip
composite handle, $75
MSRP: **$110**

Knives of Alaska

www.knivesofalaska.com

KNIVES OF ALASKA ALPHA WOLF
D2/CUB COMBO STAG

KNIVES OF ALASKA MAGNUM
ALASKAN GUT HOOK

KNIVES OF ALASKA SUPER
PRO PACK WOOD SAW

FIXED BLADE KNIVES

ALPHA WOLF D2/CUB COMBO STAG

Blade Length: 3.75 in./2.75 in.
Blade Material: D2 Tool steel/440C
Length: 7.9 in./6.5 in.
Handle: Stag
Weight: 5.2 oz.
Features: Double drawn heat tempered; vegetable tanned oil leather sheath
Options: With Muskrat companion knife instead of the Cub, $305
MSRP: **$295**

MAGNUM ALASKAN GUT HOOK G10

Blade Length: 4.5 in.
Blade Material: D2 Tool steel
Length: 9.5 in.
Handle: G10
Weight: 6 oz.
Features: Ceramic-peened non glare finish; vegetable tanned oil leather sheath
Options: Suregrip composite handle, $175
MSRP: **$175**

SUPER PRO PACK WOOD SAW

Blade Length: 4.5 in. Magnum Alaskan/2.75 in. Cub/2.75 in. Muskrat
Blade Material: D2 Tool steel

Dimensions (Closed): 8 in. x 6 in. x 3 in.
Handle: Knives–Suregrip composite; axe–hickory
Weight (Total): 34.5 oz.

Features: Ceramic-peened non glare finish; cordura knife pack; includes sharpening stone
Options: With bone saw, $270
MSRP: **$270**

TRIPLE COMBO STAG

Blade Length: 6.5 in. Brown Bear Cleaver/3.5 in. Light Hunter/2.75 in. Cub
Blade Material: D2 Tool steel Cleaver; D2 Tool steel Light Hunter Mini Skinner/Cleaver; 440C Cub
Length (Max): 10.4 in.
Handle: Stag
Weight (Total): 28 oz.
Features: Ceramic-peened non glare finish; Light Hunter includes gut hook; leather combo belt sheath
Options: Sure grip composite handle, $299
MSRP: $599

KNIVES OF ALASKA
TRIPLE COMBO STAG

Ontario Knife Company

www.ontarioknife.com

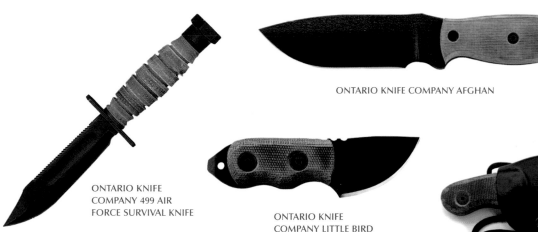

ONTARIO KNIFE COMPANY AFGHAN

ONTARIO KNIFE
COMPANY 499 AIR
FORCE SURVIVAL KNIFE

ONTARIO KNIFE
COMPANY LITTLE BIRD

ONTARIO KNIFE COMPANY
LITTLE BIRD SHEATH

FIXED BLADE KNIVES

499 AIR FORCE SURVIVAL KNIFE

Blade Length: 5 in.
Blade Material: 1095 steel
Length: 9.5 in.
Handle: Leather
Weight: 13.4 oz.
Features: Zinc Phosphate coated blade; leather sheath with sharpening stone in outer pouch; leather tie downs; steel butt cap; saw teeth on spine
Options: None
MSRP: $70

AFGHAN 9419OM

Blade Length: 5 in.
Blade Material: 5160 steel
Length: 10 in.
Handle: G10
Weight: 19.9 oz.
Features: Black powder coat blade; MOLLE compatible nylon sheath includes plastic insert and utility pouch
Options: None
MSRP: $133

LITTLE BIRD 9413OM

Blade Length: 1.75 in.
Blade Material: 1095 steel
Length: 4 in.
Handle: G10
Weight: 3.8 oz.
Features: Black powder coat blade; Kydex sheath
Options: None
MSRP: $42

Ontario Knife Company

www.ontarioknife.com

ONTARIO KNIFE COMPANY
NIGHT STALKER

ONTARIO KNIFE COMPANY
P3 ARMY QUARTERMASTER

ONTARIO KNIFE COMPANY
P4 USMC COMBAT

ONTARIO KNIFE
COMPANY RAK

NIGHT STALKER 9420BM

Blade Length: 6 in.
Blade Material: 5160 steel
Length: 11.75 in.
Handle: Micarta
Weight: 22.6 oz.
Features: Black powder coat blade; MOLLE compatible nylon sheath includes plastic insert and utility pouch
Options: None
MSRP: **$151**

P3 ARMY QUARTERMASTER 6310

Blade Length: 6 in.
Blade Material: 440A Stainless steel
Length: 10.75 in.
Handle: Stacked leather
Weight: 12.8 oz.
Features: Leather sheath
Options: None
MSRP: **$150**

P4 USMC COMBAT 6311

Blade Length: 7 in.
Blade Material: 440A Stainless steel
Length: 10.75 in.
Handle: Stacked leather
Weight: 12.8 oz.
Features: Black powder coat blade; Kydex sheath
Options: None
MSRP: **$150**

RAK 9414BCHS

Blade Length: 6 in.
Blade Material: 1095 steel
Length: 12 in.
Handle: Black Paracord
Weight: 16.3 oz.
Features: Black powder coat blade; MOLLE compatible nylon sheath; includes plastic insert and utility pouch
Options: Tan or Olive Drab Paracord; G10 or Micarta handle; plain or partially serrated edge blade
MSRP: **$95**

Ontario Knife Company

www.ontarioknife.com

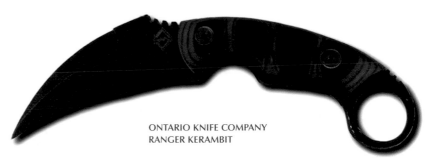

ONTARIO KNIFE COMPANY
RANGER KERAMBIT

RANGER KERAMBIT 9466

Blade Length: 3.5 in.
Blade Material: 5160 High Carbon steel
Length: 7.5 in.
Handle: Micarta
Weight: 12 oz.
Features: Black powder coat blade; Kydex sheath
Options: None
MSRP: **$208**

RANGER SHANK ORANGE G10 9410OM

Blade Length: 6.5 in.
Blade Material: 1095 steel
Length: 10.4 in.
Handle: Micarta
Weight: 8.6 oz.
Features: Black powder coat blade; nylon sheath
Options: None
MSRP: **$90**

ONTARIO KNIFE
COMPANY RANGER SHIV

RANGER SHIV 9411TCH

Blade Length: 4.5 in.
Blade Material: 1095 steel
Length: 8.4 in.
Handle: Tan Paracord
Weight: 5.9 oz.
Features: Black powder coat blade; nylon sheath
Options: None
MSRP: **$64**

ONTARIO KNIFE COMPANY RAT-5

RAT-5 8638

Blade Length: 4.75 in.
Blade Material: 1095 steel
Length: 10.75 in.
Handle: Micarta
Weight: 19.2 oz.
Features: Black powder coat blade; lined Cordura sheath includes plastic insert and utility pouch; triangular pommel edge
Options: None
MSRP: **$160**

ONTARIO KNIFE COMPANY RBS-9

RBS-9 9446BMRD

Blade Length: 9 in.
Blade Material: 1075 steel
Length: 14.9 in.
Handle: Micarta
Weight: 19.7 oz.
Features: Black powder coat blade; Kydex sheath
Options: None
MSRP: **$103**

ONTARIO KNIFE COMPANY RANGER SHANK ORANGE

FIXED BLADE KNIVES

Ontario Knife Company

www.ontarioknife.com

RS4 TAN MICARTA SERRATED 9415TMS

Blade Length: 4.5 in.
Blade Material: 5160 steel
Length: 10.25 in.
Handle: Micarta
Weight: 20.3 oz.
Features: Black powder coat blade; MOLLE compatible nylon sheath includes Kydex insert and utility pouch
Options: None
MSRP: $121

ONTARIO KNIFE RS4 TAN MICARTA SERRATED

Puma® Knife Company USA

pumaknifecompanyusa.com

PUMA® 4 STAR GRENADILL

PUMA® BOATMAN GUARD

PUMA® BOATMAN GUARD SHEATH

PUMA® BOCK

4 STAR GRENADILL 126005

Blade Length: 3.8 in.
Blade Material: 440C
Length: 8.1 in.
Handle: Grenadill wood
Weight: 7 oz.
Features: Handmade; leather sheath
Options: None
MSRP: $450

BOATMAN GUARD 136389

Blade Length: 5.1 in.
Blade Material: N680 steel
Length: 11 in.
Handle: Rubber

Weight: 7.7 oz.
Features: Blade includes line cutter, nail extractor, screwdriver, and edged pommel; hard nylon click-in sheath
Options: Available w/o guard, $275; Frogman w/Spearpoint blade, $275; Seahunter w/Drop point blade with or w/o guard, $275
MSRP: $275

BOCK 112590

Blade Length: 4.5 in.
Blade Material: 440C
Length: 9.1 in.
Handle: Stag
Weight: 5.2 oz.
Features: Hard leather sheath
Options: None
MSRP: $160

Puma® Knife Company USA

pumaknifecompanyusa.com

PUMA® KEILER

PUMA® KEILER SHEATH

PUMA® LEATHER HUNTER

PUMA® MUFFEL

PUMA® MUFFEL SHEATH

FIXED BLADE KNIVES

KEILER 112596
Blade Length: 3.7 in.
Blade Material: 420 Stainless
Length: 9.1 in.
Handle: Stag
Weight: 4.3 oz.
Features: Hard leather sheath
Options: None
MSRP: $160

LEATHER HUNTER 806374
Blade Length: 5.3 in.
Blade Material: 440C Stainless

Length: 10.4 in.
Handle: Leather
Weight: 10.5 oz.
Features: Handmade; leather sheath
Options: None
MSRP: $300

MUFFEL 112593
Blade Length: 3.9 in.

Blade Material: 420 Stainless
Length: 8.5 in.
Handle: Stag
Weight: 3.1 oz.
Features: Hard leather sheath
Options: None
MSRP: $100

Puma® Knife Company USA

pumaknifecompanyusa.com

PUMA® PRO HUNTER

PUMA® WAIDBLATT

PUMA® WHITE HUNTER SPECIAL EDITION

PRO HUNTER 116800
Blade Length: 3.6 in.
Blade Material: 440C Stainless
Length: 7.5 in.
Handle: Stag
Weight: 3.7 oz.
Features: Handmade; naturally dropped stag antlers; custom proofed Rockwell hardness; gut hook blade; leather sheath
Options: None
MSRP: $127

WAIDBLATT 113588
Blade Length: 7.9 in.
Blade Material: 1.4116 Stainless
Length: 12.8 in.
Handle: Stag
Weight: 19.6 oz.
Features: Forged guard and butt cap; naturally dropped stag antlers; custom proofed Rockwell hardness; leather sheath
Options: None
MSRP: $1,000

WHITE HUNTER SPECIAL EDITION 116075
Blade Length: 5.9 in.
Blade Material: 440C Stainless
Length: 11 in.
Handle: Stag
Weight: 12.3 oz.
Features: Handmade; naturally dropped stag antlers; nickel silver bolsters; leather sheath
Options: Standard White Hunter, $380
MSRP: $540

QUEEN CUTLERY 2050A 73ASB BEAR HEAD

QUEEN CUTLERY 2058A 98ASB SKINNER

QUEEN CUTLERY 3215 4190GMB PREMIUM HUNTER

2050A 73ASB BEAR HEAD

Blade Length: 4 in.
Blade Material: D2 steel
Overall Length: 8 in.
Handle: Aged Honey Stag Bone
Weight: 3.2 oz.
Features: Leather sheath
Options: None
MSRP: $88

2058A 98ASB SKINNER

Blade Length: 4 in.
Blade Material: D2 steel
Overall Length: 7.75 in.
Handle: Aged Honey Stag Bone
Weight: 3.2 oz.
Features: Leather sheath
Options: None
MSRP: $95

3215 4190GMB PREMIUM HUNTER

Blade Length (Max): 3.75 in.
Blade Material: NA
Overall Length: 8 in.
Handle: Gold redwood burl
Weight: 5.3 oz.
Features: Embossed leather sheath; mirror polished blade
Options: Spalted maple burl; oak wood handle
MSRP: $78

Schrade

www.schradeknives.com

SCHRADE BOOT KNIFE

SCHRADE EXTREME
SURVIVAL PACKAGE

SCHRADE EXTREME
SURVIVAL KNIFE

FIXED BLADE KNIVES

BOOT KNIFE 162OT
Blade Length (Max): 3.8 in.
Blade Material: 400 Series Stainless steel
Overall Length: 7.8 in.
Handle: Delrin
Weight: 3.9 oz.
Features: Leather sheath; mirror polished blade
Options: None
MSRP: $35

EXTREME SURVIVAL SCHF5
Blade Length (Max): 1.7 in.
Blade Material: 400 Series Stainless steel
Overall Length: 5.1 in.
Handle: Aluminum
Weight: 2.6 oz.
Features: Neck chain; pocket clip carry; knuckle guard sheath
Options: Partially serrated blade (SCHF5S)
MSRP: $34

SCHRADE FRONTIER SKINNER SCST1

FRONTIER SKINNER SCST1
Blade Length (Max): 3.7 in.
Blade Material: 400 Series Stainless steel
Overall Length: 9.7 in.
Handle: Stag

Weight: NA
Features: Leather sheath
Options: Spike, bowie, and skinner blades
MSRP: $80

Schrade

www.schradeknives.com

SCHRADE LARGE CORBY SCOR

LARGE CORBY SCOR
Blade Length (Max): 12. in.
Blade Material: 400 Series Stainless steel
Overall Length: 17.6 in.
Handle: Micarta
Weight: 14.1 oz.
Features: Leather sheath; double hand guard; Stainless steel pommel
Options: None
MSRP: **$80**

LARGE MACHETE SCHLM
Blade Length (Max): 14 in.
Blade Material: 400 Series Stainless steel
Overall Length: 19 in.
Handle: Aluminum/rubber overmold
Weight: 35.2 oz.
Features: Leather sheath
Options: None
MSRP: **$45**

SCHRADE LARGE MACHETE SCHLM

SCHRADE MINI PRO HUNTER

MINI PRO HUNTER PH2W
Blade Length (Max): 2.8 in.
Blade Material: 400 Series Stainless steel
Overall Length: 6.9 in.
Handle: Desert ironwood
Weight: 3.5 oz.
Features: Leather sheath
Options: 3.6-inch blade (Pro Hunter PHW)
MSRP: **$40**

SMALL MACHETE
Blade Length (Max): 12.5 in.
Blade Material: 400 Series Stainless steel
Overall Length: 18 in.
Handle: PP
Weight: 15.4 oz.
Features: PE/EVA synthetic sheath
Options: 16.5-inch blade (SCHMACH22)
MSRP: **$32**

SCHRADE SMALL MACHETE

FIXED BLADE KNIVES

Schrade

www.schradeknives.com

X-TIMER SCH550
Blade Length (Max): 1.7 in.
Blade Material: 400 Series Stainless steel
Overall Length: 5.1 in.
Handle: Aluminum
Weight: 2.6 oz.
Features: Kydex sheath
Options: None
MSRP: $34

SCHRADE X-TIMER

SOG Knives

sogknives.com

SOG DAGGERT 2

SOG DEMO

SOG GUNNY FIXED
BLADE KNIFE

DAGGERT 2 D26B-K
Blade Length: 6.6 in.
Blade Material: AUS 8
Length: 11.85 in.
Handle: Kraton
Weight: 8.5 oz.
Features: Bead blasted finish blade; upper edge partially serrated; Kydex sheath
Options: Black TiNi coated blade, $191; 5.65-inch black TiNi blade (D25T), $171
MSRP: $155

DEMO SSD01
Blade Length: 7.2 in.
Blade Material: AUS8
Length: 11.8 in.
Handle: Kraton
Weight: 12.3 oz.
Features: Titanium Nitride finish blade; leather sheath
Options: None
MSRP: $235

GUNNY FIXED BLADE KNIFE GFX01L
Blade Length: 7 in.
Blade Material: VG10
Length: 12.2 in.
Handle: Cocobolo wood; stingray skin; nickel
Weight: 14.1 oz.
Features: Leather sheath; display box; signed; limited to 1,000 serialized pieces
Options: None
MSRP: $750

SOG JUNGLE WARRIOR

SOG KIKU DAGGER KU-03

JUNGLE WARRIOR F14-N

Blade Length: 9.75 in.
Blade Material: 8Cr13Mov
Length: 15.25 in.
Handle: Kraton
Weight: 16.5 oz.
Features: Black oxide finish blade; DigiGrip handle; nylon sheath with utilily pouch
Options: None
MSRP: $80

SOG KIKU KU-01

KIKU DAGGER KU-03

Blade Length: 8.6 in.
Blade Material: OU 31 steel
Length: 13.75 in.
Handle: Green canvas Micarta
Weight: 16 oz.
Features: Limited edition leather sheath; presentation box; micro fine steel blade; HRc 64
Options: Tanto blade; black grip
MSRP: $3,625

SOG NW RANGER

KIKU KU-01

Blade Length: 7.5 in.
Blade Material: OU 31 steel
Length: 12.5 in.
Handle: Green canvas Micarta
Weight: 21 oz.
Features: Limited edition leather sheath; presentation box; micro fine steel blade; HRc 64
Options: Tanto blade; black grip
MSRP: $2,590

SOG PENTAGON MINI

SOG RECON BOWIE 2.0

NW RANGER S240-L

Blade Length: 5.2 in.
Blade Material: AUS 8
Length: 9.9 in.
Handle: Kraton
Weight: 6.2 oz.
Features: Leather sheath
Options: Black Titanium Nitride blade (S241), $114
MSRP: $99

PENTAGON MINI M14K

Blade Length: 3.5 in.
Blade Material: AUS 8
Length: 7.75 in.
Handle: Kraton
Weight: 3.3 oz.
Features: Plain and serrated edge; powder coat finish; Kydex sheath
Options: 5-inch blade (M14N), $104
MSRP: $88

RECON BOWIE 2.0 SRB01

Blade Length: 6.8 in.
Blade Material: AUS 8
Length: 11.4 in.
Handle: Kraton
Weight: 11.4 oz.
Features: Vietnam War era style; leather sheath
Options: None
MSRP: $235

FIXED BLADE KNIVES

SOG Knives

sogknives.com

SOG REVOLVER HUNTER

SOG REVOLVER SEAL

SOG SUPER SOG BOWIED

SOG THE FORCE

SOG THROWING KNIVES

FIXED BLADE KNIVES

REVOLVER HUNTER
FX20-N
Blade Length: 4.75 in.
Blade Material: 440A steel
Length: 10 in.
Handle: Glass reinforced nylon
Weight: 6 oz.
Features: Plain edge and gut hook blade; double tooth saw; hard nylon sheath; push panel lock in handle; lanyard loop
Options: None
MSRP: $42

REVOLVER SEAL FX21-N
Blade Length: 4.75 in.
Blade Material: 440A steel
Length: 10 in.
Handle: Glass reinforced nylon
Weight: 6 oz.
Features: Titanium Nitride finish blades; plain edge and double tooth saw; nylon sheath; push panel lock in handle; lanyard loop
Options: None
MSRP: $42

SUPER SOG BOWIED
SB1T-L
Blade Length: 7.5 in.
Blade Material: AUS 8
Length: 12.9 in.
Handle: Epoxied leather washers
Weight: 17.4 oz.
Features: Titanium Nitride coated blade; leather sheath w/ sharpening stone and pouch
Options: None
MSRP: $311

THE FORCE SE38
Blade Length: 6 in.
Blade Material: 154CM
Length: 11.25 in.
Handle: GRN
Weight: 10.5 oz.
Features: Titanium Nitride finish blade; nylon MOLLE sheath
Options: None
MSRP: $180

THROWING KNIVES
F04T-N
Blade Length: 4.4 in.
Blade Material: 420 steel
Length: 10 in.
Handle: 420 steel
Weight: 5.3 oz. (each)
Features: Package of three knives; black oxide coated blades; nylon sheath holds all three knives
Options: None
MSRP: $57

SOG TIGER SHARK 2.0

SOG VULCAN

TIGER SHARK 2.0 TE01-N

Blade Length: 9 in.
Blade Material: AUS 8
Length: 15.25 in.
Handle: Glass reinforced nylon
Weight: 16.3 oz.
Features: Powder coat finish blade; cryogenically heat treated; nylon sheath; removable handguard and rear point

Options: Black TiNi coated blade (TE02),$248; 5.65-inch black TiNi blade (D25T), $171
MSRP: **$192**

VULCAN VL51-L

Blade Length: 5.3 in.
Blade Material: VG10

Length: 10.4 in.
Handle: Glass reinforced nylon
Weight: 8.4 oz.
Features: Three grind blade; Titanium Nitride finish; leather sheath
Options: Satin finish blade (VL50), $233
MSRP: **$285**

Spyderco Knives

www.spyderco.com

SPYDERCO BILL MORAN
DROP POINT BLACK BLADE

SPYDERCO
BUSHCRAFT

BILL MORAN DROP POINT BLACK BLADE FB02BB

Blade Length: 3.94 in.
Blade Material: VG10
Length: 8.01 in.
Handle: Glass reinforced nylon
Weight: 3 oz.
Features: Kraton inserts on handle; Titanium Carbon Nitride finish; Boltaron G-clip belt or pack sheath
Options: Satin finish blade (FB02), $125; upswept blade, black or satin (FB01), $125–$140
MSRP: **$140**

BUSHCRAFT FB26G

Blade Length: 4 in.
Blade Material: O-1 Tool steel
Length: 8.75 in.
Handle: G10
Weight: 7.75 oz.
Features: Black leather sheath; inspired by Bushmen survival skills
Options: None
MSRP: **$280**

Spyderco Knives

www.spyderco.com

SPYDERCO MULE TEAM 11

SPYDERCO CASPIAN 2 SALT

SPYDERCO SHREMPP ROCK

SPYDERCO STREET BEAT

SPYDERCO TEMPERANCE 2

CASPIAN 2 SALT FB22BK
Blade Length: 4.3 in.
Blade Material: H-1
Length: 7.1 in.
Handle: Fiberglass reinforced nylon
Weight: 2.9 oz.
Features: One piece construction; corrosion resistant for divers and kayaking, etc.; FRN sheath features retention contours and nylon straps
Options: None
MSRP: $120

MULE TEAM 11 MT11
Blade Length: 3.3 in.
Blade Material: M390
Length: 7.6 in.
Handle: M390
Weight: 2.7 oz.
Features: No handle scales or sheath; budget priced invitation to personal design

Options: None
MSRP: $75

ROCK FB20FBK
Blade Length: 6.75 in.
Blade Material: VG10
Length: 12.25 in.
Handle: Fiberglass reinforced nylon
Weight: 9.1 oz.
Features: Drop handle minimizes fatigue; Boltaron G-clip belt or pack sheath
Options: None
MSRP: $235

STREET BEAT FB15
Blade Length: 3.5 in.
Blade Material: VG10
Length: 7.2 in.

Handle: Micarta
Weight: 3.2 oz.
Features: Blade/handle of equal weight; Boltaron G-clip belt or pack sheath
Options: None
MSRP: $265

TEMPERANCE 2 FB05P2
Blade Length: 4.9 in.
Blade Material: VG10
Length: 9.75 in.
Handle: Canvas Micarta
Weight: 6.75 oz.
Features: Boltaron G-clip belt or pack sheath
Options: None
MSRP: $330

Spyderco Knives

www.spyderco.com

WARRIOR FB25BK

Blade Length: 5.7 in.
Blade Material: H-1
Length: 10.6 in.
Handle: Fiberglass reinforced nylon
Weight: 8.2 oz.
Features: Corrosive resistant; ballistic nylon sheath; MOLLE compatible; 3 percent of sales go to Special Operations Warrior Foundation, www.specialops.org
Options: Black blade (FB25BBK), $450
MSRP: **$400**

SPYDERCO WARRIOR

SureFire

www.surefire.com

ECHO FIXED-BLADE COMBAT/UTILITY KNIFE EW-05

Blade Length: 4.5 in.
Blade Material: CPM S30V
Length: 8.9 in.
Handle: Micarta
Weight: 5.1 oz.
Features: Injection molded sheath; integrated DMT diamond sharpener
Options: None
MSRP: **$200**

SUREFIRE ECHO FIXED-BLADE COMBAT/UTILITY KNIFE

Tops Knives

www.topsknives.com

ALERT XL ALRTXL-01

Blade Length: 1.4 in.
Blade Material: 1095 High Carbon alloy
Length: 5.5 in.
Handle: Skeleton handle
Weight: 4 oz.
Features: Black traction coat blade; Kydex sheath; belt loop hook or neck chain
Options: XL03 offers Micarta scales
MSRP: **$65**

TOPS ALERT XL

Tops Knives

www.topsknives.com

BAGDAD BOX CUTTER BBC01

Blade Length: 2.25 in.
Blade Material: 1095 High Carbon alloy
Length: 4.9 in.
Handle: Skeletonized
Weight: 4.3 oz.
Features: Black traction coat blade; Kydex sheath; belt loop hook or neck chain
Options: Partially serrated blade, +$15; camo finish blade, +$30
MSRP: **$69**

BAGDAD BULLET BAGD-03

Blade Length: 3.5 in.
Blade Material: 1095 High Carbon alloy
Length: 6.25 in.
Handle: G10
Weight: 4.4 oz.
Features: Black traction coat blade; Kydex sheath w/ multi position steel clip
Options: Partially serrated blade, +$15; tactical gray color blade, +$30; black G10 handle
MSRP: **$99**

B.E.S.T. BLACK EAGLE STRIKE TEAM BE5020HP

Blade Length: 7 in.
Blade Material: 154CM-CRYO
Length: 12 in.
Handle: Canvas Micarta
Weight: 22 oz.
Features: Double heat treated blade; traction coat blade; ballistic nylon sheath
Options: Partially serrated blade, +$15; camo finish, +$30; treaded grip, +$30
MSRP: **$299**

C.A.T COVERT ANTI-TERRORISM 201

Blade Length: 3.25 in.
Blade Material: 1095 High Carbon alloy
Length: 7.25 in.
Handle: Skeletonized
Weight: 4.1 oz.
Features: Black traction coat blade; Kydex sheath w/ rotating steel clip
Options: Partially serrated blade, +$15; camo coat blade, +$30; Code Yellow coat blade, +$10; black G10 handle
MSRP: **$69**

FIXED BLADE KNIVES

TOPS BAGDAD BOX CUTTER

TOPS BAGDAD BULLET

TOPS B.E.S.T. BLACK EAGLE STRIKE TEAM

TOPS C.A.T. COVERT ANTI-TERRORISM

TOPS CHEETAH XL

TOPS DEVILS ELBOW XL

TOPS PATHFINDER Q134

TOPS POWER EAGLE PE-12

CHEETAH XL CH262-XL
Blade Length: 4 in.
Blade Material: 1095 High Carbon alloy
Length: 8 in.
Handle: Linen Micarta
Weight: 7.7 oz.
Features: Tactical gray color blade; Kydex sheath w/ rotating steel clip
Options: Partially serrated blade +$15; camo finish blade, +$30; 3.25-inch blade (CH262), $79; 3.25-inch Stainless steel blade; cord wrapped handle (CH262-SKEL), $69
MSRP: $149

DEVILS ELBOW XL DEV-01
Blade Length: 2.1 in.
Blade Material: 1095 High Carbon alloy
Length: 6 in.
Handle: Linen Micarta
Weight: 4.2 oz.
Features: Black traction coat blade; Kydex sheath w/ rotating steel clip
Options: Partially serrated blade, +$15; camo finish blade, +$30
MSRP: $99

PATHFINDER Q134 PFS-01
Blade Length: 4 in.
Blade Material: 1095 High Carbon alloy
Length: 9.25 in.
Handle: Linen Micarta
Weight: 10.6 oz.
Features: Tactial gray color blade; Kydex sheath
Options: Tan nylon sheath
MSRP: $199

POWER EAGLE PE-12
Blade Length: 12 in.
Blade Material: 51-60 spring steel
Length: 17.6 in.
Handle: Canvas Micarta
Weight: 25.6 oz.

Features: Black traction coat blade; elastic hand lanyard; nylon sheath
Options: Partially serrated blade, +$15; camo finish blade, +$30; Micarta scales, treaded or plain, +$30
MSRP: $200

FIXED BLADE KNIVES

Tops Knives

www.topsknives.com

TOPS RANGER
SHORT-STOP

RANGER SHORT-STOP RSS01

Blade Length: 3.1 in.
Blade Material: 1095 High Carbon alloy
Length: 6.25 in.
Handle: Linen Micarta
Weight: 6 oz.
Features: Black traction coat blade;
Options: Partially serrated blade, +$15; camo finish blade, +$30
MSRP: **$119**

WALKABOUT MICARTA WAB-01

Blade Length: 3.6 in.
Blade Material: 1095 High Carbon alloy
Length: 8.75 in.
Handle: Linen Micarta
Weight: 6.7 oz.
Features: Black traction coat blade; Kydex sheath w/ rotating steel clip
Options: Partially serrated blade, +$15; camo finish, +$30; treaded grip, +$30
MSRP: **$129**

TOPS WALKABOUT
MICARTA

WOLF PUP WP010

Blade Length: 2.5 in.
Blade Material: 1095 High Carbon alloy
Length: 5.25 in.
Handle: Micarta
Weight: 4 oz.
Features: Black traction coat blade; Kydex sheath w/ rotating steel clip
Options: Partially serrated blade, +$15; camo finish, +$30; treaded grip, +$30; 3.5-inch Blade XL (WO011), $129
MSRP: **$75**

TOPS WOLF PUP

FIXED BLADE KNIVES

Zero Tolerance Knives

zerotoleranceknives.com

ZERO TOLERANCE ALL-BLACK FIXED BLADE

ZERO TOLERANCE BLACK FIXED BLADE

ZERO TOLERANCE FIXED BLADE COMBAT KNIFE 0160

ZERO TOLERANCE FIXED BLADE COMBAT KNIFE 0170

ZERO TOLERANCE RANGER GREEN FIXED BLADE

ZERO TOLERANCE S30V BAYONET

ALL-BLACK FIXED BLADE 0100
Blade Length: 5.75 in.
Blade Material: CPM3V Tool steel
Length: 10.5 in.
Handle: G10
Weight: 11.4 oz.
Features: Tungsten DLC coated blade; nylon and Kydex sheath
Options: None
MSRP: $325

BLACK FIXED BLADE 0150
Blade Length: 3.5 in.
Blade Material: S30V
Length: 7.5 in.
Handle: G10
Weight: 3.6 oz.
Features: Kydex sheath; belt or MOLLE carry; PVD coated blade
Options: None
MSRP: $160

FIXED BLADE COMBAT KNIFE 0160
Blade Length: 5 in.
Blade Material: 14C28N
Length: 10 in.
Handle: G10
Weight: 8 oz.
Features: Tungsten DLC coated blade; Kydex sheath
Options: None
MSRP: $130

FIXED BLADE COMBAT KNIFE 0170
Blade Length: 5.7 in.
Blade Material: 14C28N
Length: 11.5 in.
Handle: G10
Weight: 11 oz.
Features: Tungsten DLC coated blade; Kydex sheath
Options: None
MSRP: $150

RANGER GREEN FIXED BLADE 0121
Blade Length: 4.25 in.

Blade Material: S30V
Length: 8 in.
Handle: G10/Titanium
Weight: 9.2 oz.
Features: Tungsten DLC coated blade; Kydex sheath; belt or MOLLE carry; cord cutter notch
Options: None
MSRP: $250

S30V BAYONET ZT-9
Blade Length: 7.5 in.
Blade Material: S30V
Length: 12.5 in.
Handle: G10
Weight: 19.4 oz.
Features: Stone washed finish blade; polymer sheath/nylon harness
Options: None
MSRP: $325

FOLDING KNIVES

Folding Knives

Folding blade knives have always been a handy tool but not always the safest one to use. If that seems like harsh criticism, let's put it in perspective. We're not that far removed from the Industrial Revolution, and it took years for safety devices to become mandatory. The immediate objective of the new machines was to increase production and do the work of many. The issue of making them safe to operate, or be around, was addressed later. The same could be said for folding knives. The safe use of early folding knives relied solely upon the user. Cutting with force applied in the proper direction held the blade open. Skill and vigilance were your best safety mechanism against the blade folding shut accidentally. In this light fixed blade knives were considered safer only because you always knew where the cutting edge was going to be.

Today, there are at least two major developments that have made folding blade knives vastly more popular than fixed blade knives. The first is the development of the locking blade. Slip-joint knives may be better than ever, but the surety of a mechanical lock has allowed consumers to handle folding knives with greater confidence by feeling more in control of the blade. You can handle a folding blade knife administratively all day long without ever seeing the blade edge. The other development that has created a boom in sales is the acceptance of the locking folder as a means of personal defense and rescue in case of emergency. In terms of emergency application, this reaches well beyond the need to extricate yourself or someone else from a wrecked automobile. The threat of terrorist attack has created the desire for the citizen to have some manner of survival tool easily at hand.

In terms of personal defense, the very concept of defending oneself has become more widely accepted. One reason may be an erosion of confidence in the police or the government to provide protection. Another is the fact that states that issue concealed handgun licenses are seeing lower violent crime statistics than states or municipalities that forbid citizens the tools to fend for themselves.

You may have noticed that gun shows are increasingly advertised as gun and knife shows. That's further evidence that tactical knives and combat folders are driving sales. Even some of the hardcore traditional "camp knife" or "pocket knife" manufacturers are beginning to make noise about offering lock blade knives aimed at the personal defense market. Elsewhere in this book you will find a comprehensive description of handling knives for self defense. Features such as locks, thumb studs, and grip material all play a part in their effectiveness. In the pages that follow you'll be able to match features to meet your needs. We hope the specifications charts will help you narrow down your choices, whether the knife is going to be used for self defense, cutting linoleum, skinning a deer, spaying cattle, gutting a bird, splicing wire, dividing and measuring grains of aspirin, loosening a knot of wet rope, cutting a leather pattern, installing a shotgun choke tube, or just playing a game of mumblety-peg in the backyard.

A. G. Russell™

www.agrussell.com

3 ⅝ INCH GUNSTOCK CQ14 CO/YD/BR

Blade Length: 2.9 in.
Blade Material: 8Cr13MoV
Length (Open/Closed): 6.5 in./3.6 in.
Handle: Cocobolo, Delrin, or Rucarta™
Lock: Lockback
Weight: 3 oz.
Features: Oversized nail nick for opening; braided leather thong
Options: Cocobolo handle scales (CQ14 CO), $55; Yellow Delrin handle scales (CQ14YD), $45; Black Rucarta™ scales (CQ14BR), $50
MSRP: . . . .$45–$55

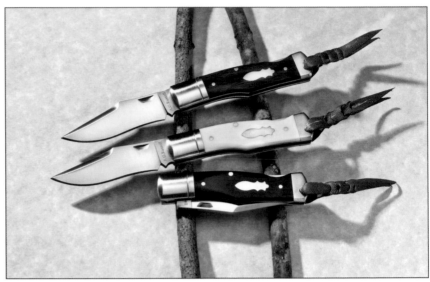

A. G. RUSSELL™ 3 ⅝ INCH GUNSTOCK

A. G. RUSSELL™ ACIES TITANIUM FRAME LOCK

ACIES TITANIUM FRAME LOCK RUS-UF12ZDP

Blade Length: 3.6 in.
Blade Material: ZDP-189
Length (Open/Closed): 8.1 in./4.5 in.
Handle: Titanium (Ti6A14V)
Lock: Frame lock
Weight: 4.8 oz.
Features: Licensed Hinderer stabilizer on frame lock; right side pocket clip; thumb stud open
Options: Tip up or tip down pocket clip upon request
MSRP $375

A. G. RUSSELL™ DOG LEG TRAPPER

DOG LEG TRAPPER RUS-JT13 CO/ES

Blade Length (Max): 2.75 in.
Blade Material: VG10
Length (Open/Closed): 6.2 in./3.45 in.
Handle: Cocobolo or European Stag
Lock: None (slip joint)
Weight: 3.6 oz.
Features: Scales fashioned from European Red Deer antler
Options: Cocobolo handle scales (RUS-JT13 CO), $165; European Stag handle scales (RUS-JT13 ES), $195
MSRP: . . . .$165–$195

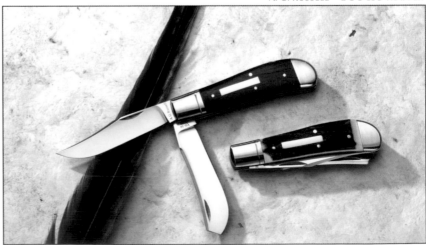

DOZIER TAB LOCK TRAPPER RUS-TD12G10

Blade Length: 3.75 in.
Blade Material: D2
Length (Open/Closed): 8.5 in./4.75 in.
Handle: G-10
Lock: Dozier tab lock
Weight: 5 oz.
Features: Thumb stud opening; right side pocket clip
Options: None
MSRP **$145**

A. G. RUSSELL™ DOZIER TAB LOCK TRAPPER

A. G. RUSSELL™ FEATHERLIGHT™

FEATHERLIGHT™ K93C/B KYD

Blade Length: 3.1 in.
Blade Material: AUS8
Length (Open/Closed): 7 in./3.9 in.
Handle: Zytel®
Lock: AGR one hand lock
Weight: 1.5 oz.
Features: Kydex neck sheath with chain; thumb hole open
Options: Clip point (K93C) or general purpose blade (K93B); ATS-34 hardened steel blade
MSRP: **$50**

SEAMASTER AGSA-118TI

Blade Length (Max): 3.25 in.
Blade Material: ATS-34
Length (Open/Closed): 7.25 in./4.1 in.
Handle: Titanium
Lock: Frame lock
Weight: 3.15 oz.
Features: 2.75-inch 303 Stainless Marlin spike; combination edge with serrations in front; made in Italy; *Blade Magazine* award for Most Innovative Import of the Year 2004
Options: None
MSRP: **$275**

A. G. RUSSELL™
SEAMASTER

FOLDING KNIVES

Al Mar Knives

www.almarknives.com

AL MAR EAGLE
ULTRA-LIGHT PLAIN

AL MAR FALCON
COCOBOLO TALON
1003 CT

AL MAR FALCON
ULTRALIGHT 40%
SERRATED

AL MAR HAWK
ULTRALIGHT 40%
SERRATED

AL MAR HAWK
ULTRALIGHT TALON

AL MAR MINI SERE
2000 MS2K

AL MAR MINI SERE 2000
MS2KB

EAGLE ULTRA-LIGHT PLAIN 1005UBK2
Blade Length: 4 in.
Blade Material: Steel AUS-8
Length (Open/Closed): 9 in./5 in.
Handle: Linen Micarta
Lock: Al Mar front lock
Weight: 2 oz.
Features: Dual stainless steel thumb studs; ambidextrous clip
Options: Black or stainless, combo blade; polished Micarta scales
MSRP: $165

FALCON COCOBOLO TALON 1003 CT
Blade Length: 3.15 in.
Blade Material: AUS 8 Steel
Length (Open/Closed): 7.15 in./4 in.
Handle: Cocobolo Wood
Lock: Al Mar front lock
Weight: 3 oz.
Features: Talon blade
Options: None
MSRP: $219

FALCON ULTRALIGHT 40% SERRATED 1003UBK4
Blade Length: 3.15 in.
Blade Material: AUS 8 Steel
Length (Open/Closed): 7.15 in./4 in.
Handle: Linen Micarta
Lock: Al Mar front lock
Weight: 1.25 oz.
Features: Reversible clip
Options: Plain edge or Talon blade
MSRP: $165

HAWK ULTRALIGHT 40% SERRATED 1002UBK4
Blade Length: 2.75 in.
Blade Material: AUS-8
Length (Open/Closed): 6 in./3.25 in.
Handle: Linen Micarta
Lock: Al Mar front lock
Weight: 0.95 oz.
Features: Dual stainless steel thumb studs; ambidextrous clip
Options: Black or stainless blade; polished Micarta scales
MSRP: $145

HAWK ULTRALIGHT TALON 1002UBK2T
Blade Length: 2.75 in.
Blade Material: AUS-8
Length (Open/Closed): 6 in./3.25 in.
Handle: Linen Micarta
Lock: Al Mar front lock
Weight: 2 oz.
Features: Dual stainless steel thumb studs; ambidextrous clip
Options: Black or stainless combo blade; polished Micarta scales
MSRP: $145

MINI SERE 2000 MS2K
Blade Length: 3 in.
Blade Material: VG10 Stainless steel
Length (Open/Closed): 7 in./4 in.
Handle: Textured G10
Lock: Liner lock
Weight: 3.5 oz.
Features: Dual thumb studs; cobalt stainless steel blade; reversible deep pocket clip; pillar construction
Options: None
MSRP: $285

MINI SERE 2000 MS2KB
Blade Length: 3 in.
Blade Material: VG10 Stainless steel
Length (Open/Closed): 7 in./4 in.
Handle: Textured G10
Lock: Liner lock
Weight: 3.5 oz.
Features: Dual thumb studs; cobalt stainless steel blade with black ceramic coating; reversible deep pocket clip; pillar construction
Options: None
MSRP: $285

FOLDING KNIVES

Al Mar Knives

www.almarknives.com

AL MAR NOMAD ND2

AL MAR OSPREY ABALONE

AL MAR SERE 2000 S2K

AL MAR PAYARA AM-PM2

AL MAR SHRIKE SKE-2G

AL MAR STOUT LITTLE BACKUP SLB 1

AL MAR TALON HAWK CLASSIC BROWN MICARTA

NOMAD ND2

Blade Length: 3 in.
Blade Material: VG10 Stainless steel
Length (Open/Closed): 7 in./4 in.
Handle: Textured G10
Lock: Liner lock
Weight: 3.5 oz.
Features: Dual thumb studs; cobalt stainless steel blade; heat treated liner; pillar construction
Options: None
MSRP: $285

OSPREY ABALONE 1001AB

Blade Length: 1.65 in.
Blade Material: Steel AUS-8
Length (Open/Closed): 3.95 in./1.3 in.
Handle: Abalone
Lock: Al Mar front lock
Weight: 0.95 oz.
Features: Stainless steel liner; leather pouch
Options: Stag, bone, cocobolo wood, stainless steel, or mother of pearl handle
MSRP: $195

PAYARA AM-PM2

Blade Length: 4 in.
Blade Material: VG-10
Length (Open/Closed): 8.5 in./4.5 in.
Handle: Textured G10
Lock: Liner lock
Weight: 6 oz.
Features: Dual thumb studs, stainless steel clip; named after fish that feed on the piranha; designed for the outdoorsman
Options: None
MSRP: $265

SERE 2000 S2K

Blade Length: 3.6 in.
Blade Material: VG10 Stainless steel
Length (Open/Closed): 8.5 in./4.9 in.
Handle: Textured G10
Lock: Liner lock
Weight: 6 oz.
Features: Dual thumb studs; cobalt stainless steel blade; satin finish; named for Army Sere School; reversible deep pocket clip; pillar construction

Options: Black ceramic finish, add $10
MSRP: $295

SHRIKE SKE-2G

Blade Length: 4 in.
Blade Material: VG10 Stainless steel
Length (Open/Closed): 8.5 in./4.5 in.
Handle: Textured G10
Lock: Liner lock
Weight: 6 oz.
Features: Dual thumb studs; Stainless steel clip; trailing point blade; a Rexroat design
Options: None
MSRP: $255

STOUT LITTLE BACKUP SLB 1

Blade Length: 1.75 in.
Blade Material: AUS 8 steel
Length (Open/Closed): 4.6 in./2.85in.
Handle: Linen Micarta
Lock: Liner lock
Weight: 1.5 oz.
Features: Knife can double as a money clip
Options: None
MSRP: $145

TALON HAWK CLASSIC BROWN MICARTA 1002UBN2T

Blade Length: 2.75 in.
Blade Material: AUS-8
Length (Open/Closed): 6 in./3.25 in.
Handle: Micarta
Lock: Al Mar front lock
Weight: 0.95 oz.
Features: Stainless steel liner; leather pouch
Options: Stag, bone, cocobolo wood, Stainless steel, or mother of pearl handle
MSRP: $120

Benchmade

www.benchmade.com

BENCHMADE 5300
AUTO PRESIDIO

BENCHMADE AUTO SPIKE

BENCHMADE INFIDEL

BENCHMADE OPPORTUNIST

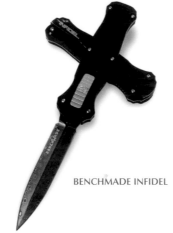

BENCHMADE
LEOPARD CUB

INFIDEL 3300-81 OTF

Blade Length: 3.95 in.
Blade Material: Damascus
Length (Open/Closed): 8.91 in./5 in.
Handle: 6061-T6 aluminum
Lock: Out the Front Double Auto
Weight: 5 oz.
Features: Double edged Damascus blade; presidio handle; heat treated hardware; Gold Class; limited run of 50 pieces
Options: None
MSRP: **$850**

LEOPARD CUB 612-101

Blade Length: 2.87 in.
Blade Material: Damascus
Length (Open/Closed): 6.78 in./3.81 in.
Handle: Skeletonized aluminum
Lock: Liner lock
Weight: 3.70 oz.
Features: Delbert Ealy Lion pattern blade; blue anodized Jeweled liner; Gold Class; limited run of 100 pieces
Options: None
MSRP: **$1,200**

5300 AUTO PRESIDIO

Blade Length: 3.44 in.
Blade Material: 154CM
Length (Open/Closed): 8.3 in./4.86 in.
Handle: 6061-T6 aluminum
Lock: Axis pull release
Weight: 5.8 oz.
Features: Integrated safety
Options: Coated or SS; plain or combo edge blade
MSRP: . . . . **$240–$255**

AUTO SPIKE 1000-101

Blade Length: 3.41 in.
Blade Material: Damascus
Length (Open/Closed): 9.24 in./4.52 in.
Handle: Titanium
Lock: Push button auto
Weight: 4 oz.
Features: Devin Thomas Reptilian Damascus Manual safety; titanium clip and spacers; Gold Class; limited run of 100 pieces
Options: None
MSRP: **$1,200**

OPPORTUNIST 440TICF-71

Blade Length: 2.99 in
Blade Material: S30V Stainless steel
Length (Open/Closed): 6.83 in./3.34 in.
Handle: Titanim/Carbon fiber
Lock: Modified locking liner
Weight: 1.7 oz.
Features: Blue nickel hardware, blue Topaz thumb stud; modified Wharncliff blade; Gold class
Options: None
MSRP: **$350**

Benchmade

www.benchmade.com

BENCHMADE PINNACLE

BENCHMADE 53 MANGUS BALI-SONG

BENCHMADE 530

BENCHMADE 755 MPR

BENCHMADE 111H2O FOLDER

530

Blade Length: 3.25 in.
Blade Material: 154CM Stainless steel
Length (Open/Closed): 7.42 in./4.17 in.
Handle: Grivory
Lock: Axis
Weight: 1.9 oz.
Features: Modified spear point; ambidextrous thumb studs
Options: Black coated blade, $120
MSRP: $105

111H2O FOLDER

Blade Length: 3.45 in.
Blade Material: N680 steel
Length (Open/Closed): 8.07 in./4.62 in.
Handle: Grivory (reg)
Lock: Axis
Weight: 4.9 oz.
Features: Ambidextrous thumb stud; tip-up pocket clip
Options: Black handle
MSRP: $125

755 MPR

Blade Length: 2.9 in.
Blade Material: M390 super steel
Length (Open/Closed): 6.9 in./3.8 in.
Handle: Titanium and G10
Lock: Monolock
Weight: 5.5 oz.
Features: Tip-down pocket clip only
Options: Black coated blade, $250
MSRP: $235

BENCHMADE BLUE CLASS

PINNACLE 750-101

Blade Length: 3.65 in.
Blade Material: Damasteel
Length (Open/Closed): 8.36 in./4.71 in.
Handle: Titanium/Carbon fiber
Lock: Titanium Monolock
Weight: 4.5 oz.
Features: USA Infinity pattern blade; DLC finished hardware and clip; Gold Class; limited run of 200 pieces
Options: None
MSRP: $800

53 MANGUS BALI-SONG

Blade Length: 3.15 in.
Blade Material: D2 Tool steel
Length (Open/Closed): 7.82 in./4.67 in.
Handle: G10
Lock: Aluminum catch
Weight: 3.5 oz.
Features: Aluminum back spacer, latch, and catch; ball bearing pivot; reversible tip up pocket clip
Options: None
MSRP: $180

FOLDING KNIVES

Benchmade
www.benchmade.com

BENCHMADE AGENCY 340

BENCHMADE EMISSARY 470

BENCHMADE GRIPTILLIAN 550SHG

BENCHMADE GRIPTILLIAN 551S

FOLDING KNIVES

AGENCY 340
Blade Length: 2.38 in.
Blade Material: 440C Stainless steel
Length (Open/Closed): 5.63 in./3.25 in.
Handle: Valox
Lock: Liner
Weight: 1.65 oz.
Features: Assisted opening
Options: Black coated blade, $85
MSRP: $70

EMISSARY 470
Blade Length: 3 in.
Blade Material: S30V Stainless steel
Length (Open/Closed): 6.9 in./3.9in.
Handle: Aluminum alloy
Lock: Axis
Weight: 2.2 oz.
Features: Assisted opening with safety

Options: None
MSRP: $200

GRIPTILLIAN 550SHG
Blade Length: 3.45 in.
Blade Material: 154CM Stainless steel
Length (Open/Closed): 8.07 in./4.62 in.
Handle: Glass filled nylon
Lock: Axis
Weight: 3.25 oz.
Features: Thumb hole opening modified sheepsfoot blade
Options: Black coated blade; sand, olive drab, yellow, blue, or pink handle; 550HG offers plain edged blade; 550T training version, $80
MSRP: . . . . $105–$125

GRIPTILLIAN 551S
Blade Length: 3.45 in.
Blade Material: 154CM Stainless steel
Length (Open/Closed): 8.07 in./4.62 in.
Handle: Glass filled nylon
Lock: Axis
Weight: 3.25 oz.
Features: Ambidextrous thumb stud
Options: Handle colors, sand, olive drab, yellow, blue, and pink; plain edge or corrosion resistant blade; 551T training version, $80
MSRP: . . . . $105–$125

Benchmade

www.benchmade.com

GRIPTILLIAN 553

Blade Length: 3.45 in.
Blade Material: 154CM Stainless steel
Length (Open/Closed): 8.07 in./4.62 in.
Handle: Glass filled nylon
Lock: Axis
Weight: 3.25 oz.
Features: Thumb stud opening; tanto blade
Options: Handle colors sand and olive drab; SS or black coated blade, plain or combo edge; 557 Mini, $95–$115
MSRP: . . . . $105–$125

GRIPTILLIAN 555HG-BLU

Blade Length: 2.91 in.
Blade Material: 154CM Stainless steel

Length (Open/Closed): 6.78 in./3.87 in.
Handle: Glass filled nylon
Lock: Axis
Weight: 2.56 oz.
Features: Thumb hole opening modified sheepsfoot blade
Options: Sand, olive, drab, yellow, black, or pink handle; combo edge blade
MSRP: . . . . $95–$110

GRIPTILLIAN 556S

Blade Length: 2.91 in.
Blade Material: 154CM Stainless steel
Length (Open/Closed): 6.78 in./3.87 in.
Handle: Glass filled nylon
Lock: Axis
Weight: 2.56 oz.

Features: Ambidextrous thumb stud
Options: Handle colors, sand, olive drab, yellow, blue, and pink; 5556HG plain edge blade
MSRP: . . . . $95–$110

GRIPTILLIAN 557SBK

Blade Length: 3.45 in.
Blade Material: 154CM Stainless steel
Length (Open/Closed): 8.07 in./4.62 in.
Handle: Glass filled nylon
Lock: Axis
Weight: 3.25 oz.
Features: Ambidextrous thumb studs
Options: SS or coated blade; handle colors, sand, olive drab, and black
MSRP: . . . . $95–$115

BENCHMADE GRIPTILLIAN 553

BENCHMADE GRIPTILLIAN 555HG-BLU

BENCHMADE GRIPTILLIAN 556S

BENCHMADE GRIPTILLIAN 557SBK

FOLDING KNIVES

Benchmade

www.benchmade.com

BENCHMADE MINI-MORPHO 32 BAIL-SONG

MINI-MORPHO 32 BALI-SONG

Blade Length: 3.25 in.
Blade Material: D2 Tool steel
Length (Open/Closed): 7.64 in./4.34 in.
Handle: G10
Lock: Spring latch
Weight: 2.7 oz.
Features: Titanium blue anodized and jeweled liners; anodized laser engraved pocket clip
Options: Model 51 4.25-inch blade, $265
MSRP: **$240**

BENCHMADE OPPORTUNIST 440

BENCHMADE PAUL 230 A1

OPPORTUNIST 440

Blade Length: 2.99 in.
Blade Material: S30V Stainless steel
Length (Open/Closed): 6.83 in./3.84 in.
Handle: 6061-T6 aluminum
Lock: Liner
Weight: 1.7 oz.
Features: Stabilized wood scales
Options: None
MSRP: **$180**

PAUL 230 A1

Blade Length: 3.9 in.
Blade Material: 154CM steel
Length (Open/Closed): 9 in./5.1 in.
Handle: G10
Lock: Paul Axial
Weight: 3.8 oz.
Features: Push button manual open
Options: Coco Bolo or Ivory Micarta scales, add $10
MSRP: **$200**

PAUL 235 A2

Blade Length: 2.58 in.
Blade Material: AUS-8 steel
Length (Open/Closed): 5.97 in./3.39 in.
Handle: Carbon fiber
Lock: Paul Axial
Weight: 1.6 oz.
Features: Push button manual open; sheath included
Options: Coco Bolo or Ivory Micarta scales, no charge
MSRP: **$120**

PAUL 240 A3

Blade Length: 2.37 in.
Blade Material: 154CM steel
Length (Open/Closed): 5.8 in./3.43 in.
Handle: G10
Lock: Paul Axial
Weight: 2.1 oz.
Features: Push button manual open
Options: Coco Bolo or Ivory Micarta scales, no charge
MSRP: **$140**

BENCHMADE PAUL 235 A2

BENCHMADE PAUL 240 A3

FOLDING KNIVES

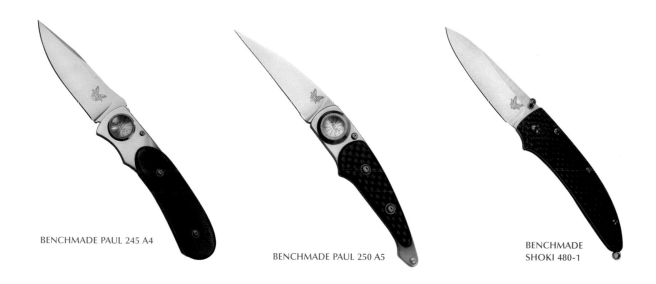

BENCHMADE PAUL 245 A4

BENCHMADE PAUL 250 A5

BENCHMADE
SHOKI 480-1

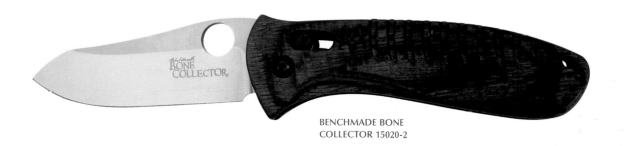

BENCHMADE BONE
COLLECTOR 15020-2

FOLDING KNIVES

PAUL 245 A4
Blade Length: 3.12 in.
Blade Material: 154CM steel
Length (Open/Closed): 7.24 in./4.12 in.
Handle: G10
Lock: Paul Axial
Weight: 3.7 oz.
Features: Push button manual open
Options: Coco Bolo or Ivory Micarta scales, add $10
MSRP: $180

PAUL 250 A5
Blade Length: 2.20 in.
Blade Material: 420HC steel
Length (Open/Closed): 5.4 in./3.2 in.
Handle: Coco Bolo
Lock: Paul Axial
Weight: 1.6 oz.
Features: Push button manual open;

sheath included
Options: Carbon fiber or Ivory Micarta scales, no charge
MSRP: $110

SHOKI 480-1
Blade Length: 2.89 in.
Blade Material: M390 super steel
Length (Open/Closed): 6.67 in./3.79 in.
Handle: Carbon fiber
Lock: Nak-Lok
Weight: 1.7 oz.
Features: Crowned Blade spine; blue anodized titanium liner; nickel plated hardware; IWA Knife of the Year 2008
Options: Model 480 offers G10/wood handle, S30V blade, $200
MSRP: $220

BENCHMADE BONE COLLECTOR

15020-2
Blade Length: 3.36 in.
Blade Material: D2 Tool steel
Length (Open/Closed): 8.2 in./4.84 in.
Handle: Walnut
Lock: Axis
Weight: 5.59 oz.
Features: Thumbhole opening
Options: Black G10, black/green G10 combo edge blade
MSRP: . . . . $150–$155

Benchmade

www.benchmade.com

BENCHMADE BONE COLLECTOR 15030-1

BENCHMADE 523 PRESIDIO ULTRA

BENCHMADE 860BK BEDLAM

BENCHMADE 913D2 NITROUS

BENCHMADE 915 TRIAGE

15030-1
Blade Length: 2.95 in.
Blade Material: D2 Tool steel
Length (Open/Closed): 7.08 in./4.13 in.
Handle: Walnut
Lock: Axis
Weight: 3.46 oz.
Features: Thumbhole opening
Options: Black G10, walnut handle; combo edge blade
MSRP: . . . . **$135–$140**

BENCHMADE BLACK CLASS FOLDING KNIVES

523 PRESIDIO ULTRA
Blade Length: 3.42 in.
Blade Material: 154CM Stainless steel
Hardness/Grind: 58-61RC/Hollow
Length (Open/Closed): 8.29 in. /4.87 in.
Handle: 6061T-6 aluminum
Lock: Axis
Weight: 5.62 oz.
Features: Dual thumb studs
Options: Available w/ drop point, tanto, plain, or serrated, coated or stainless blade, $185–$200; Models 522/527 Presidio Ultras use 440C steel and Noryl GTX handles, $95–$125;

Trainer, 520T, also available; Model 525 offers 2.97-inch blade
MSRP: **$185**

860BK BEDLAM
Blade Length: 3.95 in.
Blade Material: 154CM Stainless steel
Hardness/Grind: 58-61 HRC/Hollow
Length (Open/Closed): 9.71 in./5.76 in.
Handle: G10
Lock: Axis
Weight: 5.1 oz.
Features: Stainless steel liners; reversible clip
Options: Plain or serrated, coated or stainless blade, $220–235
MSRP: **$235**

913D2 NITROUS
Blade Length: 3.7 in.
Blade Material: D2 Tool steel
Hardness/Grind: 60-62 HRC/Hollow
Length (Open/Closed): 8.38 in./4.68 in.
Handle: Black/Green G10
Lock: Liner
Weight: 5.59 oz.
Features: Dual thumb studs; nitrous assist opening; titanium liners
Options: Modified drop point; plain edge stainless finish, $150
MSRP: **$165**

915 TRIAGE
Blade Length: 3.5 in.
Blade Material: N680 steel
Hardness/Grind: 57-59 HRC/Hollow
Length (Open/Closed): 8.2 in./4.7 in.
Handle: G10
Lock: Axis
Weight: 5.1 oz.
Features: 440C steel hook shaped safety cutter; carbide glass break; dual thumb studs; stainless steel liners, reversible clip
Options: Black or orange handle; sheath, black or coyote, add $25
MSRP: . . . . **$165–$180**

BENCHMADE 950SBK RIFT

BENCHMADE 2550 MINI REFLEX

BENCHMADE 3150 IMPEL

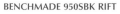

BENCHMADE 3300 INFIDEL

BENCHMADE 3550SBK

950SBK RIFT

Blade Length: 3.67 in.
Blade Material: 154CM Stainless steel
Hardness/Grind: 58-61 HRC/Hollow
Length (Open/Closed): 8.27 in./4.8 in.
Handle: G10
Lock: Axis
Weight: 5.1 oz.
Features: Stainless steel liners; reversible clip
Options: Plain or serrated, coated or stainless blade, $185–$200
MSRP: $200

BENCHMADE BLACK CLASS AUTOMATIC OPENING

2550 MINI REFLEX

Blade Length: 3.16 in.
Blade Material: 154CM steel
Length (Open/Closed): 7.32 in./4.36 in.
Handle: 6061 T-6 aluminum

Lock: Push button
Weight: 2.7 oz.
Features: Automatic opening; integrated safety
Options: Plain edge, $190
MSRP: $205

3150 IMPEL

Blade Length: 1.98 in.
Blade Material: S30V Stainless steel
Length (Open/Closed): 5.03 in./3.06 in.
Handle: Aluminum/G10
Lock: Push button
Weight: 2.1 oz.
Features: Automatic opening; integrated safety
Options: Coated blade, $175
MSRP: $160

3300 INFIDEL

Blade Length: 3.91 in.
Blade Material: D2 Tool steel
Length (Open/Closed): 8.91 in./5.06 in.
Handle: 6061 T-6 aluminum

Lock: Thumb slide
Weight: 4.9 oz.
Features: Automatic opening; integrated cleaning port; double-edged spear point
Options: Coated blade; 3310 offer single edge blade, coated, combo or plain edge, $450–$460; Mini-Infidel 3350, 3.1-inch double-edged blade, $380
MSRP: $450

3550SBK

Blade Length: 2.98 in.
Blade Material: 154CM steel
Length (Open/Closed): 7.1 in./4.1 in.
Handle: 6061 T-6 aluminum
Lock: Push button
Weight: 2.8 oz.
Features: Automatic opening; integrated safety
Options: Model 3550 offers plain edge SS blade, $190
MSRP: $205

FOLDING KNIVES

Benchmade

www.benchmade.com

BENCHMADE 3800BK NTK

5270 MINI AUTO PRESIDIO ULTRA

Blade Length: 2.97 in.
Blade Material: 440C Stainless steel
Length (Open/Closed): 7.12 in./4.15 in.
Handle: Noryl GTX
Lock: Axis pull release
Weight: 3.1 oz.
Features: Automatic opening; integrated safety
Options: Coated or SS, plain or combo edge blade; 5220 Presidion Ultra offers 3.5-inch blade, $205–$220
MSRP: . . . . **$185–$200**

3800BK NTK

Blade Length: 3.9 in.
Blade Material: D2 Tool steel
Length (Open/Closed): 8.78 in./4.88 in.
Handle: Nylon
Lock: Double action liner
Weight: 5.8 oz.
Features: Automatic opening; integrated safety; dual thumb studs; Stainless steel liners
Options: Combo edge, coated, or SS
MSRP: **$215**

BENCHMADE 5270 MINI AUTO PRESIDIO ULTRA

8600BK AUTO BEDLAM

Blade Length: 4 in.
Blade Material: 154Cm Stainless steel
Length (Open/Closed): 9.76 in./5.76 in.
Handle: G10
Lock: Axis pull release
Weight: 4.8 oz.
Features: Automatic opening; integrated safety
Options: Coated combination edge, no charge
MSRP: **$275**

9101SBK AGENCY

Blade Length: 3.6 in.
Blade Material: 154CM Stainless steel
Length (Open/Closed): 8.3 in./4.7 in.
Handle: 6061 T-6 aluminum
Lock: Push button
Weight: 4.2 oz.
Features: Automatic opening; integrated safety
Options: Plain edge blade; 9500 offers 2.95-inch blade, $205
MSRP: **$250**

BENCHMADE 8600BK AUTO BEDLAM

BENCHMADE 9101SBK AGENCY

9555S AUTO RIFT
Blade Length: 3.67 in.
Blade Material: 154Cm Stainless steel
Length (Open/Closed): 8.27 in./4.6 in.
Handle: G10
Lock: Axis pull release
Weight: 4.8 oz.
Features: Automatic opening; integrated safety; reverse tanto blade
Options: Plain, combo edge, coated, or SS
MSRP: $240

BENCHMADE 9555S AUTO RIFT

Blackhawk!
www.blackhawk.com

BLACKHAWK! CQD MKI 15M301BK

BLACKHAWK! CQD MKI 15M401BK

BLACKHAWK! CRUCIBLE II FOLDER

BLACKHAWK! HAWKPOINT

CQD MKI 15M301BK
Blade Length: 3.75 in.
Blade Material: 440C Stainless steel
Length (Open/Closed): 9.5 in./5.75 in.
Handle: Aluminum
Lock: Button lock
Weight: 7.8 oz.
Features: Black PVD coated blade; secondary safety; carbide glass breaker; seat belt/cord cutter; reversible clip
Options: Combo edge blade (15M301BK)
MSRP: $250

CQD MKI 15M401BK
Blade Length: 3.3 in.
Blade Material: 440C Stainless steel
Length (Open/Closed): 7.95 in./4.65 in.

Handle: Aluminum/rubber
Lock: Button lock
Weight: 4.4 oz.
Features: Black PVD coated blade; secondary safety; carbide glass breaker; reversible spring steel clip
Options: Combo edge blade (15M411bK)
MSRP: $250

CRUCIBLE II FOLDER 15C201BK
Blade Length: 3.25 in.
Blade Material: AUS8A Stainless steel
Length (Open/Closed): 8 in./4.75 in.
Handle: Textured G10
Lock: Liner lock
Weight: 6.25 oz.

Features: Black PVD coated blade; reversible pocket clip
Options: Combo edge blade (15C211)
MSRP: $90

HAWKPOINT 15HP01BK
Blade Length: 2.375 in.
Blade Material: AUS8A Stainless steel
Length (Open/Closed): 5.625 in./3.25 in.
Handle: Fiberglass/nylon
Lock: Liner lock
Weight: 4 oz.
Features: Black PVD coated blade; right side pocket clip tip-down
Options: Combo edge blade (15HP11BK)
MSRP: $45

FOLDING KNIVES

Blackhawk!

www.blackhawk.com

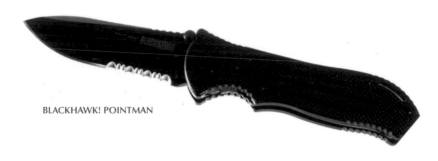

BLACKHAWK! POINTMAN

POINTMAN 15PM11BK

Blade Length: 3.4 in.
Blade Material: AUS8A Stainless steel
Length (Open/Closed): 7.8 in./4.4 in.
Handle: Textured G10
Lock: Liner lock
Weight: 6.25 oz.
Features: Black PVD coated blade; reversible pocket clip
Options: Plain edge blade (15PM01BK)
MSRP: $99

Blade Tech

www.blade-tech.com

BLADE TECH BLACKWOLF

BLADE TECH KATANA LITE

BLADE TECH GANYANA LITE

BLADE TECH PRO HUNTER MAGNUM

BLACKWOLF

Blade Length: 3.6 in.
Blade Material: S30V steel
Length (Open/Closed): 8.5 in./4.9 in.
Handle: G10 Nylon
Lock: Liner
Weight: 4.8 oz.
Features: Reversible pocket clip; V-hole opening; DLC coated blade
Options: None
MSRP: $220

GANYANA LITE

Blade Length: 2.75 in.
Blade Material: AUS 8 steel
Length (Open/Closed): 6.75 in./3.4 in.
Handle: Fiberglass reinforced nylon
Lock: Liner lock
Weight: 2.6 oz.
Features: Reversible pocket clip; thumbhole opening
Options: Handle colors orange, green, or black
MSRP: $27

KATANA LITE

Blade Length: 6.75 in.
Blade Material: AUS 8 steel
Length (Open/Closed): 6.75 in./3.4 in.
Handle: Fiberglass reinforced nylon
Lock: Liner lock
Weight: 2.6 oz.
Features: Reversible pocket clip; V-hole opening
Options: Handle colors gray or black
MSRP: $27

PRO HUNTER MAGNUM

Blade Length: 3.6 in.
Blade Material: S30V steel
Length (Open/Closed): 8.5 in./4.9 in.
Handle: Linen Micarta
Lock: Liner lock
Weight: 4.8 oz.
Features: Reversible pocket clip; thumbhole opening
Options: Handle colors orange, green, or black
MSRP: $200

FOLDING KNIVES

Blade Tech

www.blade-tech.com

BLADE TECH RATEL LITE

BLADE TECH U.L.U.

RATEL LITE
Blade Length: 1.9 in.
Blade Material: AUS 8 steel
Length (Open/Closed): 4.9 in./3.1 in
Handle: Fiberglass reinforced nylon
Lock: Liner lock
Weight: 2.1 oz.
Features: Reversible pocket clip;
V-hole opening
Options: Handle colors black, gray, or
pink
MSRP: $24

U.L.U.
Blade Length: 3.75 in.
Blade Material: AUS 8 Steel
Length (Open/Closed): 8.6 in./4.9 in.
Handle: Aluminum w/rubber inserts
Lock: Liner lock
Weight: 2.1 oz.

Features: Universal Locking Utility;
handle can be locked directly above
blade
Options: Handle colors black or
orange
MSRP: $60

Böker USA

www.boker.de/us/

2011 ANNUAL DAMASCUS COLLECTOR'S KNIFE
Blade Length: 2.6 in.
Blade Material: Damascus stainless
steel
Length (Open/Closed): 6.25 in./3.65
in.
Handle: Desert ironwood
Lock: Liner lock
Weight: 3.6 oz.
Features: Hand forged 300 layer rain
drop pattern; nail nick opening
Options: None
MSRP: $600

CONGRESS 110720
Blade Length (Max): 2.1 in.
Blade Material: High Carbon steel
Length (Open/Closed): 5.7 in./3.6 in.
Handle: Smooth red bone
Lock: None
Weight: 3.2 oz.
Features: Four blades; opposing hing-
es; nail nick open
Options: Stag and bone handles
MSRP: $40

DINOSAUR GENTLEMAN'S KNIFE
Blade Length: 2 in.
Blade Material: Stainless steel
Length (Open/Closed): 6.25 in./3.65 in.
Handle: Sauropod bone
Lock: Lockback
Weight: 1.75 oz.
Features: Handle scales made from
petrified dinosaur bone
Options: None
MSRP: $400

BÖKER CONGRESS

BÖKER 2011 ANNUAL DAMASCUS
COLLECTOR'S KNIFE

BÖKER DINOSAUR
GENTLEMAN'S KNIFE

Böker USA
www.boker.de/us/

BÖKER HADDOCK DLC

BÖKER ILLUMINATION TOP LOCK

BÖKER ILLUMINATION TURBINE

BÖKER MAGNUM DEEP BLUE

BÖKER MAGNUM DEFILADE

BÖKER MAGNUM ELK HUNTING FOLDER

FOLDING KNIVES

HADDOCK DLC 110617DLC
Blade Length: 3.4 in.
Blade Material: N690BO steel
Length (Open/Closed): 7.6 in./4.2 in.
Handle: G10
Lock: Titanium frame lock
Weight: 4 oz.
Features: Titanium back liners; CNC machined handles; nail nick open; two-way clip
Options: None
MSRP: $300

ILLUMINATION TOP LOCK110018
Blade Length: 3.25 in.
Blade Material: 4043 Stainless steel
Length (Open/Closed): 7.25 in./4.6 in.
Handle: Aluminum
Lock: Button (non-auto)
Weight: 4 oz.
Features: Handle glows in the dark; Cordura belt sheath
Options: None
MSRP: $175

ILLUMINATION TURBINE 110126
Blade Length: 3 in.
Blade Material: X-15 TN steel
Length (Open/Closed): 7 in./4.1 in.
Handle: AIMgSi/G10 inlay
Lock: Liner lock
Weight: 4.5 oz.
Features: Blade glows in the dark; thumb stud and flipper; Cordura belt sheath
Options: None
MSRP: $280

MAGNUM DEEP BLUE 01SC156
Blade Length: 2.4 in.
Blade Material: 440 Stainless steel
Length (Open/Closed): 5.9 in./3.5 in.
Handle: Rosewood
Lock: Frame lock
Weight: 1.5 oz.
Features: Lanyard hole and pocket clip
Options: None
MSRP: $19

MAGNUM DEFILADE
Blade Length: 3 in.
Blade Material: 440 Stainless steel
Length (Open/Closed): 7.1 in./4.1 in.
Handle: Aluminum
Lock: Liner lock
Weight: 3.2 oz.
Features: Titanium coated blade
Options: None
MSRP: $22

MAGNUM ELK HUNTING FOLDER
Blade Length: 2.6 in.
Blade Material: 440 Stainless steel
Length (Open/Closed): 6 in./3.4 in.
Handle: Rosewood and walnut
Lock: Liner lock
Weight: 2.8 oz.
Features: Pocket clip; nail nick open
Options: None
MSRP: $22

MAGNUM FIRST RESPONDER 01SC157

Blade Length: 2.75 in.
Blade Material: 440 Stainless steel
Length (Open/Closed): 6.6 in./3.9 in.
Handle: Synthetic
Lock: Liner lock
Weight: 3.3 oz.
Features: Seatbelt cutter; glass break; can opener; pocket clip
Options: None
MSRP: $25

MAGNUM FISHBONE

Blade Length: 3.25 in.
Blade Material: 440 Stainless steel
Length (Open/Closed): 8.5 in./5.25 in.
Handle: Aluminum
Lock: Liner lock
Weight: 5.8 oz.
Features: Milled grip; titanium coated blade
Options: None
MSRP: $22

MAGNUM SMOOTHIE

Blade Length: 3.4 in.
Blade Material: 440 Stainless steel
Length (Open/Closed): 8 in./4.6 in.
Handle: Pakka wood
Lock: Liner lock
Weight: 4.3 oz.
Features: Thumb stud; no pocket clip
Options: None
MSRP: $22

MOKUME DAMASCUS 110144DAM

Blade Length: 3.1 in
Blade Material: Damascus stainless steel
Length (Open/Closed): 7 in./3.9 in.
Handle: Imbuia wood
Lock: Back lock
Weight: 4.3 oz.
Features: Thomas forged 150 Typhoon pattern; Japanese Mokume bolsters; presentation box
Options: None
MSRP: $550

PLUS CARBON

Blade Length: 2.9 in.
Blade Material: 440C Stainless steel
Length (Open/Closed): 6.9 in./4 in.
Handle: Carbon fiber
Lock: Push button (non-auto)
Weight: 2.5 oz.
Features: Titanium liners; two tone blade
Options: None
MSRP: $100

PLUS ELEGANCE

Blade Length: 2.6 in.
Blade Material: 440C Stainless steel
Length (Open/Closed): 6 in./3.4 in.
Handle: Titanium and G10
Lock: Push button (non-auto)
Weight: 2 oz.
Features: Titanium liners
Options: None
MSRP: $80

BÖKER MAGNUM FIRST RESPONDER

BÖKER MOKUME DAMASCUS

BÖKER MAGNUM FISHBONE

BÖKER MAGNUM SMOOTHIE

BÖKER PLUS CARBON

BÖKER PLUS ELEGANCE

FOLDING KNIVES

Böker USA

www.boker.de/us/

PLUS KAL 10S

Blade Length: 3.5 in.
Blade Material: 440C Stainless steel
Length (Open/Closed): 8.1 in./4.6 in.
Handle: Aluminum
Lock: Liner lock
Weight: 6 oz.
Features: Raised palm support; finger choil; thumbhole open; belt pouch
Options: None
MSRP: **$45**

PLUS KAL 10T

Blade Length: 3.5 in.
Blade Material: 440C Stainless steel
Length (Open/Closed): 8.1 in./4.6 in.
Handle: Aluminum
Lock: Liner lock
Weight: 6 oz.
Features: Raised palm support and finger choil; thumbhole; belt pouch
Options: KAL 10S spear point
MSRP: **$45**

PLUS LOCKBACK BUBINGA

Blade Length: 3.6 in.
Blade Material: 440C Stainless steel
Length (Open/Closed): 8.25 in./7.5 in.
Handle: Bubinga wood
Lock: Lockback
Weight: 4.5 oz.
Features: Stainless steel bolsters; nail nick opening
Options: None
MSRP: **$50**

PLUS NOPAL

Blade Length: 2.1 in.
Blade Material: 440C Stainless steel
Length (Open/Closed): 5.5 in./3.4 in.
Handle: G10
Lock: Push button (non-auto)
Weight: 3 oz.
Features: Wharncliff straight edge blade; finger choils; removable pocket clip
Options: None
MSRP: **$50**

PLUS RESURRECTION GEN 2

Blade Length: 3.25 in.
Blade Material: 440C Stainless steel
Length (Open/Closed): 9 in./5.75 in.
Handle: G10
Lock: Liner lock

BÖKER PLUS KAL 10S

BÖKER PLUS KAL 10T

BÖKER PLUS LOCKBACK BUBINGA

BÖKER PLUS RESURRECTION GEN 2

BÖKER PLUS NOPAL

BÖKER PLUS TD YELLOW

Weight: 4.5 oz.
Features: Reversible clip; ambidextrous thumb studs
Options: Mini (01BO410), $40
MSRP: **$95**

PLUS TD YELLOW

Blade Length: 3 in.
Blade Material: AUS 8 steel

Length (Open/Closed): 7.1 in./4.1 in.
Handle: Zytel
Lock: Back lock
Weight: 3 oz.
Features: Thumbhole; reversible clip
Options: Black grip and blade; plain or combo edge blade
MSRP: **$40**

FOLDING KNIVES

Böker USA

BÖKER PLUS TITAN DROP

BÖKER STOCKMAN

BÖKER TRAPPER

PLUS TITAN DROP

Blade Length: 3.75 in.
Blade Material: 440C Stainless steel
Length (Open/Closed): 8.4 in./4.65 in.
Handle: Bead blasted Titanium
Lock: Back lock
Weight: 4.5 oz.
Features: Ultra thin profile; reversible clip
Options: None
MSRP: **$65**

STOCKMAN 110725

Blade Length (Max): 2.75 in.
Blade Material: High Carbon steel
Length (Open/Closed): 6.75 in./4 in.
Handle: Jigged black bone
Lock: None
Weight: 3.2 oz.
Features: Three blades; dual hinge and single hinge; nail nick open
Options: Stag handle, $90; medium, Mini Stockman, $20–$35
MSRP: **$40**

TRAPPER 110732

Blade Length(Max): 3.1 in.
Blade Material: High Carbon steel
Length (Open/Closed): 7.3 in./4.25 in.
Handle: Smooth red bone
Lock: None
Weight: 3.2 oz.
Features: Dual blade; single hinge; nail nick open
Options: Synthetic and bone handles
MSRP: **$40**

Buck Knives

016 LUX PRO

Blade Length: 2.5 in.
Blade Material: S30V steel
Length (Open/Closed): 6.25 in./3.75 in.
Handle: Stainless steel and Carbon fiber
Lock: Liner lock
Weight: 3.3 oz.
Features: Titanium coated blade; flipper; removable pocket clip
Options: Stainless steel grip; 123C26 Sandvik steel blade (015), $75; 420HC steel blade (014), $58
MSRP: **$125**

BUCK 016 LUX PRO

Buck Knives

www.buckknives.com

BUCK 110 CHAIRMAN FOLDING HUNTER

BUCK 110RD ECOLITE

BUCK 183 BOONE AND CROCKET ALPHA CROSSLOCK

BUCK 222 SILVER CREEK VERSA

BUCK 271 ALPHA DORADO

BUCK 306YW DUET

110 CHAIRMAN FOLDING HUNTER
Blade Length: 3.75 in.
Blade Material: 420HC steel
Length (Open/Closed): 8.65 in./4.9 in.
Handle: Cherrywood dymondwood
Lock: Back lock
Weight: 7.2 oz.
Features: Leather sheath; nickel silver bolsters; signature
Options: None
MSRP: **$100**

110RD ECOLITE
Blade Length: 3.75 in.
Blade Material: 420HC steel
Length (Open/Closed): 8.65 in./4.9 in.
Handle: PaperStone
Lock: Back lock
Weight: 4.1 oz.
Features: Nylon sheath
Options: Green or red handle
MSRP: **$45**

183 BOONE AND CROCKET ALPHA CROSSLOCK
Blade Length: 3 in.
Blade Material: 420HC steel
Length (Open/Closed): 7.6 in./4.6 in.
Handle: Rubber coated aluminum
Lock: Liner lock
Weight: 4 oz.
Features: Nylon sheath; saw and gut hook
Options: None
MSRP: **$108**

222 SILVER CREEK VERSA
Blade Length: 4 in.
Blade Material: 420HC steel
Length (Open/Closed): 8.75 in./4.75 in.
Handle: Polypropylene/rubber
Lock: Liner lock
Weight: 4.3 oz.
Features: Titanium coated blade; thumb stud, lanyard; stainless steel guard
Options: None
MSRP: **$40**

271 ALPHA DORADO
Blade Length: 2.5 in.
Blade Material: 12C27 Mod Sandvik
Length (Open/Closed): 6.5 in./4 in.
Handle: Rosewood dymondwood
Lock: Liner lock
Weight: 4.3 oz.
Features: Leather sheath
Options: Charcoal dymondwood handle; nylon sheath; 3.5-inch blade (Folding Alpha Hunter)
MSRP: **$94**

306YW DUET
Blade Length: 3.75 in.
Blade Material: 420HC steel
Length (Open/Closed): 8.65 in./2.6 in.
Handle: Yellow Delrin
Lock: Slip joint
Weight: 1 oz.
Features: Spring loaded scissors; nickel silver bolsters
Options: Pink, charcoal, or black handle
MSRP: **$45**

FOLDING KNIVES

BUCK 770OR FLASHPOINT

BUCK 766YW REVEL

BUCK 870BK BONES

BUCK TOPS CSAR T 095

BUCK VANTAGE
FORCE PRO 847

766YW REVEL
Blade Length: 2.5 in.
Blade Material: 420HC steel
Length (Open/Closed): 6.25 in./3.75 in.
Handle: Aluminum/rubber inlay
Lock: Liner lock
Weight: 2.4 oz.
Features: Carabiner/bottle opener; slide/flipper opening; blade locks open and closed
Options: Blue, black, or yellow handle
MSRP: $30

770OR FLASHPOINT
Blade Length: 2.9 in.
Blade Material: 420HC steel
Length (Open/Closed): 7.4 in./4.5 in.
Handle: Aluminum/rubber inlay
Lock: Liner lock
Weight: 4 oz.
Features: Carabiner/bottle opener; push button/flipper opening; blade locks open and closed

Options: Blue, black, or orange handle
MSRP: $53

870BK BONES
Blade Length: 3 in.
Blade Material: 420HC steel
Length (Open/Closed): 7.6 in./4.6 in.
Handle: Stainless steel
Lock: Liner lock
Weight: 4.4 oz.
Features: Black oxide coated blade; removable pocket clip
Options: Tiger camo; plain or combination edge; 2.1-inch blade (869), $28
MSRP: $39

TOPS CSAR T 095
Blade Length: 3.5 in.
Blade Material: 154CM
Length (Open/Closed): 8.5 in./5 in.
Handle: G10
Lock: Liner lock
Weight: 7.1 oz.

Features: Zirblast finish blade; reversible pocket clip; MOLLE compatible nylon sheath
Options: Rubber grip (090), $110; First Responder w/ glass break and seat belt cutter (091), $140
MSRP: $160

VANTAGE FORCE PRO 847
Blade Length: 3.25 in.
Blade Material: S30V steel
Length (Open/Closed): 7.65 in./4.4 in.
Handle: G10
Lock: Liner lock
Weight: 7.1 oz.
Features: Black oxide coated blade; flipper; removable, reversible pocket clip
Options: Aluminum grip (846), $95; glass reinforced nylon grip (845), $65; plain or combination edge blade
MSRP: $135

Camillus Knives

www.camillusknives.com

CAMILLUS 6.75"
FOLDING 18669

CAMILLUS 6.75"
FOLDING 18671

CAMILLUS
8" FOLDING

CAMILLUS 8.25" FOLDING 18519

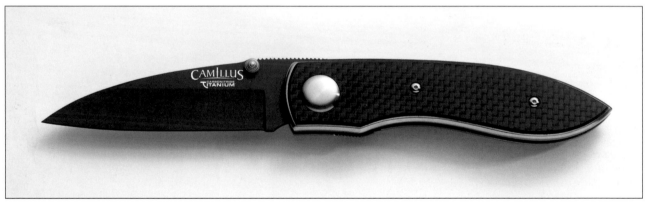

6.75" FOLDING 18669
Blade Length: 2.9 in.
Blade Material: VG10
Length (Open/Closed): 6.75 in./3.85 in.
Handle: G10
Lock: Liner lock
Weight: 4.2 oz.
Features: Carbonitride Titanium coated blade; pocket clip
Options: None
MSRP: $70

6.75" FOLDING 18671
Blade Length: 3 in.
Blade Material: VG10
Length (Open/Closed): 6.75 in./3.75 in.
Handle: G10

Lock: Liner lock
Weight: 6.1 oz.
Features: Carbonitride Titanium coated blade; pocket clip
Options: None
MSRP: $74

8" FOLDING 18513
Blade Length: 3.25 in.
Blade Material: AUS8
Length (Open/Closed): 8 in./4.75 in.
Handle: Aluminum
Lock: Liner lock
Weight: 7.5 oz.
Features: Carbonitride Titanium coated blade; pocket clip

Options: None
MSRP: $44

8.25" FOLDING 18519
Blade Length: 3.5 in.
Blade Material: AUS8
Length (Open/Closed): 8.25 in./4.75 in.
Handle: Aluminum/carbon fiber
Lock: Liner lock
Weight: 6.6 oz.
Features: Carbonitride Titanium coated blade; pocket clip
Options: None
MSRP: $61

CAMILLUS 8.25" FOLDING 18672

8.25" FOLDING 18672
Blade Length: 3.5 in.
Blade Material: VG10
Length (Open/Closed): 8.25 in./4.75 in.
Handle: G10
Lock: Liner lock
Weight: 7.5 oz.
Features: Carbonitride Titanium coated blade; pocket clip
Options: 2.85 in. blade (18673), $66
MSRP: **$83**

CAMMILUS 9" CUDA NO. 18533

9" CUDA NO. 18533
Length: 3.75 in.
Blade Material: VG10
Length (Open/Closed): 9 in./5.25in.
Handle: G10
Lock: Liner lock
Weight: 7 oz.
Features: Carbonitride Titanium coated blade; pocket clip;quick release button
Options: None
MSRP: **$59**

CAMILLUS FOLDING 6.5" MARLIN SPIKE

FOLDING 6.5" MARLIN SPIKE 18670
Blade Length: 2.75 in.
Blade Material: VG10
Length (Open/Closed): 6.5 in./3.75 in.
Handle: G10
Lock: Liner lock
Weight: 5.9 oz.
Features: Carbonitride Titanium coated blade; pocket clip; locking spike
Options: None
MSRP: **$74**

CAMILLUS TIGER SHARP FOLDING, BLUE

TIGER SHARP FOLDING, BLUE 18563
Blade Length: 2.5 in.
Blade Material: AUS8
Length (Open/Closed): 6.5 in./4 in.
Handle: Aluminum

Lock: Liner lock
Weight: 5.8 oz.
Features: Titanium bonded blade surface; replaceable blades, plain, and serrated supplied; pocket clip
Options: Blue handle (18562)
MSRP: **$52**

FOLDING KNIVES

Case Knives

www.wrcase.com

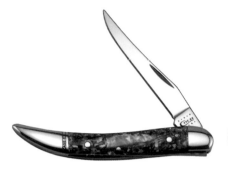

CASE ABALONE SMALL TEXAS TOOTHPICK

CASE AMBER BONE TRAPPERLOCK

CASE BLUE BONE TRAPPER

CASE CALIBER CAMO 118

CASE CHANGER SET

FOLDING KNIVES

ABALONE SMALL TEXAS TOOTHPICK 12002
Blade Length (Max): 2.25 in.
Blade Material: Stainless steel
Length (Open/Closed): 5.25 in./3 in.
Handle: Abalone
Lock: None
Weight: 1 oz.
Features: Nail mark opening; case XX embossed bolster
Options: Stag; Mother of Pearl assorted color bone handles
MSRP: $174

AMBER BONE TRAPPERLOCK 024
Blade Length (Max): 4 in.
Blade Material: Chrome Vanadium
Length (Open/Closed): 7.4 in./3.4 in.
Handle: Bone
Lock: Liner lock
Weight: 3.4 oz.
Features: Thumb stud opening
Options: Stag; red or black G10; decorative and commemorative handles
MSRP: $106

BLUE BONE TRAPPER 2800
Blade Length (Max): 3.8 in.
Blade Material: Stainless steel
Length (Open/Closed): 7.9 in./4.1 in.
Handle: Bone
Lock: None
Weight: 4 oz.
Features: Nail mark; clip and spey blades
Options: Stag; abalone; assorted bone handles
MSRP: $64

CALIBER CAMO 118
Blade Length: 2.75 in.
Blade Material: Stainless steel
Length (Open/Closed): 6.5 in./3.75 in.
Handle: Zytel
Lock: Back lock
Weight: 1.2 oz.
Features: Nail mark opening
Options: Black handle (156)
MSRP: $21

CHANGER SET 6004
Blade Length: 3.5 in.
Blade Material: Stainless steel
Length (Open/Closed): 8.5 in./5 in.
Handle: Amber bone
Lock: Back lock
Weight: 12 oz.
Features: Clip; gut hook; drop point and saw blades; leather belt pouch
Options: Collectible gift tin
MSRP: $93

CASE CHESTNUT BONE CV MEDIUM STOCKMAN

CASE DARK RED BONE CV RUSS LOCK

CASE ELVIS PRESLEY HUMPBACK HALF WHITTLER

CASE EXECUTIVE LOCKBACK 004

CHESTNUT BONE CV MEDIUM STOCKMAN 7008
Blade Length (Max): 2.3 in.
Blade Material: Chrome Vanadium
Length (Open/Closed): 5.9 in./3.6 in.
Handle: Bone
Lock: None
Weight: 2.5 oz.
Features: Nail mark opening; clip, sheepsfoot, and pen blades
Options: None
MSRP: **$61**

DARK RED BONE CV RUSS LOCK 6994
Blade Length (Max): 2 in.
Blade Material: Chrome Vanadium
Length (Open/Closed): 6.25 in./4.25 in.
Handle: Bone
Lock: Russ lock
Weight: 2.7 oz.
Features: One hand opening
Options: Stag; assorted bone handles; celebrity commemorative handles
MSRP: **$74**

ELVIS PRESLEY HUMPBACK HALF WHITTLER 17507
Blade Length (Max): 2.36 in.
Blade Material: Stainless steel
Length (Open/Closed): 6 in./3.6 in.
Handle: Jigged red bone
Lock: None
Weight: 2.4 oz.
Features: Commemorative wooden guitar box; clip and pen blade
Options: None
MSRP: **$235**

EXECUTIVE LOCKBACK 004
Blade Length (Max): 2.4 in.
Blade Material: Stainless steel
Length (Open/Closed): 5.5 in./3.1 in.
Handle: Brushed stainless
Lock: Back lock
Weight: 2.3 oz.
Features: Nail mark opening; lanyard hole
Options: 2.2-inch and 2.5-inch blade
MSRP: **$37**

HAWKBILL PRUNER 2244
Blade Length (Max): 3 in.
Blade Material: Stainless steel
Length (Open/Closed): 7 in./4 in.
Handle: Rosewood
Lock: None
Weight: 1.7 oz.
Features: Nail mark opening
Options: Zytel; G10; jigged bone; yellow synthetic; John Deere handle
MSRP: **$72**

HUMPBACK STOCKMAN 11923
Blade Length (Max): 2.4 in.
Blade Material: Stainless steel
Length (Open/Closed): 6 in./3.6 in.
Handle: Mother of Pearl
Lock: None
Weight: 1.7 oz.

CASE HAWKBILL PRUNER

CASE HUMPBACK STOCKMAN

Features: Nail mark opening; spear, spey, and pen blades; case XX embossed bolster
Options: None
MSRP: **$287**

FOLDING KNIVES

Case Knives

www.wrcase.com

CASE IMAGE XX PALMETTE WHITTLER

CASE IMAGE XX WAR TRAPPER

CASE MEDIUM NAVY BLUE BONE CONGRESS

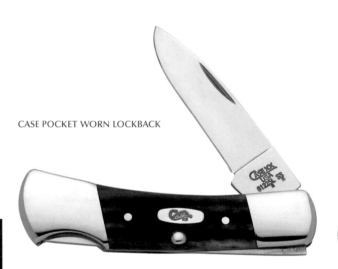

CASE POCKET WORN LOCKBACK

CASE POCKET WORN MINI POCKET LOCK

FOLDING KNIVES

IMAGE XX PALMETTE WHITTLER 6827

Blade Length (Max): 2.2 in.
Blade Material: Stainless steel
Length (Open/Closed): 5.7 in./3.5 in.
Handle: Bone
Lock: None
Weight: 2.1 oz.
Features: Nail mark opening clip, short clip, and pen blades
Options: None
MSRP: $108

IMAGE XX WAR TRAPPER 7071

Blade Length (Max): 3.8 in.
Blade Material: Stainless steel
Length (Open/Closed): 7.9 in./4.1 in.
Handle: Bone
Lock: None
Weight: 4 oz.
Features: Op. Enduring Freedom on handle; clip and spey blade

Options: None
MSRP: $80

MEDIUM NAVY BLUE BONE CONGRESS 7061

Blade Length (Max): 2.3 in.
Blade Material: Stainless steel
Length (Open/Closed): 5.9 in./3.6 in.
Handle: Bone
Lock: None
Weight: 2.3 oz.
Features: Nail mark opening; spear, coping, sheepsfoot, and pen blades
Options: None
MSRP: $89

POCKET WORN LOCKBACK 2758

Blade Length: 2.25 in.
Blade Material: Stainless steel
Length (Open/Closed): 5.25 in./3 in.
Handle: Bone

Lock: Lockback
Weight: 1.9 oz.
Features: Nail mark opening; stainless bolsters
Options: Abalone; Cayenne bone; white synthetic; jigged blue bone; smooth oak wood handle
MSRP: $70

POCKET WORN MINI POCKET LOCK 9723

Blade Length (Max): 2.8 in.
Blade Material: Stainless steel
Length (Open/Closed): 6.4 in./3.6 in.
Handle: Green bone
Lock: Lockback
Weight: 2 oz.
Features: Nail mark opening
Options: Jigged bone; synthetic Derlin; stag; Mother of Pearl handles
MSRP: $74

POCKET WORN RED BONE SWAY BACK GENT 2746 AND 5526

Blade Length (Max): 2.3 in.
Blade Material: Stainless steel
Length (Open/Closed): 5.5 in./3.2 in.
Handle: Bone
Lock: None
Weight: 1.8 oz.
Features: Nail mark opening; wharncliffe blade
Options: Mother of Pearl assorted bone handles; 3.5-inch blade; wharncliffe and pen blades (5526)
MSRP: $147

SLIM LOCK 5129

Blade Length (Max): 2.6 in.
Blade Material: BG-42 Stainless steel
Length (Open/Closed): 6.1 in./3.5 in.
Handle: Mammoth Ivory
Lock: Case slim lock
Weight: 2.3 oz.
Features: Thumb stud opening
Options: Mother of Pearl; bone and English walnut handles
MSRP: $513

XX VAULT CHEETAH 057

Blade Length (Max): 4 in.
Blade Material: Chrome Vanadium
Length (Open/Closed): 8.4 in./4.4 in.
Handle: Synthetic
Lock: Back lock
Weight: 3.5 oz.
Features: Nail mark opening; swing guard
Options: Stag or bone handles; rain drop Damascus blade
MSRP: $74

XX VAULT DOCTOR'S KNIFE 11382

Blade Length (Max): 3 in.
Blade Material: Stainless steel
Length (Open/Closed): 6.75 in./3.75 in.
Handle: Antique bone
Lock: None
Weight: 2.3 oz.
Features: Nail mark opening; spear and spatula blades
Options: Bone, barn board, or stag handles; single spear point blade
MSRP: $73

CASE POCKET WORN RED BONE SWAY BACK GENT 2746

CASE POCKET WORN RED BONE SWAY BACK GENT 5526

CASE SLIM LOCK

CASE XX VAULT CHEETAH

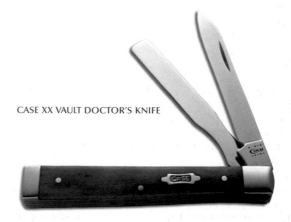

CASE XX VAULT DOCTOR'S KNIFE

FOLDING KNIVES

Chris Reeve Knives

www.chrisreeve.com

SMALL SABENZA 21 INTEGRAL LOCK
Blade Length: 2.9 in.
Blade Material: S35V SS
Length (Open/Closed): 6.9 in./4 in.
Handle: 6A14V Titanium
Lock: Frame lock
Weight: 3 oz.
Features: Integrated frame lock; lanyard; anodized thumb stud; stone washed blade; sand blasted handle
Options: Thumb stud colors; graphics on handles; wood inlaid grips; Damascus blade
MSRP: **$330**

CHRIS REEVE SMALL SABENZA 21 INTEGRAL LOCK

CHRIS REEVE TI LOCK

TI LOCK
Blade Length: 3.25 in.
Blade Material: CPM S35V SS
Length (Open/Closed): 7.25 in./4 in.
Handle: 6A14V Titanium
Lock: Ti-Lock
Weight: 3 oz.

Features: Ambidextrous lock; lanyard; 6A14V pocket clip
Options: None
MSRP: **$475**

Cold Steel

www.coldsteel.com

AK47 TLAK
Blade Length: 3.5 in.
Blade Material: AUS8A
Length (Open/Closed): 9 in./5.5 in.
Handle: G10
Lock: Tri-Ad back lock
Weight: 5.5 oz.
Features: Reversible pocket clip
Options: 2.75-inch blade (26TMAK)
MSRP: **$120**

COUNTER POINT II 10AMC
Blade Length: 3 in.
Blade Material: AUS8A
Length (Open/Closed): 6.9 in./3.9 in.
Handle: Grivory
Lock: Tri-Ad back lock
Weight: 2.2 oz.
Features: Pocket clip
Options: 4-inch blade (10ALC)
MSRP: **$60**

COLD STEEL AK47 TLAK

COLD STEEL COUNTER POINT II

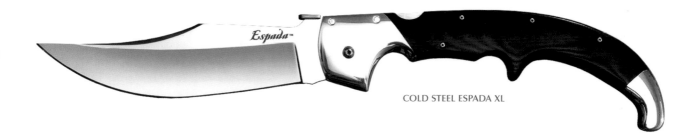

COLD STEEL ESPADA XL

ESPADA XL 62NX
Blade Length: 7.5 in.
Blade Material: AUS8A
Length (Open/Closed): 16.75 in./9.25 in.
Handle: G10/7075 aluminum
Lock: Tri-Ad back lock
Weight: 15 oz.
Features: Pocket clip
Options: 3.5-inch or 5.5-inch plain edge blade
MSRP: $470

COLD STEEL G10 ESPADA MEDIUM

G10 ESPADA MEDIUM 62NM
Blade Length: 3.5 in.
Blade Material: AUS8A
Length (Open/Closed): 8.5 in./5 in.
Handle: G10
Lock: Tri-Ad back lock
Weight: 5.5 oz.
Features: Bead blasé finish; pocket clip
Options: 5.5-inch or 7.5-inch blade
MSRP: $120

HOLD OUT II 11HLS
Blade Length: 4 in.
Blade Material: AUS8A
Length (Open/Closed): 9 in./5 in.
Handle: G10
Lock: Tri-Ad back lock
Weight: 4.2 oz.
Features: Pocket clip
Options: 3-inch blade plain (11HM); 3-inch blade serrated (11HMS)
MSRP: $105

COLD STEEL HOLD OUT II

MINI LAWMAN 58ALM
Blade Length: 2.5 in.
Blade Material: AUS8A
Length (Open/Closed): 5.9 in./3.4 in.
Handle: G10
Lock: Tri-Ad back lock
Weight: 2.6 oz.

COLD STEEL MINI LAWMAN

Features: Pocket clip; Teflon coated
Options: 3.5-inch blade (58AL)
MSRP: $80

FOLDING KNIVES

Cold Steel

www.coldsteel.com

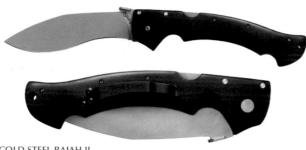

COLD STEEL MINI TUFF LITE

COLD STEEL PARADOX

COLD STEEL POCKET BUSHMAN

COLD STEEL RAJAH II

COLD STEEL RECON 1

FOLDING KNIVES

MINI TUFF LITE 20MT
Blade Length: 2 in.
Blade Material: AUS8A
Length (Open/Closed): 5 in./3 in.
Handle: Grivory
Lock: Tri-Ad back lock
Weight: 1.7 oz.
Features: Pocket clip
Options: Serrated blade (20MTS)
MSRP: $35

PARADOX 24P
Blade Length: 4.5 in.
Blade Material: AUS8A
Length (Open/Closed): 9.5 in./5 in.
Handle: 6061 aluminum
Lock: Ballisong
Weight: 6.1 oz.
Features: Pocket clip
Options: Grivory grip (24PG); 5.5-inch
blade (24PA)
MSRP: $130

POCKET BUSHMAN 95FB
Blade Length: 4.5 in.
Blade Material: 4116 Krupp SS
Length (Open/Closed): 10.25 in./5.75
in.
Handle: 420 Stainless steel
Lock: Ram safe
Weight: 6.1 oz.
Features: One piece steel handle;
pocket clip
Options: None
MSRP: $40

RAJAH II 62KG
Blade Length: 6 in.
Blade Material: AUS8A
Length (Open/Closed): 14 in./8 in.
Handle: Grivory

Lock: Tri-Ad back lock
Weight: 13.4 oz.
Features: Pocket clip
Options: 3.5-inch blade; plain or ser-
rated
MSRP: $160

RECON 1 27TLC
Blade Length: 4 in.
Blade Material: AUS8A
Length (Open/Closed): 9.4 in./5.4 in.
Handle: G10
Lock: Tri-Ad back lock
Weight: 4.7 oz.
Features: Pocket clip; Teflon coated
Options: 50/50; plain; serrated; tanto/
clip
MSRP: $105

COLD STEEL SPARTAN

COLD STEEL TI LITE

SPARTAN 21S
Blade Length: 4.5 in.
Blade Material: AUS8A
Length (Open/Closed): 10.5 in./6 in.
Handle: Grivory
Lock: Tri-Ad back lock
Weight: 7.5 oz.
Features: Pocket clip
Options: None
MSRP: **$95**

TI LITE 26AST
Blade Length: 4 in.
Blade Material: AUS8A
Length (Open/Closed): 8.75 in./4.75 in.
Handle: 7075 aluminum
Lock: Leaf spring
Weight: 4.6 oz.
Features: Pocket clip
Options: 6-inch blade (26ASTX)
MSRP: **$120**

COLD STEEL VAQUERO

VAQUERO 29TLVS
Blade Length: 4 in.
Blade Material: AUS8A
Length (Open/Closed): 9.25 in./5.25 in.
Handle: Grivory
Lock: Tri-Ad back lock
Weight: 4.7 oz.
Features: Reversible pocket clip
Options: Plain edge blade (26TLV)
MSRP: **$70**

VOYAGER EXTRA LARGE CLIP POINT PLAIN E 29TXC
Blade Length: 5.5 in.
Blade Material: AUS8A
Length (Open/Closed): 12.25 in./7.25 in.
Handle: Grivory
Lock: Tri-Ad back lock
Weight: 7.2 oz.
Features: Reversible pocket clip
Options: Plain edge blade (26TLV)
MSRP: **$88**

COLD STEEL VOYAGER EXTRA LARGE CLIP POINT PLAIN E

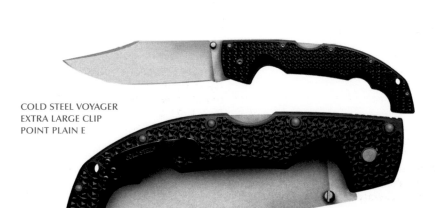

FOLDING KNIVES

Columbia River Knife and Tool

www.crkt.com

CRKT EROS

CRKT GLIDE LOCK 7415

CRKT HISSATSU FOLDER

CRKT K.I.S.S. ASSIST 5655

CRKT M16 13DFSG

CRKT M16 13SFGL

FOLDING KNIVES

EROS K455TXP

Blade Length: 3 in.
Blade Material: Acuto +
Length (Open/Closed): 7 in./4 in.
Handle: 6AL4V Titanium
Lock: Frame lock
Weight: 1.4 oz.
Features: Assisted opening; ball bearing hinge; pocket clip
Options: 2-inch blade (K450TXP), $150
MSRP: $200

GLIDE LOCK 7415

Blade Length: 2.875 in.
Blade Material: Aus 4
Length (Open/Closed): 6.5 in./3.6 in.
Handle: CPL composite
Lock: Bolster lock
Weight: 1.6 oz.
Features: TiNitride coated blade
Options: Coral handle (7410)
MSRP: $60

HISSATSU FOLDER 2903

Blade Length: 3.875 in.
Blade Material: AUS 8

Length (Open/Closed): 8.75 in./5 in.
Handle: Zytel
Lock: Liner lock
Weight: 5.8 oz.
Features: Black Teflon coated blade; assisted opening can be deactivated; automatic lock; pocket clip
Options: Partial serrated blade (2903Q)
MSRP: $100

K.I.S.S. ASSIST 5655

Blade Length: 2.75 in.
Blade Material: AUS 4
Length (Open/Closed): 6.25 in./3.5 in.
Handle: 4202J/Carbon fiber
Lock: Frame lock
Weight: 2.5 oz.
Features: Assisted opening with safety lock; pocket clip
Options: Plain edge blade (5650)
MSRP: $60

M16 13DFSG

Blade Length: 3.5 in.
Blade Material: 8Cr14MoV

Length (Open/Closed): 8.25 in./4.75 in.
Handle: G10
Lock: Locking liner
Weight: 4 oz.
Features: Dual hilt/flipper opening; veff serrated TiNitride coated blade; auto lock open; 4-position pocket clip
Options: None
MSRP: $60

M16 13SFGL

Blade Length: 3.5 in.
Blade Material: 8Cr14MoV
Length (Open/Closed): 8.25 in./4.6 in.
Handle: G10
Lock: Locking liner
Weight: 4 oz.
Features: Dual hilt/flipper opening; veff serrated TiNitride coated blade; auto lock open; 4-position pocket clip
Options: None
MSRP: $60

Columbia River Knife and Tool

www.crkt.com

CRKT M16 14T

M16 14T

Blade Length: 3.875 in.
Blade Material: Aus 8
Length (Open/Closed): 9.25 in./5.4 in.
Handle: Titanium
Lock: Locking liner
Weight: 5.7 oz.
Features: Single flipper opening; one position clip; auto lock open
Options: None
MSRP: **$150**

M16 14ZER

Blade Length: 3.75 in.
Blade Material: AUS 8
Length (Open/Closed): 9.25 in./5.5 in.
Handle: Zytel
Lock: Locking liner
Weight: 6.2 oz.
Features: Flipper opening; glass breaker; seatbelt cutter; 4-position pocket clip
Options: None
MSRP: **$90**

CRKT M16 14ZER

M16 ZYTEL 03Z

Blade Length: 3.5 in.
Blade Material: Aus 4
Length (Open/Closed): 8.25 in./4.75 in.
Handle: Zytel
Lock: Locking liner
Weight: 3.5 oz.
Features: Single flipper opening; one position clip; auto lock open
Options: Partially serrated blade (M160-13Z)
MSRP: **$60**

CRKT M16 ZYTEL 03Z

M21 14SFG

Blade Length: 3.875 in.
Blade Material: 8Cr14MoV
Length (Open/Closed): 9.25 in./5.4 in.
Handle: G10
Lock: Locking liner
Weight: 6.1 oz.
Features: Dual hilt/flipper opening; veff serrated TiNitride coated blade; auto lock open; 4-position pocket clip
Options: None
MSRP: **$80**

CRKT M21 14SFG

FOLDING KNIVES

Columbia River Knife and Tool

www.crkt.com

NIRK NORVO 5170

Blade Length: 2.75 in.
Blade Material: 4Cr15MoVNi
Length (Open/Closed): 6.25 in./3.75 in.
Handle: 2Cr13
Lock: Lockback
Weight: 2.5 oz.
Features: Pocket clip
Options: Partial serrated blade (5175)
MSRP: **$25**

CRKT NIRK NORVO 5170

NIRK TIGHE 5250

Blade Length: 3.9 in.
Blade Material: AUS8
Length (Open/Closed): 9.1 in./5.25 in.
Handle: 420J2
Lock: Lockback
Weight: 5.1 oz.
Features: Pocket clip; flipper open
Options: Partially serrated blade (5175)
MSRP: **$150**

CRKT NIRK TIGHE 5250

NOTORIOUS 1168K

Blade Length (Max): 3.5 in.
Blade Material: 8Cr14MoV
Length (Open/Closed): 8 in./4.5 in.
Handle: Stainless steel/G10
Lock: Frame lock
Weight: 5 oz.
Features: Black oxide finish; veff serrated edge; pocket clip
Options: None
MSRP: **$70**

CRKT NOTORIOUS

SAMPA 5335K

Blade Length: 3.125 in.
Blade Material: AUS 8
Length (Open/Closed): 7.25 in./4.25 in.
Handle: 6061 aluminum
Lock: Liner lock
Weight: 2.7 oz.
Features: TiNitridet coated blade; pocket clip; flipper opening; IKBS ball bearing hinge
Options: Satin finish blade
MSRP: **$110**

CRKT SAMPA

TEXAS TOOTHPICK 6061

Blade Length: 2.75 in.
Blade Material: High Carbon SS
Length (Open/Closed): 5.75 in./3 in.
Handle: Bone
Lock: None (slip joint)
Weight: 1.6 oz.

CRKT TEXAS TOOTHPICK 6061

Features: Polished nickel bolster and pins
Options: 2.25 in. blade (6060), $30
MSRP: **$30**

DARK OPS STRATOFIGHTER
FOLDER SPEAR PT.

DARK OPS STRATOFIGHTER
TANTO COVERT

STRATOFIGHTER FOLDER SPEAR PT. DOH115

Blade Length: 4.5 in.
Blade Material: CTV2 Stainless steel
Length (Open/Closed): 10.2 in./5.7 in.
Handle: T6160 aluminum
Lock: RaptorLok TM back lock
Weight: 8.6 oz.
Features: CrisisCross TM cross bolt safety; reversible pocket clip; window break pommel; quartz impregnated grip inserts; titanium carbon nitride finish
Options: Hard anodized IR invisible finish; stiletto point blade, (DOH109)
MSRP: **$269**

STRATOFIGHTER TANTO COVERT DOH109

Blade Length: 3.7 in.
Blade Material: CTV2 Stainless steel
Length (Open/Closed): 8.6 in./4.9 in.
Handle: T6160 aluminum
Lock: RaptorLok TM back lock
Weight: 7.1 oz.
Features: CrisisCross TM cross bolt safety; reversible pocket clip; window break pommel; Titanium Carbon Nitride finish
Options: Hard anodized IR invisible finish; modified clip point blade
MSRP: **$229**

Emerson Knives

www.emersonknives.com

FOLDING KNIVES

A100 BT

Blade Length: 3.6 in.
Blade Material: 154CM
Length (Open/Closed): 8.4 in./4.8 in.
Handle: G10
Lock: Locking liner
Weight: 4.3 oz.
Features: Ambidextrous opening; pocket clip
Options: Plain or partially serrated; black or satin finish
MSRP: **$195**

EMERSON A100 BT

Emerson Knives

www.emersonknives.com

EMERSON AMERICAN
HARDWARE RELIANT W

EMERSON COMBAT KARAMBIT BT

EMERSON COMMANDER BTS

EMERSON CQC 13 BT

EMERSON GENTLEMAN JIM

EMERSON JAPANESE
HARDWARE TRAVELER B1PS

AMERICAN HARDWARE RELIANT W
Blade Length: 3.2 in.
Blade Material: 154CM
Length (Open/Closed): 7.8 in./4.6 in.
Handle: G10
Lock: Liner lock
Weight: 4.3 oz.
Features: Remote pocket opening or thumbhole open; pocket clip
Options: Black or stonewash finish; 3-inch clip point blade (Traveler); 3.2-inch clip point blade (Endeavor)
MSRP: $198

COMBAT KARAMBIT BT
Blade Length: 2.6 in.
Blade Material: 154CM
Length (Open/Closed): 6.8 in./4.2 in.
Handle: G10
Lock: Liner lock
Weight: 3.6 oz.
Features: Remote pocket opening or thumbhole open; pocket clip
Options: Black or satin finish
MSRP: $258

COMMANDER BTS
Blade Length: 3.75 in.
Blade Material: 154CM
Length (Open/Closed): 8.75 in./5 in.
Handle: G10
Lock: Locking liner
Weight: 4.9 oz.
Features: Remote pocket opening or ambidextrous thumb stud; pocket clip
Options: Plain or partially serrated; black or satin finish
MSRP: $240

CQC 13 BT
Blade Length: 3.85 in.
Blade Material: 154CM
Length (Open/Closed): 9 in./4.8 in.
Handle: G10
Lock: Locking liner
Weight: 5 oz.
Features: Remote pocket opening or ambidextrous thumb stud; pocket clip
Options: Plain or partially serrated; black or satin finish
MSRP: $248

GENTLEMAN JIM
Blade Length: 3.75 in.
Blade Material: 154CM
Length (Open/Closed): 8.55 in./4.8 in.
Handle: G10
Lock: Locking liner
Weight: 4.2 oz.
Features: Remote pocket opening or thumbhole open; pocket clip
Options: None
MSRP: $240

JAPANESE HARDWARE TRAVELER B1PS
Blade Length: 3 in.
Blade Material: AUS8
Length (Open/Closed): 7 in./4 in.
Handle: Zytel
Lock: Back lock
Weight: 1.5 oz.
Features: Scratch resistant finish.
Options: Plain or serrated edge; 3.4-inch clip point blade (Endeavor); 3.4-inch tanto point blade (Reliant)
MSRP: $80

EMERSON MINI CQC HORSEMAN

EMERSON SUPER KARAMBIT

Emerson Knives

www.emersonknives.com

MINI CQC HORSEMAN
Blade Length: 3.54 in.
Blade Material: 154CM
Length (Open/Closed): 8.35 in./4.8 in.
Handle: G10
Lock: Liner lock
Weight: 4.4 oz.
Features: Remote pocket opening or thumbhole open; pocket clip
Options: Black or satin finish
MSRP: **$196**

POLICE SARK BTS
Blade Length: 3.5 in.
Blade Material: 154CM
Length (Open/Closed): 8.2 in./4.7 in.
Handle: G10
Lock: Liner lock
Weight: 4.1 oz.
Features: Remote pocket opening or thumbhole open; pocket clip
Options: Black or satin finish; plain or serrated edge blade
MSRP: **$205**

SEARCH AND RESCUE SARK BTS
Blade Length: 3.5 in.
Blade Material: 154CM
Length (Open/Closed): 8.2 in./4.7 in.
Handle: G10
Lock: Liner lock
Weight: 4.1 oz.
Features: Remote pocket opening or thumbhole open; pocket clip
Options: Black or satin finish; plain or serrated edge blade; left hand model available
MSRP: **$205**

SUPER COMMANDER
Blade Length: 4 in.
Blade Material: 154CM
Length (Open/Closed): 9.5 in./5.5 in.
Handle: G10
Lock: Liner lock

EMERSON POLICE SARK BTS

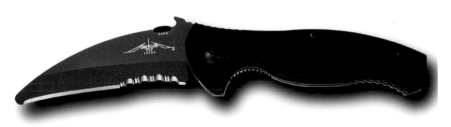

EMERSON SEARCH AND RESCUE SARK BTS

EMERSON SUPER COMMANDER

Weight: 6.2 oz.
Features: Remote pocket opening or thumbhole open; pocket clip
Options: Black or satin finish; plain or serrated edge blade
MSRP: **$313**

SUPER KARAMBIT
Blade Length: 3.4 in.
Blade Material: 154CM

Length (Open/Closed): 8.4 in./5 in.
Handle: G10
Lock: Liner lock
Weight: 4.8 oz.
Features: Remote pocket opening or thumbhole open; pocket clip
Options: Black or satin finish
MSRP: **$302**

FOLDING KNIVES

Gerber Gear Knives

www.gerbergear.com

GERBER 06 AUTO 22

GERBER APPLEGATE
COMBAT FOLDER

GERBER BEAR GRYLLS FOLDER 31

GERBER CONTRAST
DROP POINT

GERBER DMF DUAL MULTI
FUNCTION AUTO TANTO

06 AUTO 22 01397
Blade Length: 3.7 in.
Blade Material: S30V
Length (Open/Closed): 8.5 in./4.8 in.
Handle: 6061-T6 aluminum
Lock: Auto lock
Weight: 7 oz.
Features: Oversize release button; stainless steel pommel; manual safety
Options: Tanto partially serrated edge blade; non-automatic F.A.S.T. assisted opening
MSRP: $250

APPLEGATE COMBAT FOLDER 45780
Blade Length: 4.48 in.
Blade Material: 154CM
Length (Open/Closed): 10.6 in./5.64 in.
Handle: Glass filled nylon
Lock: Roto lock
Weight: 7.4 oz.

Features: Double edged partially serrated
Options: Applegate Covert series; 3.79-inch blade
MSRP: $128

BEAR GRYLLS FOLDER 31 000752
Blade Length: 3.63 in.
Blade Material: High Carbon steel
Length (Open/Closed): 7.3 in./4 in.
Handle: Rubber
Lock: Lockback
Weight: 2.4 oz.
Features: Pocket clip; dual thumb studs
Options: None
MSRP: $29

CONTRAST DROP POINT 30-000595
Blade Length: 3 in.
Blade Material: Stainless steel

Length (Open/Closed): 7.1 in./4.3 in.
Handle: G10/Stainless steel
Lock: Frame lock
Weight: 3.7 oz.
Features: Dual thumb studs
Options: Partially serrated edge blade
MSRP: $37

DMF DUAL MULTI FUNCTION AUTO TANTO 30-000379
Blade Length: 3.5 in.
Blade Material: S30V
Length (Open/Closed): 7.35 in./4.45 in.
Handle: G10
Lock: Wedge lock
Weight: 6.7 oz.
Features: Auto opening; manual safety; dual thumb studs; pommel striker
Options: Modified clip point (30-000378), $69; manual operation (31-000583), $70
MSRP: $300

EMERSON ALLIANCE 22 07158

Blade Length: 3.44 in.
Blade Material: 154CM
Length (Open/Closed): 8.7 in./5.39 in.
Handle: 6061-T6 aluminum
Lock: Cross bolt
Weight: 6 oz.
Features: Automatic opening w/ safety; ballistic Nylon sheath; black oxide coated blade
Options: None
MSRP: **$239**

GERBER EMERSON ALLIANCE 22

EZ OUT DPSF 01648G

Blade Length: 3.5 in.
Blade Material: S30V
Length (Open/Closed): 8 in./4.5 in.
Handle: Glass-filled nylon/rubber inserts
Lock: Lockback
Weight: 2.8 oz.
Features: Thumbhole open
Options: None
MSRP: **$40**

GERBER EZ OUT DPSF

KIOWA 22 01405

Blade Length: 3 in.
Blade Material: High Carbon Stainless steel
Length (Open/Closed): 7.4 in./4.37 in.
Handle: Glass-filled nylon
Lock: Liner lock
Weight: 3.4 oz.
Features: Dual thumb studs
Options: None
MSRP: **$53**

GERBER KIOWA 22

Grayman Knives

graymanknives.com

GRAYMAN DUA BEADBLAST/DLC COATING

DUA BEADBLAST/DLC COATING

Blade Length: 3 in.
Blade Material: S30V
Length (Open/Closed): 4 in./7 in.
Handle: Titanium/G10
Lock: Frame lock
Weight: 5 oz.
Features: Titanium construction with G10 coated handle on non-locking side

Options: Beadblast or DLC coating
MSRP: **$255/285**

Hogue Elishewitz Extreme Knives

www.elishewitzknives.com

HOGUE TACTICAL FOLDER DROP BLADE

HOGUE TACTICAL FOLDER TANTO BLADE

TACTICAL FOLDER DROP BLADE 34170
Blade Length: 3.5 in.
Blade Material: 154CM
Length (Open/Closed): 8 in./4.5 in.
Handle: Aluminum
Lock: Button lock
Weight: 4.5 oz.
Features: Auto-engage safety manual release; cryogenically heat treated stonewash finish blade; heat-treated safety button and pivot; ambidextrous thumb studs; tip up/tip down pocket clip
Options: Green aluminum handle; G10/Damascus pattern handle, $220; 4-inch blade aluminum handle, $220; 4-inch blade G10/Damascus pattern handle, $240
MSRP: **$200**

TACTICAL FOLDER TANTO BLADE 34161
Blade Length: 3.5 in.
Blade Material: 154CM
Length (Open/Closed): 8 in./4.5 in.
Handle: 6061-T6 aluminum
Lock: Button lock
Weight: 4.4 oz.
Features: Auto-engage safety manual release; cryogenically heat treated stonewash finish blade; heat-treated safety button and pivot; ambidextrous thumb studs; tip up/tip down pocket clip
Options: Black aluminum handle; G10/Damascus pattern handle, $220; 4-inch blade aluminum handle, $220; 4-inch blade G10/Damascus pattern handle, $240
MSRP: **$200**

KA-BAR Knives

www.kabar.com

DESERT MULE FOLDER 3053
Blade Length: 3.8 in.
Blade Material: AUS 8A
Length (Open/Closed): 9.1 in./5.25 in.
Handle: Zytel/Kraton inserts
Lock: Lockback
Weight: 7.2 oz.
Features: Teflon coat blade; nylon sheath; vertical or horizontal carry; reversible pocket clip
Options: Plain or serrated edge blade; black or desert tan handle
MSRP: **$70**

KA-BAR DESERT MULE FOLDER

KA-BAR DOG'S
HEAD LOCKBACK

DOG'S HEAD LOCKBACK 3112
Blade Length: 3 in.
Blade Material: 440C
Length (Open/Closed): 6.9 in./3.9 in.

Handle: American Chestnut
Lock: Lockback
Weight: 2.4 oz.
Features: Nail mark opening
Options: None
MSRP: **$127**

KA-BAR Knives

www.kabar.com

KA-BAR DOG'S HEAD THREE
BLADE STOCKMAN

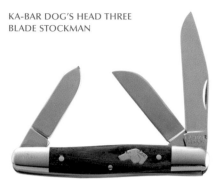

KA-BAR DOG'S
HEAD TWO
BLADE TRAPPER

KA-BAR FIN FOLDING HAWKBILL TANTO

KA-BAR FIN MOJO FOLDER

KA-BAR JOHNSON ADVENTURER
BLADES PIGGY BLACK FOLDER

DOG'S HEAD THREE BLADE STOCKMAN 3313

Blade Length: 3 in.
Blade Material: 440C
Length (Open/Closed): 6.9 in./3.9 in.
Handle: American Chestnut
Lock: None (slip joint)
Weight: 3.2 oz.
Features: Nail mark opening; clip, spey, and sheepsfoot point blades
Options: None
MSRP: $160

DOG'S HEAD TWO BLADE TRAPPER 3211

Blade Length (Max): 3.1 in.
Blade Material: 440C
Length (Open/Closed): 7.4 in./4.3 in.
Handle: American Chestnut
Lock: None (slip joint)
Weight: 4 oz.
Features: Nail mark opening; clip and spey point blades

Options: None
MSRP: $123

FIN FOLDING HAWKBILL TANTO 5553

Blade Length: 2.75 in.
Blade Material: AUS 8A
Length (Open/Closed): 6.9 in./4.25 in.
Handle: Stainless steel
Lock: Frame lock
Weight: 5.6 oz.
Features: Reversible pocket clip; black EDP coating
Options: Drop or tanto point blade; plain edge or serrated
MSRP: $68

FIN MOJO FOLDER 5548

Blade Length: 3.4 in.
Blade Material: 5Cr Stainless steel
Length (Open/Closed): 8.1 in./4.7 in.

Handle: G10
Lock: Liner lock
Weight: 4.8 oz.
Features: Pocket clip; thumb stud opening;
Options: Partially serrated edge blade
MSRP: $40

JOHNSON ADVENTURER BLADES PIGGY BLACK FOLDER 5597

Blade Length: 3.4 in.
Blade Material: AUS 8A
Length (Open/Closed): 7.9 in./4.5 in.
Handle: GFN-PA66
Lock: Lockback
Weight: 3.2 oz.
Features: Reversible pocket clip
Options: Clip or tanto point blade
MSRP: $41

FOLDING KNIVES

KA-BAR Knives

www.kabar.com

KA-BAR K-2 GILA

KA-BAR TDI 2483

KA-BAR WARTHOG FOLDER

K-2 GILA 3077
Blade Length: 3.75 in.
Blade Material: 3Cr13
Length (Open/Closed): 8.6 in./5 in.
Handle: Aluminum
Lock: Liner lock
Weight: 5.6 oz.
Features: Teflon coat blade; thumbhole open; pocket clip
Options: None
MSRP: $21

TDI 2483
Blade Length: 3.6 in.
Blade Material: 5Cr Stainless steel
Length (Open/Closed): 7.5 in./3.9 in.
Handle: G10
Lock: Liner lock
Weight: 5.6 oz.
Features: Thumbhole open; pocket clip
Options: Plain or serrated edge blade
MSRP: $42

WARTHOG FOLDER 3073
Blade Length: 3 in.
Blade Material: 3Cr13
Length (Open/Closed): 7.5 in./4.5 in.
Handle: G10
Lock: Liner lock
Weight: 7.2 oz.
Features: Teflon coat blade; pocket clip
Options: Plain or serrated edge blade
MSRP: $19

Kershaw Knives

www.kershawknives.com

KERSHAW 1920 SELECT FIRE

KERSHAW ASSET 1930ST

KERSHAW BABY BOA

1920 SELECT FIRE
Blade Length: 3.4 in.
Blade Material: 8CR13MOV
Length (Open/Closed): 7.6 in./4.25 in.
Handle: Glass filled nylon
Lock: Liner lock
Weight: 5 oz.
Features: Bit driver and 4-piece bit set
Options: None
MSRP: $35

ASSET 1930ST
Blade Length: 3.25 in.
Blade Material: 8CR13MOV
Length (Open/Closed): 7.9 in./4.6 in.
Handle: Glass-filled nylon
Lock: Liner lock
Weight: 3.8 oz.
Features: SpeedSafe assisted opening; thumb stud; flipper; pocket clip;
Options: Plain edged blade (1930)
MSRP: $40

BABY BOA 1585BR
Blade Length: 2 in.
Blade Material: Sandvik 14C28N
length (Open/Closed): 4.75 in./2.75 in.
Handle: 6061-T6 aluminum
Lock: None
Weight: 1.2 oz.
Features: SpeedSafe assisted opening; thumb stud; flipper; pocket clip; red/black anodized handle; each pattern unique
Options: None
MSRP: $80

FOLDING KNIVES

KERSHAW BLACKHORSE II

KERSHAW BRAWLER 1990

BLACKHORSE II 1060
Blade Length: 3.75 in.
Blade Material: 8CR13MOV
Length (Open/Closed): 8.6 in./4.9 in.
Handle: Co-Polymer
Lock: Back lock
Weight: 4.6 oz.
Features: Sheath carry; nylon realtree camo handle
Options: Black grip (1060A)
MSRP: **$40**

BRAWLER 1990
Blade Length: 3.25 in.
Blade Material: 8CR13MOV
Length (Open/Closed): 7.4 in./4.1 in.
Handle: 410 Stainless steel
Lock: Liner lock
Weight: 3.8 oz.
Features: SpeedSafe assisted opening; thumb stud; flipper; pocket clip
Options: None
MSRP: **$40**

KERSHAW CHIVE 1600BLK

KERSHAW DOUBLE DUTY

CHIVE 1600BLK
Blade Length: 1.95 in.
Blade Material: 420HC
Length (Open/Closed): 4.85 in./2.9 in.
Handle: 410 Stainless steel
Lock: None
Weight: 1.9 oz.
Features: SpeedSafe assisted opening; thumb stud; flipper; pocket clip; DLC coated blade and handle
Options: Ti Oxide rainbow; anodized aluminum; Stainless steel blade; handle coatings, $58–$85
MSRP: **$85**

DOUBLE DUTY 4390
Blade Length (Max): 2.75 in.
Blade Material: AUS 6A
Length (Open/Closed): 6.85 in./4.1 in.
Handle: Nickel/Staminawood
Lock: Liner lock
Weight: 3.1 oz.
Features: Thumb stud for one hand opening; nail mark; clip and spey point blades
Options: None
MSRP: **$100**

KERSHAW ECHELON 1880

KERSHAW HALF TON 1445

ECHELON 1880
Blade Length: 3.25 in.
Blade Material: Sandvik 14C28N
Length (Open/Closed): 7.25 in./4 in.
Handle: G10
Lock: Liner lock
Weight: 2.6 oz.
Features: SpeedSafe assisted opening; thumb stud; reversible pocket clip
Options: None
MSRP: **$90**

HALF TON 1445
Blade Length: 2.5 in.
Blade Material: 8CR13MOV
Length (Open/Closed): 6.1 in./3.6 in.
Handle: Glass filled nylon/santoprene inserts
Lock: Liner lock
Weight: 1.2 oz.
Features: Thumb stud; pocket clip
Options: 3.5-inch blade (1446), $35; 3-inch blade G10 handle (1447), $24
MSRP: **$20**

FOLDING KNIVES

Kershaw Knives
www.kershawknives.com

KERSHAW JUNKYARD DOG
(JYD) II COMPOSITE BLADE

KERSHAW NORTHSIDE
HUNTER

KERSHAW PACKRAT

KERSHAW RAINBOW LEEK

FOLDING KNIVES

JUNKYARD DOG (JYD) II COMPOSITE BLADE 1725CB
Blade Length: 3.75 in.
Blade Material: Sandvik 14C28N w/ copper accent
Length (Open/Closed): 8.6 in./4.9 in.
Handle: G10
Lock: Frame lock
Weight: 5.2 oz.
Features: Thumb stud; flipper; pocket clip
Options: Non-composite blade; liner lock; plain edge or partially serrated blade, $85
MSRP: $130

NORTHSIDE HUNTER 1090
Blade Length: 4.5 in.
Blade Material: 8CR13MOV

Length (Open/Closed): 8.4 in./4.9 in.
Handle: Santoprene
Lock: Back lock
Weight: 4.7 oz.
Features: Sheath carry; nylon
Options: Gut hook blade (1090GH)
MSRP: $40

PACKRAT 1665
Blade Length: 3.25 in.
Blade Material: Sandvik 14C28N
Length (Open/Closed): 7.25 in./4.1 in.
Handle: G10
Lock: Liner lock
Weight: 3 oz.
Features: SpeedSafe assisted opening; thumb stud; flipper; pocket clip

Options: Plain edge or partially serrated blade
MSRP: $90

RAINBOW LEEK 1660VIB
Blade Length: 3 in.
Blade Material: 14C28N
Length (Open/Closed): 4 in./7 in.
Handle: 410 Stainless steel
Lock: Frame lock
Weight: 3 oz.
Features: SpeedSafe assisted opening; thumb stud; pocket clip; Ti Oxide coated blade and handle
Options: Partially serrated blade (1660VIBST)
MSRP: $100

KERSHAW RAKE 1780CB

KERSHAW RIPCORD 3200

KERSHAW RIPCORD
3200 SHEATH

KERSHAW SHALLOT BLACK SERRATED

KERSHAW SHOTGUN
SHELL 12GAD

RAKE 1780CB
Blade Length: 3.5 in.
Blade Material: CPM D-2/Sandvik 14C28N
Length (Open/Closed): 8.1 in./4.6 in.
Handle: G10
Lock: None
Weight: 1.2 oz.
Features: SpeedSafe assisted opening; thumb stud; flipper; pocket clip
Options: None
MSRP: **$140**

RIPCORD 3200
Blade Length: 3.45 in.
Blade Material: Sandvik 14C28N
Length (Open/Closed): 7.85 in./4.4 in.
Handle: 6061-T6 aluminum/Trac Tek inserts
Lock: Button lock
Weight: 4.2 oz.
Features: OTF (Out the Front) opening; interacts w/ Kydex sheath to open and close; tungsten DLC coated blade
Options: None
MSRP: **$120**

SHALLOT BLACK SERRATED 1840CKTST
Blade Length: 3.5 in.
Blade Material: Sandvik 14C28N
Length (Open/Closed): 7.9 in./4.4 in.
Handle: 410 Stainless steel
Lock: Frame lock
Weight: 1.2 oz.
Features: SpeedSafe assisted opening; thumb stud; flipper; pocket clip; DLC coated blade and handle
Options: Satin finish; plain edge blade
MSRP: **$100**

SHOTGUN SHELL 12GAD
Blade Length (Max): 2 in.
Blade Material: AUS 6A
Length (Open/Closed): 4.6 in./2.6 in.
Handle: Rosewood/brass
Lock: None
Weight: 1.2 oz.
Features: Nail mark opening; 2-inch nail file
Options: None
MSRP: **$20**

FOLDING KNIVES

Kershaw Knives

www.kershawknives.com

KERSHAW SKYLINE 1760OR

KERSHAW SPEEDFORM II

KERSHAW SQUAW CREEK

KERSHAW TALON II

KERSHAW TANTO BLUR

SKYLINE 1760OR
Blade Length: 3.1 in.
Blade Material: Sandvik 14C28N
Length (Open/Closed): 7.3 in./4.25 in.
Handle: G10
Lock: Liner lock
Weight: 2.3 oz.
Features: Thumb stud; flipper; pocket clip
Options: Black G10 handle
MSRP: $65

SPEEDFORM II 3550
Blade Length: 3.25 in.
Blade Material: ELMAX reg trademark
Length (Open/Closed): 7.4 in./4.1 in.
Handle: G10
Lock: Liner lock
Weight: 3.2 oz.
Features: Thumb stud; flipper; pocket

clip; blade formed from powdered steel; 2009 Knife of the Year, *BLADE Magazine*
Options: None
MSRP: $140

SQUAW CREEK 2150
Blade Length: 2 in.
Blade Material: AUS6A
Length (Open/Closed): 4.6 in./2.6 in.
Handle: Satin stainless/rosewood
Lock: Back lock
Weight: 1.4 oz.
Features: Nail nick open
Options: None
MSRP: $30

TALON II 1425
Blade Length: 2.9 in.
Blade Material: Sandvik 14C28N

Length (Open/Closed): 6.9 in./4 in.
Handle: G10
Lock: Liner lock
Weight: 3.2 oz.
Features: SpeedSafe assisted opening; thumb stud; flipper; pocket clip
Options: None
MSRP: $100

TANTO BLUR 1670
Blade Length: 3.25 in.
Blade Material: Sandvik 14C28N
Length (Open/Closed): 7.25 in./4.1 in.
Handle: 6061-T6 aluminum w/soft inserts
Lock: Liner lock
Weight: 3 oz.
Features: SpeedSafe assisted opening; thumb stud; flipper; pocket clip
Options: Plain edge or partially serrated blade; black or stainless finish blade, $95–$100; 530V stainless plain edge blade, stonewash finish, $140
MSRP: $95

Kershaw Knives

www.kershawknives.com

KERSHAW WILDCAT RIDGE

KERSHAW WILDCAT RIDGE
ROCKY MT. ELK FOUNDATION

WILDCAT RIDGE 3140JB

Blade Length: 3.5 in.
Blade Material: 8CR13MOV
Length (Open/Closed): 8.4 in./4.9 in.
Handle: Satin stainless/jigged bone
Lock: Back lock
Weight: 7.6 oz.
Features: Nail nick open
Options: ABS or hardwood inlaid scales; RMEF Insigina model includes sheath and blade guard; portion of proceeds to Rocky Mtn. Elk Foundation
MSRP: **$50**

WILDCAT RIDGE ROCKY MT. ELK FOUNDATION 3140WRMEF

Blade Length: 3.5 in.
Blade Material: 8CR13MOV
Length (Open/Closed): 8.5 in./4.9 in.
Handle: Hardwood/stainless steel
Lock: Back lock
Weight: 7.2 oz.
Features: Sheath or blade guard carry
Options: Jigged bone handle; grooved ABS inlaid handle
MSRP: **$50**

Ontario Knife Company

www.ontarioknife.com

8902 JPT 3R ROUND HANDLE

Blade Length (Max): 3.2 in.
Blade Material: AUS 8A
Length (Open/Closed): 8 in./4.8in.
Handle: Zytel
Lock: Liner lock
Weight: 6.3 oz.
Features: Thumb stud, lanyard, pocket clip.
Options: Black or natural stainless color blade; plain or partially serrated edge; drop point or tanto point blade
MSRP: **$70**

ONTARIO KNIFE COMPANY 8902 JPT 34
ROUND HANDLE

8917 JPT 4ST SQUARE HANDLE

Blade Length (Max): 3.2 in.
Blade Material: AUS 8A
Length (Open/Closed): 8 in./4.8 in.
Handle: Zytel
Lock: Liner lock
Weight: 6.3 oz.
Features: Thumb stud; lanyard; pocket clip
Options: Black or natural stainless color blade; plain or partially serrated edge; drop point or tanto point blade
MSRP: **$70**

ONTARIO KNIFE COMMPANY 8917 JPT
4ST SQUARE HANDLE

FOLDING KNIVES

Ontario Knife Company

www.ontarioknife.com

ONTARIO KNIFE COMPANY
APACHE TAC 1 DUTY

ONTARIO KNIFE COMPANY CAMP KNIFE

ONTARIO KNIVE COMPANY RANDALLS RAT FOLDER

ONTARIO KNIFE COMPANY RETRIBUTION 1

ONTARIO KNIFE COMPANY UTILITAC 8787 JPT 2B GREEN

APACHE TAC 1 DUTY 8720

Blade Length (Max): 3.75 in.
Blade Material: 440C Stainless steel
Length (Open/Closed): 8.5 in./4.75 in.
Handle: G10
Lock: Button
Weight: 3.1 oz.
Features: Dual thumb stud; pocket clip
Options: None
MSRP: $155

CAMP KNIFE 8980

Blade Length (Max): 3.25 in.
Blade Material: 420HC
Length (Open/Closed): 7 in./3.6 in.
Handle: Stainless steel
Lock: None
Weight: 3.5 oz.
Features: Flat head screwdriver; awl; can opener; cap lifter; nail notch open
Options: None
MSRP: $65

RANDALLS RAT FOLDER 8847

Blade Length: 3.5 in.
Blade Material: AUS8
Length (Open/Closed): 8.5 in./5 in.
Handle: Nylon 6
Lock: Liner lock
Weight: NA

Features: Reversible, tip-up tip-down pocket clip
Options: Plain or partially serrated edge blade; black or satin Stainless finish blade; OD green or desert tan handle, $26
MSRP: $21

RETRIBUTION 1 8782

Blade Length (Max): 4.3 in.
Blade Material: N690Co
Length (Open/Closed): 10.6 in./6 in.
Handle: Micarta
Lock: Liner lock
Weight: 6.3 oz.
Features: Black nylon belt sheath
Options: 3.9-inch blade (8781)
MSRP: $250

UTILITAC 8787 JPT 2B GREEN

Blade Length (Max): 4 in.
Blade Material: 440 Stainless steel
Length (Open/Closed): 7.1 in./4 in.
Handle: Zytel
Lock: Liner lock
Weight: 6.3 oz.
Features: Thumb stud; pocket clip
Options: Black or green handle; black or natural stainless color blade; plain or partially serrated edge
MSRP: $50

FOLDING KNIVES

Ontario Knife Company

www.ontarioknife.com

XM STRIKE FIGHTER

Blade Length (Max): 3.75 in.
Blade Material: 154CM Stainless steel
Length (Open/Closed): 8.5 in./4.8 in.
Handle: 6061-T6 aluminum
Lock: Button
Weight: 3.1 oz.
Features: Auto opening; button release safety lock when closed; Tribocoat R40 finish blade
Options. None
MSRP: $392

XM1 D DESERT CAMO PLAIN EDGE 8760

Blade Length (Max): 3.4 in.
Blade Material: N690Co
Length (Open/Closed): 8 in./4.6 in.
Handle: 6061-T6 aluminum
Lock: Liner lock
Weight: 6.3 oz.
Features: Thumb stud; reversible pocket clip
Options: Partially serrated blade (8765)
MSRP: $265

XTREME RESCUE 8763

Blade Length (Max): 3.4 in.
Blade Material: N690Co
Length (Open/Closed): 8 in./4.6 in.
Handle: 6061-T6 aluminum
Lock: Liner lock
Weight: 6.4 oz.
Features: Thumb stud; reversible pocket clip; strap cutter; glass break; Torx

ONTARIO KNIFE COMPANY XM STRIKE FIGHTER

ONTARIO KNIFE COMPANY XM1 D DESERT CAMO PLAIN EDGE

ONTARIO KNIFE COMPANY XTREME RESCUE

wrench; set of replaceable blades
Options: Tan, black, or green handle
MSRP: $250

Puma® Knife Company USA

www.pumaknifecompanyusa.com

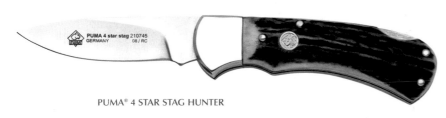

PUMA® 4 STAR STAG HUNTER

4 STAR STAG HUNTER 210745

Blade Length: 2.6 in.
Blade Material: 440A
Length (Open/Closed): 6.6 in./4 in.
Handle: Stag
Lock: Lockback
Weight: 4.1 oz.
Features: Sheath sold separately
Options: 2-inch blade, 4 Star Mini, $56
MSRP: $75

Puma® Knife Company USA

www.pumaknifecompanyusa.com

PUMA® JAGDMESSER

PUMA® WAIDMESSER

JAGDMESSER 210943
Blade Length: 3.1 in.
Blade Material: 440A
Length (Open/Closed): 7.6 in./4.5 in.
Handle: Stag
Lock: Lockback
Weight: 6 oz.
Features: Drop point blade; saw; corkscrew
Options: 3.5-inch drop point blade, with additional gutting blade, $360
MSRP: **$448**

WAIDMESSER 113597
Blade Length: 4.3 in.
Blade Material: 440C
Length (Open/Closed): 13 in./9.1 in.
Handle: Stag
Lock: None
Weight: 7.6 oz.
Features: Unique fixed blade knife with saw; gutting blade and corkscrew in handle
Options: Swing out saw only; Waidmesser II, $280
MSRP: **$400**

Queen Cutlery

www.queencutlery.com

QUEEN CUTLERY 042160 F&W
SOWBELLY

QUEEN CUTLERY 70A COUNTRY COUSIN

042160 F&W SOWBELLY
Blade Length (Max): 2.7 in.
Blade Material: ATS 34 steel
Length (Open/Closed): 6.4 in./3.7 in.
Handle: Moring Ash Worm Groove Bone
Lock: None
Weight: 3.3 oz.
Features: Clip and spey blade; brass pins and liners; file and wire shield; limited production run
Options: None
MSRP: **$137**

70A COUNTRY COUSIN
Blade Length (Max): 3.15 in.
Blade Material: D2 steel
Length (Open/Closed): 7.75 in./3.6 in.
Handle: Delrin
Lock: None
Weight: 2.1 oz.
Features: Brass pins and liner
Options: Yellow handle (70B)
MSRP: **$44**

Queen Cutlery

www.queencutlery.com

QUEEN CUTLERY 2034A ILACSB SWING GUARD LOCK

QUEEN CUTLERY 3314 8445CZ SMALL LOCKBACK

QUEEN CUTLERY 3700 16P MINI TOOTHPICK

QEEN CUTLERY 390146AB WARNCLIFF

QUEEN CUTLERY
PRESIDENT'S CHOICE

QUEEN CUTLERY 7200 RANGER STAG

2034A ILACSB SWING GUARD LOCK

Blade Length (Max): 3.5 in.
Blade Material: D2 steel
Length (Open/Closed): 8 in./4.5 in.
Handle: Aged Honey Bone Amber Stag
Lock: Lockback
Weight: 3.6 oz.
Features: Stainless steel pins and springs; nickel bolster; brass liners
Options: Curly Zebra hardwood handle, 33001LCZ
MSRP: $116

3314 8445CZ SMALL LOCKBACK

Blade Length (Max): 2.1 in.
Blade Material: D2 steel
Length (Open/Closed): 5 in./2.9 in.
Handle: Curly Zebra African hardwood
Lock: Lockback
Weight: 1.6 oz.
Features: Stainless steel pins and springs; nickel bolster; brass liners
Options: None
MSRP: $71

3700 16P MINI TOOTHPICK

Blade Length (Max): 2.25 in.
Blade Material: D2 steel
Length (Open/Closed): 5.25 in./3 in.
Handle: Mother of Pearl
Lock: None
Weight: 1.1 oz.
Features: Stainless steel pins and springs; nickel bolster; brass liners
Options: None
MSRP: $92

390146AB WHARNCLIFF

Blade Length (Max): 2 in.
Blade Material: D2 steel
Length (Open/Closed): 5.1 in./3.1 in.
Handle: Abalone
Lock: None
Weight: 1.1 oz.
Features: Stainless steel pins and springs; nickel bolster; brass liners
Options: None
MSRP: $115

7200 RANGER STAG

Blade Length (Max): 2.5 in.
Blade Material: Damascus steel
Length (Open/Closed): 6.1 in./ 3.6 in.
Handle: Stag
Lock: Liner lock
Weight: 3.2 oz.
Features: Numbered and signed
Options: Bone, pearl, or abalone handle
MSRP: $225

PRESIDENT'S CHOICE

Blade Length (Max): 3 in.
Blade Material: D2 steel
Length (Open/Closed): 7.1 in./4.1 in.
Handle: Sanbar Stag
Lock: None
Weight: 3.6 oz.
Features: Gold-filled laser-engraved blades; limited edition
Options: Magnetic display stand
MSRP: $228

FOLDING KNIVES

Remington Cutlery

www.remington.com

REMINGTON ELITE SKINNER
SERIES II 2 BLADE STAG

REMINGTON SPORTSMAN
SERIES FAST FOLDER LARGE/
MEDIUM

ELITE SKINNER SERIES II 2 BLADE STAG 19752

Blade Length (Max): 3.4 in.
Blade Material: 440C
Length (Open/Closed): 7.9 in./4.5 in.
Handle: 6061 aluminum/stag
Lock: Axis lock
Weight: NA
Features: 3.25-inch saw; leather pancake style open top sheath
Options: Olive wood or genuine stag insets; three blade model adds 3.4-inch gut hook
MSRP: $150

SPORTSMAN SERIES FAST FOLDER LARGE/MEDIUM

Blade Length: 3.6 in./3.1 in.
Blade Material: 440 Stainless
Length (Open/Closed): Large: 8.6 in./5 in.; Mediums: 7.1 in./4.1 in.
Handle: Aluminum/rubber coat
Lock: Liner lock
Weight: 4.2 oz./3.6 oz.
Features: Dual thumb stud or flipper opening; partial hand-guard integral w/blade
Options: Black, orange and camo handle; advantage Max4 and mossy oak patterns
MSRP: . . . . $25/$21

Schrade

www.schradeknives.com

1ST RESPONDER SCH911DBS

Blade Length (Max): 3.5 in.
Blade Material: 4034 Stainless steel
Length (Open/Closed): 8.2 in./4.7 in.
Handle: Nylon fiber
Lock: Liner lock
Weight: 5.6 oz.
Features: M.A.G.I.C. assist opening; safety lock; belt cutter
Options: Teflon coat; full or partial serrated blade
MSRP: $80

SCHRADE 1ST RESPONDER

SCHRADE 2 BLADE LADY LEG KNIFE FLAG HANDLE SLEG1

SCHRADE BUZZSAW TRAPPER 97OT

SCHRADE FOLDING HUNTER 220OT

SCHRADE LAND SHARK 190T

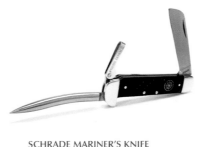

SCHRADE MARINER'S KNIFE

SCHRADE MIGHTY ANGLER LARGE FILET KNIFE MA6

2 BLADE LADY LEG KNIFE FLAG HANDLE SLEG1

Blade Length (Max): 2.1 in.
Blade Material: Stainless steel
Length (Open/Closed): 5.2 in./3.1 in.
Handle: Celluloid
Lock: None
Weight: 1.6 oz.
Features: 65th anniversary imprint; American Flag theme handle; brass pins and liner; nickel bolsters
Options: 2.1-inch or 3.8-inch clip point blade
MSRP: $20

BUZZSAW TRAPPER 97OT

Blade Length (Max): 3.7 in.
Blade Material: 400 Series Stainless
Length (Open/Closed): 7.8 in./4.1 in.
Handle: Delrin
Lock: Lockback
Weight: 4 oz.
Features: Nail nick opening; locking sawblade; field pick; tweezers
Options: None
MSRP: $38

FOLDING HUNTER 220OT

Blade Length (Max): 4 in.
Blade Material: 400 Series Stainless
Length (Open/Closed): 9.2 in./5.2 in.
Handle: Delrin
Lock: None
Weight: 8.8 oz.
Features: Nail nick opening; nylon flap over belt sheath; saw blade and hatchet
Options: None
MSRP: $39

LAND SHARK 190T

Blade Length (Max): 2.5 in.
Blade Material: 400 Series Stainless
Length (Open/Closed): 6.3 in./3.8 in.
Handle: Delrin
Lock: None
Weight: 2.6 oz.
Features: Nail nick opening
Options: None
MSRP: $14

MARINER'S KNIFE 735RPB

Blade Length (Max): 2.8 in.
Blade Material: 400 Series Stainless

Length (Open/Closed): 6.9 in./4.1 in.
Handle: Red pick bone
Lock: Lever lock
Weight: 4.4 oz.
Features: Nail nick opening; rope blade; marlin spike w/ shackle
Options: None
MSRP: $32

MIGHTY ANGLER LARGE FILET KNIFE MA6

Blade Length (Max): 5.5 in.
Blade Material: 400 Series Stainless
Length (Open/Closed): 12.2 in./6.7 in.
Handle: Wood
Lock: Lockback
Weight: 4.5 oz.
Features: Nail nick opening; finger grooves on handle
Options:4.3-inch blade (MA5)
MSRP: $22

Schrade

www.schradeknives.com

OUT THE FRONT ASSIST SCHOTFG

Blade Length (Max): 3 in.
Blade Material: 4116 Stainless steel
Length (Open/Closed): 7.6 in./4.6 in.
Handle: Zytel
Lock: Lever lock
Weight: 4.4 oz.
Features: Titanium coated blade; blade lock and slide safety
Options: Black handle; 2nd Generation OTFAs (out the front action); aluminum handles; drop and tanto point, $64; plain and partially serrated blades
MSRP: **$60**

SCHRADE OUT THE FRONT ASSIST SCHOTFG

SOG Knives

sogknives.com

SOG AEGIS MINI AE21

AEGIS MINI AE21

Blade Length: 3 in.
Blade Material: AUS 8
Length (Open/Closed): 7 in./4.25 in.
Handle: Glass reinforced nylon
Lock: Lockback
Weight: 2 oz.
Features: Assisted opening; built in safety with red visual index; rubber inserts on grip; cryogenic heat treated blade; reversible low ride pocket clip
Options: Black Titanium Nitride finish; tanto blade; 3.5-inch blade Aegis with satin; Digital Camo; Black Titanium Nitride; plain or partially serrated edge blade, $93–$114
MSRP: **$80**

ARCITECH A01

Blade Length: 3.5 in.
Blade Material: 420J2 Stainless/VG10 Core
Length (Open/Closed): 8 in./4.5 in.
Handle: Titanium/jigged bone

SOG ARCITECH A01

SOG BLINK BBA-99

Lock: Arc lock
Weight: 4.5 oz.
Features: Mirror polished laminate san mai blade; jeweled abalone thumb stud; limited production
Options: Damascus blade; carbon fiber handle, $600
MSRP: **$492**

BLINK BBA-99

Blade Length: 2.25 in

Blade Material: AUS 8
Length (Open/Closed): 5.4 in./3.2 in.
Handle: Aluminum
Lock: Lockback
Weight: 2.1 oz.
Features: Assisted opening; dual thumb studs; reversible low ride pocket clip; cryogenic heat treated blade
Options: Black Titanium Nitride finish, $70
MSRP: **$60**

SOG BLUTO BL 01

BLUTO BL 01
Blade Length: 2.25 in.
Blade Material: 420J2 Stainless steel/
VG10 Core
Length (Open/Closed): 5.5 in./3.25 in.
Handle: Aluminum
Lock: Arc lock
Weight: 3.2 oz.
Features: Flipper or thumb stud open;
reversible pocket clip
Options: Black handle (BL-03)
MSRP: **$192**

CONTRACTOR III EL30-CP
Blade Length (Max): 2.9 in.
Blade Material: 6Cr12 MoV
Length (Open/Closed): 5.75 in./2.85
in.
Handle: G10
Lock: None
Weight: 2.1 oz.
Features: Flat blade screwdriver; nail
mark opening; lanyard ring
Options: None
MSRP: **$55**

SOG CONTRACTOR III
EL30-CP

FIELDER XL FF-34
Blade Length: 4.1 in.
Blade Material: 7Cr13 Stainless
Length (Open/Closed): 9.6 in./5.5 in.
Handle: Wood
Lock: Liner lock
Weight: 8.6 oz.
Features: Left side thumbstud; right
side pocket clip
Options: 2.75-inch blade, $25; 3.5-
inch blade, $30
MSRP: **$35**

SOG FIELDER XL

FLASH I STGFSA-97
Blade Length: 2.5 in.
Blade Material: AUS 8
Length (Open/Closed): 5.75 in./3.25
in.
Handle: Aluminum
Lock: Piston lock
Weight: 1.6 oz.
Features: Assisted opening; built-in
safety with red visual index; reversible
low ride pocket clip
Options: Glass reinforced handle;
satin finish; plain or half serrated edge
blade; blue, black, or pink handle
MSRP: **$120**

SOG FLASH I STGFSA-97

FOLDING KNIVES

SOG Knives

sogknives.com

SOG FLASH RESCUE OFSA-6

SOG GUNNY FOLDING KNIFE GFL01-L

SOG MICRON 2.0 FF93 CP

SOG NAUTICAL FFCP-23

FLASH RESCUE OFSA-6
Blade Length: 3.5 in.
Blade Material: AUS 8
Length (Open/Closed): 8 in./4.5 in.
Handle: Glass reinforced nylon
Lock: Piston lock
Weight: 3.1 oz.
Features: Half serrated sheepsfoot blade; assisted opening with safety lock; dual thumb studs; reversible low ride pocket clip; cryogenic heat treated blade
Options: Black handle (FSA6), $75; black Titanium Nitride coated blade (TFSA-6), $87
MSRP: **$70**

GUNNY FOLDING KNIFE GFL01-L
Blade Length: 4 in.
Blade Material: VG10
Length (Open/Closed): 9.1 in./4.1 in.
Handle: Cocobolo; stingray; nickel
Lock: Lockback
Weight: 1.4 oz.
Features: Commemorative Gunny coin inlaid in handle; signed piece; limited to 1,000 serialized pieces; leather sheath
Options: None
MSRP: **$500**

MICRON 2.0 FF93 CP
Blade Length (Max): 2.25 in.
Blade Material: 420 Steel
Length (Open/Closed): 5 in./2.75 in.
Handle: Stainless steel
Lock: Lockback
Weight: 1.4 oz.
Features: Bead blast finish; ultra slim for pocket carry
Options: Tanto blade; black Titanium Nitride finish; 1.5-inch blade, $18
MSRP: **$26**

NAUTICAL FFCP-23
Blade Length (Max): 2.9 in.
Blade Material: 6Cr12 MoV
Length (Open/Closed): 7.1 in./4.2 in.
Handle: G10
Lock: None
Weight: 4.9 oz.
Features: Marlin spike; lanyard ring
Options: None
MSRP: **$75**

SOG SPEC ELITE I AUTO SE-52

SOG SPEC ELITE MINI SE-01

SOG TRIDENT TIGER STRIPE TF-3

SOG TWITCH XL TWI-20

SOG VULCAN MINI TANTO VL-04

SPEC ELITE I AUTO SE-52

Blade Length: 3.5 in.
Blade Material: AUS 8
Length (Open/Closed): 7.8 in./4.3 in.
Handle: Aluminum
Lock: Auto lock
Weight: 2.8 oz.
Features: Automatic opening and safety; reversible low ride pocket clip
Options: Satin finish blade (SE-51), $175; manual open, arc lock (SE-14), $155
MSRP: $190

SPEC ELITE MINI SE-01

Blade Length: 2.75 in.
Blade Material: VG10
Length (Open/Closed): 6.5 in./4.3 in.
Handle: Glass reinforced nylon
Lock: Arc lock
Weight: 2.7 oz.
Features: Reversible low ride pocket clip
Options: None
MSRP: $140

TRIDENT TIGER STRIPE TF-3

Blade Length: 3.75 in.
Blade Material: AUS 8
Length (Open/Closed): 8.5 in./4.75 in.
Handle: Glass reinforced nylon
Lock: Arc actuator
Weight: 3.6 oz.
Features: Assisted opening; built in safety with red visual index; cord cutting groove in grip; reversible low ride pocket clip; cryogenic heat treated blade
Options: Black Titanium Nitride; digital or desert camo finish; plain edged blade; 3.15-inch blade Trident Mini (TF-22), $85
MSRP: $114

TWITCH XL TWI-20

Blade Length: 3.25 in.
Blade Material: AUS 8
Length (Open/Closed): 7.5 in./4.25 in.
Handle: Aluminum
Lock: Lockback
Weight: 4.2 oz.
Features: Assisted opening and safety; flipper and dual thumb studs; cryogen-ic heat treated blade; reversible low ride pocket clip
Options: Satin finish blade; black Titanium Nitride; plain or partially serrated edge blade; 2-inch blade Twitch I; 2.7-inch blade Twitch II; graphite or aluminum handle, $62–$145
MSRP: $104

VULCAN MINI TANTO VL-04

Blade Length: 3 in.
Blade Material: 420J2 Stainless/VG10 Core
Length (Open/Closed): 7.35 in./4.35 in.
Handle: Glass reinforced nylon
Lock: Arc lock
Weight: 3.4 oz.
Features: Flipper and dual thumb studs; reversible low ride pocket clip
Options: VG10 steel blade w/ satin, $155; or black Titanium Nitride finish, $175; full-size Vulcan has 3.5-inch blade, $181–$195
MSRP: $181

Spyderco Knives

www.spyderco.com

SPYDERCO ASSIST BLACK BLADE

SPYDERCO BALANCE BY ED SCHEMPP C141

SPYDERCO BYRD CARA CARA G10

SPYDERCO BYRD CROSSBILL BY07

SPYDERCO BYRD MEADOWLARK2

SPYDERCO BYRD WINGS SLIPIT

ASSIST BLACK BLADE C79BBK

Blade Length: 3.7 in.
Blade Material: VG10
Length (Open/Closed): 8.44 in./4.8 in.
Handle: Fiberglass reinforced nylon
Lock: Lockback
Weight: 4 oz.
Features: Reversible tip wire pocket clip; Cobra Hood over opening hole assists cutting with blade partially closed; replaceable/retractable carbide glass break stored in handle
Options: Orange or black handle; natural stainless color blade, $130
MSRP: $145

BALANCE BY ED SCHEMPP C141

Blade Length: 1.9 in.
Blade Material: VG10
Length (Open/Closed): 4.44 in./2.7 in.
Handle: Stainless steel
Lock: Liner
Weight: 1.4 oz.
Features: Centered thumbhole when closed; ambidextrous tip-up/tip-down pocket clip
Options: Carbon fiber handle (C141CF), $200
MSRP: $125

BYRD CARA CARA G10 BY03G-2

Blade Length: 3.75 in.
Blade Material: 8Cr13MoV
Length (Open/Closed): 8.5 in./4.75 in.
Handle: G10
Lock: Back lock
Weight: 4.25 oz.
Features: Ambidextrous pocket clip; tip-up or tip-down
Options: Black or stainless color blade; plain edge or partially serrated blade
MSRP: $50

BYRD CROSSBILL BY07

Blade Length: 3.5 in.
Blade Material: 8Cr13MoV
Length (Open/Closed): 7.6 in./4.6 in.
Handle: Stainless steel
Lock: Lockback
Weight: 5.6 oz.
Features: Left side tip-up pocket clip
Options: Partially serrated blade
MSRP: $38

BYRD MEADOWLARK2 BY04BK2

Blade Length: 2.9 in.
Blade Material: 8Cr13MoV
Length (Open/Closed): 6.8 in./4.01 in.
Handle: Glass reinforced nylon
Lock: Back lock
Weight: 2.4 oz.
Features: Ambidextrous pocket clip; tip-up or tip-down
Options: Plain edge blade
MSRP: $30

BYRD WINGS SLIPIT BY21G

Blade Length (Max): 2.75 in.
Blade Material: 8Cr13MoV
Length (Open/Closed): 6.5 in./3.75 in.
Handle: G10/Stainless steel
Lock: None
Weight: 3.4 oz.
Features: Ambidextrous pocket clip; tip-up or tip-down; 2.75-inch sheepsfoot blade
Options: G10 handle; 3.4-inch blades (BY20G), $50
MSRP: $30

Spyderco Knives

SPYDERCO CHINESE FOLDER
GLASS FIBER HANDLE

SPYDERCO CHOKWE C132G

CHINESE FOLDER GLASS FIBER HANDLE C65CF

Blade Length: 3.2 in.
Blade Material: VG10
Length (Open/Closed): 7.2 in./4.25 in.
Handle: Glass fiber
Lock: Liner lock
Weight: 3 oz.
Features: Right side pocket clip; tip-up or tip-down
Options: None
MSRP: **$220**

CHOKWE C132G

Blade Length: 3.75 in.
Blade Material: CPM S30V
Length (Open/Closed): 8.5 in./4.75 in.
Handle: G10
Lock: Reeve integral
Weight: 3.7 oz.
Features: Locks on handle scale; lock reinforced by full length liner; dedicated to the Chokwe of Zambia; 5 percent of sales to http://keepachildalive.org
Options: None
MSRP: **$220**

CITADEL 92MM BLACK BLADE III C117BK

Blade Length: 3.1 in.
Blade Material: CPM S30V
Length (Open/Closed): 7.4 in./4.28 in.
Handle: Aluminum
Lock: Automatic
Weight: 3.6 oz.
Features: Push button opening; manual lock open or closed; ambidextrous tip up pocket clip; restricted sale to authorized personnel
Options: Natural or black finish; 83 mm compact model (C119), $240
MSRP: **$250**

SPYDERCO CITADEL
92MM BLACK BLADE III

SPYDERCO CRICKET
STAINLESS STEEL

CRICKET STAINLESS STEEL C29SS

Blade Length: 1.9 in.
Blade Material: VG10
Length (Open/Closed): 4.25 in./2.75 in.
Handle: Stainless steel
Lock: Reeve integral
Weight: 1.75 oz.
Features: Locks on handle scale
Options: None
MSRP: **$100**

Spyderco Knives

www.spyderco.com

SPYDERCO DELICA4
EMERSON OPENER

SPYDERCO DRAGONFLY2 SALT

SPYDERCO ED SHREMPP
PERSIAN FOLDER

SPYDERCO EMBASSY C121

DELICA4 EMERSON OPENER C11GYW

Blade Length: 3.75 in.
Blade Material: VG10
Length (Open/Closed): 8.75 in./5 in.
Handle: Fiberglass reinforced nylon
Lock: Lockback
Weight: 3.6 oz.
Features: Hook catches on pocket for quick opening; ambidextrous tip-up/tip-down pocket clip
Options: Trainer available
MSRP: $110

DRAGONFLY2 SALT C28YL2

Blade Length: 2.25 in.
Blade Material: H-1
Length (Open/Closed): 5.55 in./3.3 in.

Handle: Fiberglass reinforced nylon
Lock: Lockback
Weight: 1.2 oz.
Features: Corrosion resistant blade; reversible tip-up wire pocket clip
Options: Serrated Spyderedge blade
MSRP: $80

ED SHREMPP PERSIAN FOLDER C83G-2

Blade Length: 3.44 in.
Blade Material: VG10
Length (Open/Closed): 8.25 in./4.75 in.
Handle: G10
Lock: Back lock
Weight: 4.2 oz.

Features: Left side tip-up pocket clip
Options: None
MSRP: $220

EMBASSY C121

Blade Length: 3.1 in.
Blade Material: CPM S30V
Length (Open/Closed): 7.4 in./4.28 in.
Handle: Aluminum/G10
Lock: Automatic
Weight: 3.6 oz.
Features: Push button opening; manual lock open or closed; three position pocket clip; restricted sale to authorized personnel
Options: Black blade and handle
MSRP: $260

ENDURA4 BLACK BLADE C10BBK

Blade Length: 3.75 in.
Blade Material: VG10
Length (Open/Closed): 8.75 in./5 in.
Handle: Fiberglass reinforced nylon
Lock: Lockback
Weight: 3.6 oz.
Features: Titanium Carbonitride finish blade; thumbhole opening; ambidextrous tip-up/tip-down pocket clip
Options: Blue, green, foliage green, or stainless steel handles; plain or partially serrated blade; Emerson opening hook; 2.9-inch blade (Delica series); trainers available
MSRP: $115

SPYDERCO ENDURA4 BLACK BLADE

KIWI3 STAG HANDLE SLIP JOINT C75ST3

Blade Length: 2.4 in.
Blade Material: 8Cr14 MoV
Length (Open/Closed): 5.6 in./3.3 in.
Handle: Stainless steel/stag
Lock: None
Weight: 1.6 oz.
Features: Slip joint pivot; wharncliff blade
Options: Stainless steel handle (C75SS3), $30
MSRP: $55

SPYDERCO KIWI3 STAG HANDLE SLIP JOINT

LADY BUG3 HAWKBILL LYL3HB

Blade Length: 1.9 in.
Blade Material: H-1
Length (Open/Closed): 4.3 in./2.44 in.
Handle: Fiberglass reinforced nylon
Lock: Lockback
Weight: 0.6 oz.
Features: Corrosion resistant blade; smallest locking Spyderco folder; Spyderedge serrated blade; no pocket clip
Options: 2.9-inch blade (C106YL), $100
MSRP: $55

SPYDERCO MASSAD AYOOB C60G

MASSAD AYOOB C60G

Blade Length: 3.6 in.
Blade Material: VG10
Length (Open/Closed): 8.6 in./5.03 in.
Handle: G10
Lock: Lockback
Weight: 4.9 oz.
Features: Ambidextrous tip down

SPYDERCO KIWI3 STAG HANDLE SLIP JOINT C75ST3

SPYDERCO LADY BUG3 HAWKBILL

SPYDERCO MILITARY DIGICAM

SPYDERCO SAGE 2 REEVE INTEGRAL LOCK TITANIUM

pocket clip; short opening arc; David Boyle lock release
Options: None
MSRP: $250

MILITARY DIGICAM C36GPCMO

Blade Length: 4 in.
Blade Material: CPM S-30V
Length (Open/Closed): 9.5 in./5.5 in.
Handle: G10
Lock: Lockback

Weight: 4.25 oz.
Features: Right hand tip down pocket clip.
Options: Left hand model available; black handle w/ black or natural blade; partially serrated blade (G36GBK), $240; 3.44-inch blade ParaMilitary2, $170–$190
MSRP: $220

SAGE 2 REEVE INTEGRAL LOCK TITANIUM C123TI

Blade Length: 3 in.
Blade Material: CPM S30V
Length (Open/Closed): 7.1 in./4.2 in.
Handle: Titanium
Lock: Reeve integral
Weight: 3.5 oz.
Features: Locks on handle scale; ambidextrous tip-up pocket clip; 5 percent of sales donated to Colorado Alzheimer Assoc. www.aalz.org/co/
Options: None
MSRP: $265

FOLDING KNIVES

Spyderco Knives

www.spyderco.com

SAGE 3 BOLT ACTION C123GBL
Blade Length: 3 in.
Blade Material: CPM S30V
Length (Open/Closed): 7.25 in./4.3 in.
Handle: G10
Lock: Bolt action
Weight: 3.5 oz.
Features: Auto lock; manual release; 5 percent of sales donated to Colorado Alzheimer Assoc. www.aalz.org/co/
Options: None
MSRP: $260

SPYDERCO SAGE 3 BOLT ACTION

SPYDERCO SQUEAK SLIPIT

SQUEAK SLIPIT C154BK
Blade Length: 2 in.
Blade Material: N690Co
Length (Open/Closed): 5.03 in./3.1 in.
Handle: Fiberglass reinforced nylon

Lock: None
Weight: 1.6 oz.
Features: Legal where locking folders are prohibited (legal in New York);

notch joint design similar to slip joint; reversible tip-up wire pocket clip
Options: None
MSRP: $220

SureFire

www.surefire.com

CRANK FOLDING UTILITY KNIFE EW-10
Blade Length (Max): 3 in.
Blade Material: 154CM
Length (Open/Closed): 6.6 in./4 in.
Handle: Aluminum
Lock: Bar lock
Weight: 3.2 oz.
Features: Flipper/thumb stud open; right side pocket clip; cord cutter; ½-inch hex wrench; coin slot to adapt coin edge for use as a screwdriver
Options: None
MSRP: $210

SUREFIRE CRANK FOLDING UTILITY KNIFE

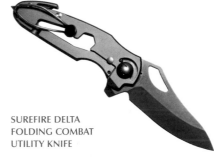

SUREFIRE DELTA FOLDING COMBAT UTILITY KNIFE

DELTA FOLDING COMBAT UTILITY KNIFE EW-04
Blade Length (Max): 3.4 in.
Blade Material: CPM S30V
Length (Open/Closed): 8 in./4.7 in.
Handle: Titanium
Lock: Frame lock
Weight: 4.6 oz.
Features: Flipper or thumb hole open; reversible pocket clip; cord cutter; slotted self seating wrench, ½-inch to ¹³⁄₆₄; window break; finger guard doubles as screwdriver
Options: None
MSRP: $445

SUREFIRE EDGE FOLDING UTILITY KNIFE

EDGE FOLDING UTILITY KNIFE EW-09
Blade Length (Max): 3.9 in.
Blade Material: 154CM
Length (Open/Closed): 8.25 in./4.9 in.
Handle: 7075 aluminum
Lock: Liner lock
Weight: 5.5 oz.

Features: Titanium liners; integral flipper/handguard as well as thumb stud or thumb hole open; right side pocket clip; integral hex wrench sizes ½ inch, ⁷⁄₁₆ inch, ³⁄₈ inch, ⁵⁄₁₆ inch, ¼ inch
Options: None
MSRP: $265

FOLDING KNIVES

TOPS FOLDER MAGNUM

TOPS FOLDER THUNDER HAWKE TANTO POINT

TOPS SERRATED FOLDER CQT 303

FOLDER MAGNUM 711
Blade Length: 4.5 in.
Blade Material: N690Co
Length (Open/Closed): 10 in./5.75 in.
Handle: G10
Lock: Liner lock
Weight: 8.7 oz.
Features: Nylon MOLLE compatible sheath; military grade Teflon coat blade
Options: None
MSRP: $229

FOLDER THUNDER HAWKE TANTO POINT
Blade Length: 3.75 in.
Blade Material: N690Co
Length (Open/Closed): 8.6 in./4.9 in.
Handle: G10
Lock: Titanium frame lock
Weight: 4 oz.
Features: Black cobalt finish
Options: Plain edge blade
MSRP: $219

SERRATED FOLDER CQT 303
Blade Length: 3.25 in.
Blade Material: 154CM
Length (Open/Closed): 7.95 in./4.7 in.
Handle: G10
Lock: Liner lock
Weight: 4 oz.
Features: Reversible tip-down pocket clip; bearing detent; bronze bushings; stainless steel liners; nickel boride finish
Options: None
MSRP: $169

Victorinox Swiss Army
www.swissarmy.com

5302FG4 ALOX FLIGHT 64GB
Blade Length: NA
Blade Material: NA
Length (Open/Closed): 3.7 in./2.3 in.
Handle: Aluminum oxide
Lock: None
Weight: 1.2 oz.
Features: No blade; 2GB to 64GB flash drive; nylon pouch
Options: Flash Alox series adds four implements
MSRP: $370

54754 SILVER TECH CLIMBER
Blade Length: 2.4 in.
Blade Material: Stainless steel
Length (Open/Closed): 3.7 in./3.6 in.
Handle: Cellidor
Lock: None
Features: 14 implements including multi-purpose hook (parcel carrier)
Options: None
MSRP: $39

VICTORINOX 5302FG4 ALOX FLIGHT 64GB

54878 ONE HAND TREKKER CAMO NS
Blade Length: 3.15 in.
Blade Material: Stainless steel
Length (Open/Closed): 8 in./4.4 in.
Handle: Cellidor
Lock: Liner lock
Weight: 4.5 oz.
Features: Twelve implements including one hand open blade and wood saw
Options: None
MSRP: $58

VICTORINOX 54754 SILVER TECH CLIMBER

VICTORINOX 54878 ONE HAND TREKKER CAMO NS

FOLDING KNIVES

Victorinox Swiss Army

www.swissarmy.com

VICTORINOX ONE HAND FIREMAN BLACK
COAT BLADE

VICTORINOX ONE HAND SENTINEL NON
SERRATED

VICTORINOX FLASH
5301 SG8 8GB RUBY

VICTORINOX RESCUE
TOOL LOCK KNIFE

VICTORINOX RESCUE TOOL RESCUE POUCH

FLASH 5301 SG8 8GB RUBY
Blade Length: 1.4 in.
Blade Material: Stainless steel
Length (Open/Closed): 3.7 in./2.3 in.
Handle: Cellidor
Lock: None
Weight: 1.9 oz.
Features: Translucent handle; eight functions including LED white light; pressurized ball point pen; nylon pouch available w/ 2GB to 64GB flash drive
Options: None
MSRP: $105

ONE HAND FIREMAN BLACK COAT BLADE
Blade Length: 3.15 in.
Blade Material: Stainless steel

Length (Open/Closed): 7.6 in./4.4 in.
Handle: Cellidor
Lock: Liner lock
Weight: NA
Features: One hand opening
Options: None
MSRP: $72

ONE HAND SENTINEL NON SERRATED
Blade Length: 2.4 in.
Blade Material: Stainless steel
Length (Open/Closed): 3.7 in./3.6 in.
Handle: Cellidor
Lock: Liner lock
Weight: 2.5 oz.
Features: One hand opening

Options: Full serrated blade; belt clip
MSRP: $32

RESCUE TOOL 53900
Blade Length (Max): 3.15 in.
Blade Material: Stainless steel
Length (Open/Closed): 7.6 in./4.4 in.
Handle: Cellidor
Lock: Liner lock
Weight: 7 oz.
Features: Luminous handle; fifteen functions include glass break, seatbelt cutter, one hand opening blade; nylon pouch
Options: None
MSRP: $95

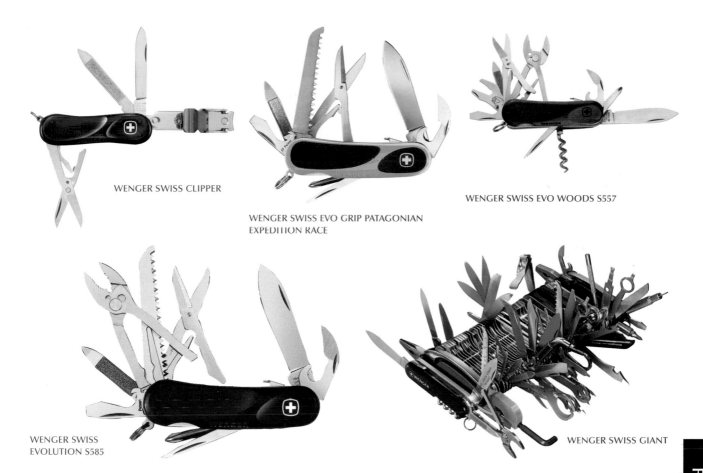

WENGER SWISS CLIPPER

WENGER SWISS EVO GRIP PATAGONIAN
EXPEDITION RACE

WENGER SWISS EVO WOODS S557

WENGER SWISS
EVOLUTION S585

WENGER SWISS GIANT

SWISS CLIPPER 16962

Blade Length: 1.75 in.
Blade Material: Stainless steel
Length (Open/Closed): 4.25 in./2.5 in.
Handle: Cellidor
Lock: None
Weight: 1.3 oz.
Features: Seven implements; eight
functions including clipper, scissors,
nail file; Purple Plum Ice translucent
handle
Options: Red, Watermelon, Pastel
Pink; stainless steel handles
MSRP: $38

SWISS EVO GRIP PATAGONIAN EXPEDITION RACE 16801

Blade Length: 2.75 in.
Blade Material: Stainless steel
Length (Open/Closed): 6 in./3.25 in.
Handle: Rubber
Lock: Back lock
Weight: 3.1 oz.

Features: Eleven implements; fifteen
functions including reamer and locking screwdriver; wire stripper
Options: None
MSRP: $75

SWISS EVO WOODS S557 16389

Blade Length: 2.5 in.
Blade Material: Stainless steel
Length (Open/Closed): 5.75 in./3.25
in.
Handle: Walnut
Lock: Back lock
Weight: 4.4 oz.
Features: Eleven implements; seven-
teen functions including pliers and
universal wrench
Options: None
MSRP: $160

SWISS EVOLUTION S585 16822

Blade Length: 2.75 in.
Blade Material: Stainless steel

Length (Open/Closed): 6 in./3.25 in.
Handle: Cellidor
Lock: Back lock
Weight: 4.1 oz.
Features: Twelve implements; eighteen
functions including tweezers, saw,
locking screwdriver
Options: None
MSRP: $80

SWISS GIANT 16999

Blade Length: 2.5 in.
Blade Material: Stainless steel
Length (Open/Closed): NA
Handle: Cellidor
Lock: Liner lock
Weight: 2 lbs.
Features: Eighty-seven implements;
141 functions including saw; spoke
wrench; divot repair tool; snap shack-
le; watch case back opening tool
Options: None
MSRP: $2,150

Wenger Swiss Army

www.wengerna.com

WENGER SWISS MIKE HORN SOUVENIR

WENGER SWISS PORSCHE
DESIGN ORIGINAL

WENGER SWISS RANGER 51

WENGER SWISS TOOL
CHEST PLUS

WENGER SWISS UELI STECK SPECIAL EDITION

FOLDING KNIVES

SWISS MIKE HORN SOUVENIR 16327
Blade Length: 2.75 in.
Blade Material: Stainless steel
Length (Open/Closed): 6 in./3.25 in.
Handle: Cellidor
Lock: None
Weight: 3.1 oz.
Features: Eleven implements; fourteen functions including wood saw, scissors, and locking screwdriver
Options: None
MSRP: $80

SWISS PORSCHE DESIGN ORIGINAL 16679
Blade Length: 2.5 in.
Blade Material: Stainless steel
Length (Open/Closed): 5.75 in./3.25 in.
Handle: Ruthenium
Lock: Back lock
Weight: 3.8 oz.
Features: Seven implements; eleven functions
Options: None
MSRP: $210

SWISS RANGER 51 16300
Blade Length: 3.9 in.
Blade Material: Stainless steel
Length (Open/Closed): 9 in./5.1 in.
Handle: Polyamide
Lock: Back lock
Weight: 3.2 oz.
Features: None
Options: None
MSRP: $43

SWISS TOOL CHEST PLUS 16906
Blade Length: 2.75 in.
Blade Material: Stainless steel
Length (Open/Closed): 6 in./3.25 in.
Handle: Cellidor
Lock: Screwdrivers only
Weight: 7.7 oz.
Features: Eighteen implements; thirty-one functions including compass; mineral crystal magnifier; universal wrench; locking screwdrivers; fish scaler; leather sheath
Option: None
MSRP: $150

SWISS UELI STECK SPECIAL EDITION 16996
Blade Length: 2.56 in.
Blade Material: Stainless steel
Length (Open/Closed): 5.56 in./3 in.
Handle: Titanium
Lock: Liner lock
Weight: 4 oz.
Features: Liner lock can be disengaged directly or by pressing button (Wenger logo); one hand opening; 7 mm, 10 mm, 13 mm Hex key wrenches; screwdriver; can opener; saw; file; ¼-inch bit adapter; flat head; Phillips head bits; wire stripper; lightweight pouch
Options: None
MSRP: $200

BLACK AUTOMATIC 0610ST

Blade Length: 3.5 in.
Blade Material: 154CM
Length (Open/Closed): 8.75 in./5.25 in.
Handle: 6061-T6 aluminum/G10
Lock: ZT push button auto lock
Weight: 5 oz.
Features: Partially serrated blade; Tungsten DLC coated blade; manual safety keeps knife closed
Options: None
MSRP: **$185**

COYOTE BROWN SPEEDSAFE 0302

Blade Length: 3.75 in.
Blade Material: S30V
Length (Open/Closed): 8.75 in./5.25 in.
Handle: G10
Lock: Frame lock
Weight: 8.6 oz.
Features: Assisted opening; Tungsten DLC coated blade w/ tiger stripes; dual thumb studs; reversible pocket clip; tip-up or tip-down carry; adjustable pivot tension
Options: Black blade, plain edge, or partially serrated (030/300ST); green handle (0301); 3.25 in. blackblade, plain edge, or partially serrated (0350/350ST).
MSRP: **$325**

HINDERER DESIGN 0551

Blade Length: 3.5 in.
Blade Material: VANAX 35
Length (Open/Closed): 8.1 in./4.6 in.
Handle: G10
Lock: Frame lock
Weight: 5.8 oz.
Features: Dual thumb studs
Options: ELMAX blade; G10 handle; glass break; and lanyard hole (0550)
MSRP: **$250**

MATTE BLACK AUTOMATIC 0650ST

Blade Length: 3.75 in.
Blade Material: 154CM
Length (Open/Closed): 8.75 in./4.9 in.
Handle: 6061-T6 aluminum/G10
Lock: CrossFire auto lock
Weight: 5.8 oz.
Features: Partially serrated blade; Tungsten DLC coated blade; manual safety keeps knife closed
Options: None
MSRP: **$200**

ZERO TOLERANCE BLACK AUTOMATIC

ZERO TOLERANCE COYOTE BROWN SPEEDSAFE 0302

ZERO TOLERANCE HINDERER DESIGN 0551

ZERO TOLERANCE HINDERER DESIGN 0550

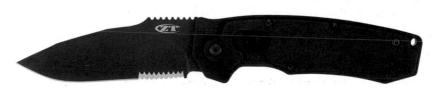

ZERO TOLERANCE MATTE BLACK AUTOMATIC

FOLDING KNIVES

Zero Tolerance Knives

zerotoleranceknives.com

ZERO TOLERANCE MATTE BLACK FOLDER

ZERO TOLERANCE MATTE BLACK TANTO SPEEDSAFE 0400

ZERO TOLERANCE S30V BLACK FOLDER

ZERO TOLERANCE S30V TALON FOLDER SPEEDSAFE

ZERO TOLERANCE S30V WIDE BLADE TANTO FOLDER

FOLDING KNIVES

MATTE BLACK FOLDER 0200
Blade Length: 4 in.
Blade Material: 154CM
Length (Open/Closed): 8.75 in./5.25 in.
Handle: G10
Lock: Liner lock
Weight: 7.8 oz.
Features: Tungsten DLC coated blade; dual thumb studs; reversible pocket clip; tip up or tip-down; adjustable pivot tension
Options: Partially serrated blade (0200ST)
MSRP: $175

MATTE BLACK TANTO SPEEDSAFE 0400
Blade Length: 3.75 in.
Blade Material: S30V
Length (Open/Closed): 8.6 in./5 in.
Handle: 6060-T6 aluminum

Lock: Liner lock
Weight: 5 oz
Features: Assisted opening; dual thumb studs; flipper; Tungsten DLC coated blade; TracTek inserts, left side only; tip-up or tip-down pocket clip right side only, adjustable pivot tension
Options: Partially serrated blade (0400ST)
MSRP: $150

S30V BLACK FOLDER 0780
Blade Length: 3.5 in.
Blade Material: S30V
Length (Open/Closed): 8.1 in./4.5 in.
Handle: G10
Lock: Liner lock
Weight: 3.6 oz.
Features: Tungsten DLC coated blade; dual thumb stud; flipper opening
Options: None
MSRP: $130

S30V TALON FOLDER SPEEDSAFE 0750
Blade Length: 3.2 in.
Blade Material: S30V
Length (Open/Closed): 7.25 in./4.25 in.
Handle: G10
Lock: Liner lock
Weight: 3.7 oz.
Features: Tungsten DLC coated blade; dual thumb stud; flipper opening
Options: None
MSRP: $130

S30V WIDE BLADE TANTO FOLDER 0700
Blade Length: 3.5 in.
Blade Material: S30V
Length (Open/Closed): 8.1 in./4.7 in.
Handle: G10
Lock: Liner lock
Weight: 4.2 oz.
Features: Stone washed finish blade; flipper opening
Options: None
MSRP: $120

Sharpeners

"A dull knife is more dangerous than a sharp knife." Maybe you've heard this before or maybe you haven't, but it's true. The reason is when you set the blade edge upon a medium you expect the blade to travel exactly where you want it. Suppose you need to slice the insulation off of a wire. The dull knife might grab for a moment then let go and send the knife flying forcefully out of control. Even if the knife was too dull to shear the cover off of the wire, it's still going to be sharp enough to cut skin or damage anything else it might come in contact with.

Let's take something delicate, like slicing a tomato, as an example. A very sharp knife will pierce the skin of the tomato and continue cutting until it stops against the cutting board. A dull knife will press on the tomato and before the skin is pierced you'll be having puree instead of slices. But cutting a tomato does not necessarily take a razor-sharp blade. A simple lateral movement will start a cut in the membrane-like skin. If you read the chapter "Folding Knives for Self Defense," you'll see Brian Hoffner making sure his combat folding knife is open by striking it on his belt—not sweeping it across the belt to lock it open but moving the knife ninety degrees in and out against the leather. That's because the teeth found along the edge of the blade will begin cutting as soon as they're moved forward or back. What if you are holding a plain-edge blade and there are no teeth or any serrations to be seen? Well, you'd to wrong to assume there is no sort of serration on a plain-blade knife. The edge of the blade is full of peaks and valleys that act as saw teeth. Some of them are visible and some are not depending on the grit material used to sharpen the edge (and we dare say the skill of the technician refining the blade). The refinement or maintenance of these so-called "teeth" are part and parcel to keeping the edge sharp enough to perform the type of work the knife will be used for.

In the following pages we present numerous tools and accessories to maintain a sharp-edged blade. The practice of maintaining a sharp edge can be a sudden necessity in the field, or it can be a home craft. Ultimately, it can prove to be a very relaxing hobby or even a source of supplemental income. It's an inexpensive skill to learn, especially if you learn on an inexpensive knife. You can learn it out of a book or just by following the directions that come with some of the kits that are widely available.

The first tool you'll need is patience. You'll also need a set of stones that are approved for the knife you are about to sharpen. Stones are marked coarse, medium, fine, and extra fine, and you'll find some that fit in between. There are natural stones and ceramic stones with open or closed cell surfaces. You must also know the proper angle at which to contact the grit surface. Some manufacturers will supply this information willingly. Others will convince you to send the knife to them for service. That's not a bad idea for most people, but the best advice is to seek out instruction. Ask around at knife stores or hardware stores and start with a softer steel blade, (around 55 HRC) fashioned in a simple configuration such as a drop point.

Working by hand is a relatively slow process depending on whether you are just keeping a sharp edge fit or beginning a reclamation process. Sharpening machines can make the job easier, but in a sense they require more skill, or at least more restraint. One of the top knife makers in the country told us that CNC machines, for example, allow you to make more mistakes faster. The same could be said of sharpening machines.

Columbia River Knife & Tool

www.crkt.com

CRKT, founded in 1994, provides a nice selection of sharpeners for all types of knives, including hunting, serrated, and gut hook knives. These sharpeners are portable, affordable, and are functional for both the novice and advanced knife owner.

EDGIE

Description: Designed by Maj. Howard Pope and Steve Jernigan.
Blade Length: 3.25 in.
Blade Material: 5Cr15MoV
Length (Open/Closed): 7.5 in./5.3 in.
Grind: High hollow
Frame: Stainless steel InterFrame with glass-filled nylon scales
Lock: Lockback
Weight: 4.3 oz.
Features: Dual-edged lockback; American Eagle wharncliffe blade grind; folder frames; removable stainless steel clips in satin finish; self-sharpening
Options: Blue or yellow insert models available
MSRP: **$39.99**

P.T.S. PELVIC TOOL/ SHARPENER

Description: Useful as a field sharpener for hunting and serrated knives, fishhook, and pelvic bone splitter.
Handle: 2CR13
Length: 4.5 in.
Weight: 3.8 oz.
Features: High carbon steel wedge with a chisel edge; no. 400 diamond grit coating; braided leather thong; handy carry pouch
Options: None
MSRP: **$39.99**

SLIDE SHARP

Description: Designed by Steve McCowen and Charles Kain.
Base Material: Hardwood
Features: Two porcelain sharpening rods
MSRP: **$34.99**

VEFF SHARP

Description: Designed by Tom Veff, this is a field and bench sharpener for serrated knives, gut hook knives, and seat belt cutters.
Handle: Anodized knurled aluminum
Rods: 2-in. straight sections (small); 6-in. flat side (large)

Blade Material: Diamond
Features: Two threaded 600-grit diamond-coated sharpening rods; smaller rod straight sections in $3/32$ in., $3/16$ in., and $1/4$ in.; larger rod has three straight sections in sizes $11/32$ in., $1/2$ in., and $5/8$ in.; nylon storage pouch
Options: None
MSRP: **$39.99**

CRKT EDGIE

CRKT P.T.S. PELVIC TOOL/SHARPENER

CRKT SLIDE SHARP

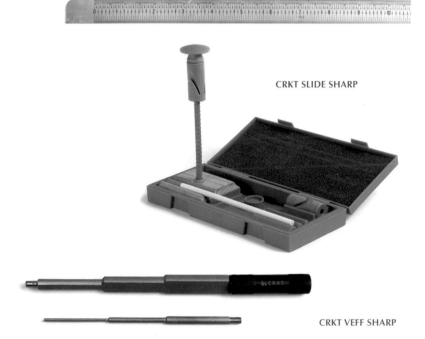

CRKT VEFF SHARP

Dan's Whetstone Company, Inc.

www.danswhetstone.com

Dan's Whetstone Company, Inc. offers a wide variety of sharpening stones for sporting goods and household use. All sharpeners are used with Novaculite, an abrasive sedimentary rock, and Dan's provides bench stones, pocket stones, Arkansas files, EZ Hones, and custom designs.

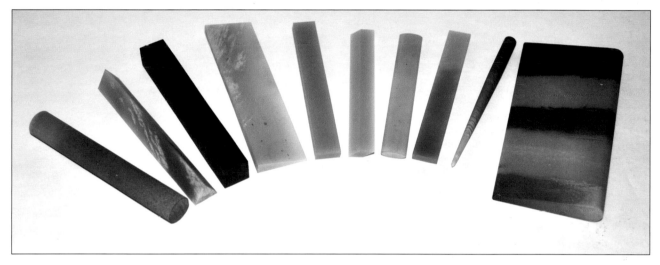

DAN'S WHETSTONE NATURAL ARKANSAS FILES & SPECIALTY TOOLS

ARKANSAS FILES

Arkansas Files come in these shapes: triangle, square, round, flat, bevel, oval, diamond, base point, and knife blade. All files are available in these classifications: Hard, True Hard, and Translucent.

FLAT FILES

Hard Select Ark Extra Fine size: 4 x ½ x ³/₁₆

True Hard Ark Extra Fine sizes: 3 x ½ x ³/₁₆; 3 ½ x ½ x ³/₁₆

Translucent Extra Fine sizes: 3 x ½ x ³/₁₆; 3 ½ x ½ x ³/₁₆

Features: Hand crafted
MSRP: . . . . $10.81–$14.83

ROUND FILES

Hard Select Ark Fine sizes: 4 x ¼; 4 x ³/₈; 4 x ½; 6 x ³/₈; 6 x ½

True Hard Ark Extra Fine sizes: 3 x ¼; 3 x ³/₈; 3 x ½; 3 ½ x ¼; 3 ½ x ³/₈; 3 ½ x ½

Translucent Extra Fine sizes: 3 x ¼; 3 x ³/₈; 3 x ½; 3 ½ x ¼, 3 ½ x ³/₈, 3 ½ x ½

Features: Hand crafted
MSRP: . . . . $12.83–$23.60

SQUARE FILES

Hard Select Ark Fine sizes: 4 x ¼; 4 x ³/₈; 4 x ½; 6 x ³/₈; 6 x ½

True Hard Ark Extra Fine sizes: 3 x ¼; 3 x ³/₈; 3 x ½; 3 ½ x ¼; 3 ½ x ³/₈; 3 ½ x ½

Translucent Extra Fine sizes: 3 x ¼; 3 x ³/₈; 3 x ½; 3 ½ x ¼, 3 ½ x ³/₈, 3 ½ x ½

Features: Hand crafted
MSRP: . . . . $10.94–$19.32

TRIANGLE FILES

Hard Select Ark Fine sizes: 4 x ¼; 4 x ³/₈; 4 x ½; 6 x ³/₈; 6 x ½

True Hard Ark Extra Fine sizes: 3 x ¼; 3 x ³/₈; 3 x ½; 3 ½ x ¼; 3 ½ x ³/₈; 3 ½ x ½

Translucent Extra Fine sizes: 3 x ¼; 3 x ³/₈; 3 x ½; 3 ½ x ¼; 3 ½ x ³/₈; 3 ½ x ½

Features: Hand crafted
MSRP: . . . . $10.93–$19.32

Dan's Whetstone Company, Inc.

www.danswhetstone.com

DAN'S WHETSTONE BLACK HARD ARKANSAS EXTRA FINE

DAN'S WHETSTONE SOFT ARKANSAS MEDIUM

DAN'S WHETSTONE
TRANSLUCENT EXTRA FINE

BENCH STONES

Bench stones come in these grades: Soft, Hard Select, True Hard, Black Hard, and Translucent.

BLACK HARD ARKANSAS EXTRA FINE

Sizes (length x width x thickness): 4 x 2 x ½; 6 x 2 x ½; 8 x 2 x ½; 4 x 2 x ¾; 6 x 2 x ¾; 8 x 2 x ¾; 10 x 2 x 1; 12 x 2 x 1
Features: Packaged in natural wood box
Options: Permanent mount in wooden box available
MSRP: . . . . $38.83–$188.22

HARD SELECT ARKANSAS FINE

Sizes (length x width x thickness): 4 x 2 x ½; 6 x 2 x ½; 8 x 2 x ½; 4 x 2 x

¾; 6 x 2 x ¾; 8 x 2 x ¾; 10 x 2 x 1; 12 x 2 x 1
Features: Packaged in natural wood box
Options: Permanent mount in wooden box available
MSRP: . . . . $15.65–$77.63

SOFT ARKANSAS MEDIUM

Sizes (length x width x thickness): 4 x 2 x ½; 6 x 2 x ½; 8 x 2 x ½; 4 x 2 x ¾; 6 x 2 x ¾; 8 x 2 x ¾; 10 x 2 x 1; 12 x 2 x 1
Features: Packaged in natural wood box
Options: Permanent mount in wooden box available
MSRP: . . . . $12.99–$52.47

TRANSLUCENT EXTRA FINE

Sizes (length x width x thickness): 4 x 2 x ½; 6 x 2 x ½; 8 x 2 x ½; 4 x 2 x

¾; 6 x 2 x ¾; 8 x 2 x ¾; 10 x 2 x 1; 12 x 2 x 1
Features: Packaged in natural wood box
Options: Permanent mount in wooden box available
MSRP: . . . . $48.95–$241.10

TRUE HARD ARKANSAS EXTRA FINE

Sizes (length x width x thickness): 4 x 2 x ½; 6 x 2 x ½; 8 x 2 x ½; 4 x 2 x ¾; 6 x 2 x ¾; 8 x 2 x ¾; 10 x 2 x 1; 12 x 2 x 1
Features: Packaged in natural wood box
Options: Permanent mount in wooden box available
MSRP: . . . . $38.83–$188.22

Dan's Whetstone Company, Inc.

www.danswhetstone.com

COMBINATION BENCH STONES

SOFT/BLACK ARKANSAS MEDIUM/EXTRA FINE

Sizes (length x width x thickness): 4 x 2 x 1; 4 x 2 ½ x 1; 6 x 2 x 1; 6 x 2 ½ x 1; 8 x 2 x 1; 8 x 2 ½ x 1; 10 x 2 ½ x 1

Features: Packaged in natural wood box

Options: Permanent mount in wooden box available

MSRP: . . . . $47.06–$154.60

SOFT /HARD SELECT ARKANSAS MEDIUM/FINE

Sizes (length x width x thickness): 4 x 2 x 1; 4 x 2 ½ x 1; 6 x 2 x 1; 6 x 2 ½ x 1; 8 x 2 x 1; 8 x 2 ½ x 1; 10 x 2 ½ x 1

Features: Packaged in natural wood box

Options: Permanent mount in wooden box available

MSRP: . . . . $23.88–$75.00

WIDE BENCH STONES

BLACK HARD ARKANSAS EXTRA FINE

Sizes (length x width x thickness): 6 x 3 x ½; 8 x 2 ½ x ½; 8 x 3 x ½; 8 x 3 x 1; 10 x 2 ½ x ½; 10 x 3 x ½; 10 x 3 x 1; 12 x 2 ½ x ½; 12 x 3 x ½; 12 x 3 x 1

Features: Packaged in natural wood box

Options: Permanent mount in wooden box available

MSRP: . . . . $100.28–$294.54

HARD SELECT ARKANSAS FINE

Sizes (length x width x thickness): 8 x 3 x 1; 10 x 3 x 1; 12 x 3 x 1

Features: Packaged in natural wood box

Options: Permanent mount in wooden box available

MSRP: . . . . $77.61–$116.42

SOFT ARKANSAS MEDIUM

Sizes (length x width x thickness): 6 x 3 x ½; 8 x 2 ½ x ½; 8 x 3 x ½; 8 x 3 x 1; 10 x 2 ½ x ½; 10 x 3 x ½; 10 x 3 x 1; 12 x 2 ½ x ½; 12 x 3 x 1

Features: Packaged in natural wood box

Options: Permanent mount in wooden box available

MSRP: . . . . $29.26–$90.08

DAN'S WHETSTONE BLACK HARD ARKANSAS EXTRA FINE 12 X 3 X 1

DAN'S WHETSTONE SOFT ARKANSAS MEDIUM 12 X 3 X 1

TRANSLUCENT EXTRA FINE

Sizes (length x width x thickness): 8 x 3 x 1; 10 x 3 x 1; 12 x 3 x 1

Features: Packaged in natural wood box

Options: Permanent mount in wooden box available

MSRP: . . . . $248.89–$373.33

Dan's Whetstone Company, Inc.

www.danswhetstone.com

BONDED ABRASIVES

Available in Silicon Carbide and Aluminum Oxide stones.

BENCH STONES
Silicon Carbide (320, 180, or 120 grit): 6 x 2 x 1
Alum Oxide (320, 180, or 120 grit): 6 x 2 x 1
MSRP: **$21.08**

COMBINATION STONE
SC 180/320 grit: 6 x 2 x 1, 8 x 2 x 1
Alum Ox 180/320 grit: 6 x 2 x 1, 8 x 2 x 1
MSRP: . . . . **$28.03–$33.18**

ROUND EDGE SLIP STONES
Alum Ox (320, 180, or 120 grit): 4 ½ x 1 ¾ x ¼ >¹/₁₆, 4 ½ x 1 ¾ x ³/₈ > ¹/₈
MSRP: **$12.74**

EZ HONES

The EZ Hone Knife Sharpening Systems are available in 4", 6", and 8" lengths. There are 3-stone models in either coarse, medium, or fine stone; there are 4-stone models in coarse, medium, fine, and extra fine stone.

ARKANSAS TRI HONE
Silicon Carbide/Soft AR/Hard: 4 x 1 ⁵/₈ x ½, 6 x 1 ⁵/₈ x ½, 8 x 1 ⁵/₈ x ½, 10 x 1 ⁵/₈ x ½
Silicon Carbide/Soft AR/Black: 4 x 1 ⁵/₈ x ½, 6 x 1 ⁵/₈ x ½, 8 x 1 ⁵/₈ x ½
Features: 1-ounce bottle honing oil
MSRP: . . . . **$22.88–$85.51**

BENCH EZ-HONE
2 stone w/ oil: Sil. Carb. & Soft Ark; 4 x 1 ⁵/₈ x ½, 6 x 1 ⁵/₈ x ½, 8 x 1 ⁵/₈ x ½
2 stone w/ oil: Sil. Carb. & Hard Ark; 4 x 1 ⁵/₈ x ½, 6 x 1 ⁵/₈ x ½, 8 x 1 ⁵/₈ x ½
2 stone w/ oil: Soft & Hard Ark; 4 x 1 ⁵/₈ x ½, 6 x 1 ⁵/₈ x ½, 8 x 1 ⁵/₈ x ½
2 stone w/ oil: Soft & True Hard Ark; 4 x 1 ⁵/₈ x ½, 6 x 1 ⁵/₈ x ½, 8 x 1 ⁵/₈ x ½
MSRP: . . . . **$19.36–$78.63**

DAN'S WHETSTONE ARKANSAS TRI HOME W/OIL

DAN'S WHETSTONE EZ-HONE

DAN'S WHETSTONE ARKANSAS STICKS

Dan's Whetstone Company, Inc.

www.danswhetstone.com

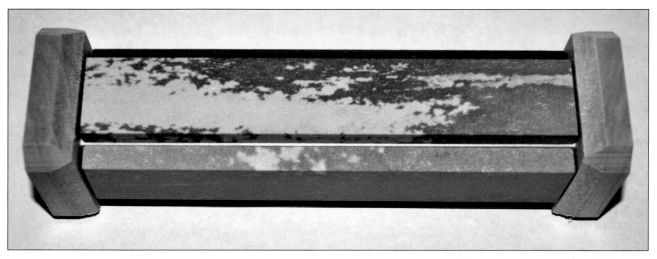

DAN'S WHETSTONE EZ-HONE 4 STONE W/ OIL

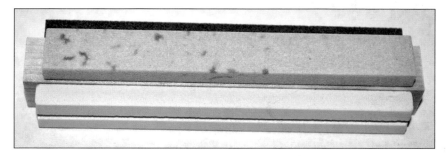

DAN'S WHETSTONE MINI-HONE

ARKANSAS STICKS

Soft Arkansas Sticks: 6 x 1 x ¼
True Hard Arkansas Sticks: 6 x 1 x ¼
Handle: Ceramic
Color: Translucent, black, or multicolored
MSRP: . . . . **$25.08–$38.45**

EZ-HONE

3 stone w/ oil: Coarse, Medium &
Fine; 4 x 1 x ¼, 6 x 1 x ¼, 8 x 1 x ¼
4 stone w/ oil: Coarse, Medium, Fine,
& Extra Fine; 4 x 1 x ¼, 6 x 1 x ¼, 8 x
1 x ¼
MSRP: . . . . **$17.87–$49.80**

MINI-HONE

3 stone w/ oil: Coarse, Medium, &
Fine; 4 x ½ x ¼
4 stone w/ oil: Coarse, Medium, Fine
& Extra Fine; 4 x ½ x ¼
MSRP: . . . . **$9.24–$16.45**

POCKET STONES

Pocket Stones come in these grades:
Soft, Hard Select, True Hard, Black
Hard, and Translucent.

BLACK HARD ARKANSAS EXTRA FINE

**Size in Leather (length x width x
thickness)**: 3 x 1 x ¼; 4 x 1 x ³⁄₈; 4 x 1
x ½; 4 x 1 ⁵⁄₈ x ½
Size in Tube (length x width x thickness): 3 x 1 x ¼; 3 x 1 x ³⁄₈; 3 x 1 x ½;
4 x 1 x ¼; 4 x 1 x ³⁄₈; 4 x 1 x ½
Features: None

TOP STONE: SOFT ARKANSAS MEDIUM; BOTTOM STONE: BLACK ARKANSAS EXTRA FINE

Options: Available with either a leather sleeve or plastic case
MSRP: . . . . **$13.35–$28.38**

Dan's Whetstone Company, Inc.

www.danswhetstone.com

HARD SELECT ARKANSAS FINE

Size in Leather (length x width x thickness): 3 x 1 x ¼; 4 x 1 x ³⁄₈; 4 x 1 x ½; 4 x 1 ⁵⁄₈ x ½

Size in Tube (length x width x thickness): 3 x 1 x ¼; 3 x 1 x ³⁄₈; 3 x 1 x ½; 4 x 1 x ¼; 4 x 1 x ³⁄₈; 4 x 1 x ½

Features: None

Options: Available with either a leather sleeve or plastic case

MSRP: . . . . $7.26–$15.05

SOFT ARKANSAS MEDIUM

Size in Leather (length x width x thickness): 3 x 1 x ¼; 4 x 1 x ³⁄₈; 4 x 1 x ½; 4 x 1 ⁵⁄₈ x ½

Size in Tube (length x width x thickness): 3 x 1 x ¼; 3 x 1 x ³⁄₈; 3 x 1 x ½; 4 x 1 x ¼; 4 x 1 x ³⁄₈; 4 x 1 x ½

Features: None

Options: Available with either a leather sleeve or plastic case

MSRP: . . . . $4.40–$8.78

TRANSLUCENT EXTRA FINE

Size in Leather (length x width x thickness): 3 x 1 x ¼; 4 x 1 x ³⁄₈; 4 x 1 x ½; 4 x 1 ⁵⁄₈ x ½

Size in Tube (length x width x thickness): 3 x 1 x ¼; 3 x 1 x ³⁄₈; 3 x 1 x ½; 4 x 1 x ¼; 4 x 1 x ³⁄₈; 4 x 1 x ½

Features: None

Options: Available with either a leather sleeve or plastic case

MSRP: . . . . $17.40–$37.97

TRUE HARD ARKANSAS EXTRA FINE

Size in Leather (length x width x thickness): 3 x 1 x ¼; 4 x 1 x ³⁄₈; 4 x 1 x ½; 4 x 1 ⁵⁄₈ x ½

Size in Tube (length x width x thickness): 3 x 1 x ¼; 3 x 1 x ³⁄₈; 3 x 1 x ½; 4 x 1 x ¼; 4 x 1 x ³⁄₈; 4 x 1 x ½

Features: None

Options: Available with either a leather sleeve or plastic case

MSRP: . . . . $13.35–$28.38

DMT® Diamond Sharpening

www.dmtsharp.com

Since 1976, DMT has been making sharpeners using monocrystalline diamonds. They offer continuous diamond surface and their trademark "polka-dot" pattern surfaces for all of their sharpening stones. Each sharpener also comes in a variety of grits.

BENCH STONES

6-INCH DIAMOND WHETSTONE™ BENCH STONES

Models: W6X, W6XP, W6C, W6CP, W6F, W6FP, W6E, W6EP

Size: 6″ x 2″ x ¾″

Grits: Black (X) diamond-extra coarse, blue (C) diamond-coarse, red (F) diamond-fine, green (E) diamond-extra fine

Surface: Interrupted diamond

Options: Plastic box; wood box; 3-stone kit

MSRP: . . . . $47–$105

8-INCH DIAMOND WHETSTONE™ BENCH STONES

Models: W8X, W8XNB, W8C, W8CNB, W8F, W8FNB, W8E, W8ENB

Size: 8″ x 2 ⁵⁄₈″ x 1 ¼″

Grits: Black (X) diamond-extra coarse, blue (C) diamond-coarse, red (F) diamond-fine, green (E) diamond-extra fine

Surface: Interrupted diamond

Options: Plastic box; wood box; no box-mat

MSRP: . . . . $73–$95

DMT® 6-INCH DIAMOND WHETSTONE™ BENCH STONES IN WOODEN BOX

DMT® 6-INCH DIAMOND WHETSTONE™ BENCH STONES IN PLASTIC CASE

DMT® 8-INCH DIAMOND WHETSTONE™ BENCH STONES IN HARDWOOD BOX

SHARPENERS

DMT® Diamond Sharpening

www.dmtsharp.com

6-INCH/ 8-INCH/ 10-INCH/ 11.5-INCH DIA-SHARP® BENCH STONE

Models: D6X, D6C, D6F, D6E, D6CX, D6FC, D6EF, D6FX; D8XX, D8X, D8C, D8F, D8E, D8EE; D10C, D10F, D10E; D11X, D11C, D11F, D11E

Sizes: 6″ x 2″ x ¼″; 8″ x 3″ x 0.375″; 10″ x 4″ x 0.375″; 11 ½″ x 2 ½″ x 0.375″

Grits: Black (X) diamond-extra coarse, blue (C) diamond-coarse, red (F) diamond-fine, green (E) diamond-extra fine, silver (XX) diamond—extra, extra coarse, tan (EE) diamond-extra, extra fine

Surface: Continuous diamond

Options: Double-sided (6-inch only)

MSRP: . . . .$34.50–$124

DMT® 6-INCH DIA-SHARP® BENCH STONE

8-INCH DUOSHARP® BENCH STONE

Models: W8CXNB, W8FCNB, W8EFNB, W8ECNB, W8CX-WB, W8FC-WB, W8EF-WB, W8EC-WBM

Size: 8″ x 2.625″ x 0.375″

Grits: Black (X) diamond-extra coarse, blue (C) diamond-coarse, red (F) diamond-fine, green (E) diamond-extra fine

Surface: Interrupted diamond

Options: DuoBase™

MSRP: . . . . $105–$115

DMT® 10-INCH DUOSHARP® BENCH STONE WITH BASE

8-INCH DUOSHARP®PLUS™ BENCH STONE

Models: WM8CX, WM8FC, WM8EF, WM8FC-WB, WM8EF-WB

Size: 6″ x 2.625″ x 0.375″

Grits: Black (X) diamond-extra coarse, blue (C) diamond-coarse, red (F) diamond-fine, green (E) diamond-extra fine

Surface: Interrupted diamond; continuous diamond

Options: DuoBase™

MSRP: . . . . $82–$95

DMT® DIAMOND WAVE™ SHARPENER

10-INCH DUOSHARP® BENCH STONE

Models: W250CXNB, W250FCNB, W250EFNB, W250ECNB, W250CX-WB, W250FC-WB, W250EF-WB, W250EC-WB

Size: 10″ x 4″ x 0.375″

Grits: Black (X) diamond-extra coarse,

blue (C) diamond-coarse, red (F) diamond-fine, green (E) diamond-extra fine

Surface: Interrupted diamond

Options: DuoBase™

MSRP: . . . . $149–$158

DIAMOND WAVE™ SHARPENER

Models: WAV F, WAV F

Size: 10″ x 2.36″ x 1.125″

Grits: Red (F) diamond-fine, green (E) diamond-extra fine

Surface: Continuous diamond

MSRP: $59.99

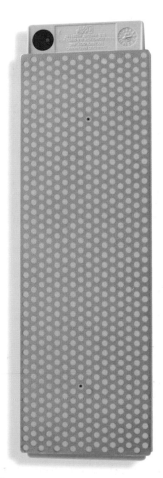

DMT® 8-INCH DUOSHARP®PLUS™ BENCH STONE

DMT® Diamond Sharpening

www.dmtsharp.com

FOLDING MODELS

DIAFOLD® DOUBLE SIDED SHARPENER
Models: FWCX, FWFC, FWEF, FWEEE
Stone size: 4.33" x 0.875" x ¼"
Size: 9 ½" open; 5" closed
Grits: Black (X) diamond-extra coarse, blue (C) diamond-coarse, red (F) diamond-fine, green (E) diamond-extra fine, tan (EE) diamond-extra, extra fine
Surface: Interrupted diamond
MSRP:$41.95

DIAFOLD® HOOK & KNIFE SHARPENER
Models: FFHWC, FFHWF
Stone Size: 4.33" x 0.875" x ¼"
Size: 9 ½" open; 5" closed
Grits: Blue (C) diamond-coarse, red (F) diamond-fine
Surface: Interrupted diamond; continuous diamond
MSRP:$31.20

DIAFOLD® SERRATED SHARPENER
Models: FSKC, FSKF, FSKE
Stone Size: ¼" to 1/16" taper x taper 4.33"
Size: 9 ½" open. 5" closed
Grits: Blue (C) diamond-coarse, red (F) diamond-fine, green (E) diamond-extra fine
Surface: Continuous diamond
MSRP:$29.55

DIAFOLD® SINGLE SIDED SHARPENER
Models: FWX, FWC, FWF, FEW
Stone Size: 4.33" x 0.875" x 0.20"
Size: 9 ½" open; 5" closed
Grits: Black (X) diamond-extra coarse, blue (C) diamond-coarse, red (F) diamond-fine, green (E) diamond-extra fine
Surface: Interrupted diamond
MSRP:$24.95

DMT® DIAFOLD® HOOK & KNIFE COARSE

DMT® DIAFOLD® DOUBLE SIDED SHARPENERS CX, FC, EF, EEE

DMT DIAFOLD® SERRATED SHARPENER FINE

DMT® DIAFOLD® SINGLE SIDED SHARPENER EXTRA-FINE

SHARPENERS

DMT® Diamond Sharpening

www.dmtsharp.com

GUIDE SHARPENING

CERAMIC STEEL SHARPENER
Model: CS2
Rod Length: 12" x ½"
Handle Length: 5"
Overall Size: 17" x 2 ½" x 2"
Grits: White (CER) ceramic
Surface: Continuous unbreakable ceramic
MSRP: **$48**

DIAMOND VEE™ SHARPENER
Model: VEE
Grit: Blue (C) diamond-coarse
Surface: Continuous diamond
MSRP: **$40.95**

DIAMOND STEEL™ SHARPENER
Models: DS4F, DS2F, DS2E, DSOF
Sizes: 14-in: 14" x 0.375"; 12-in: 12" x 0.375"; 10-in: 10" x 0.375"
Grits: Red (F) diamond-fine, green (E) diamond-extra fine
Surface: Continuous diamond
MSRP: . . . . **$40–$62**

DIAMOND-UNBREAKABLE CERAMIC TRIANGLE SHARPENER
Model: CDT62
Rod Length: 6"
Handle Length: 4.1"
Radii: 0.063", 0.125", 0.188"
Overall Size: 10 ½" x 1.13" x 1.13"
Grits: Blue (C) diamond-coarse, red (F) diamond-fine, green (E) diamond-extra fine, white (CER) ceramic
Surface: Continuous diamond; continuous unbreakable ceramic
MSRP: **$62**

DIA-STRIKE™ DIAMOND BROADHEAD SHARPENER
Models: D-STRIKE E, D-STRIKE F, D-STRIKE EF
Grits: Red (F) diamond-fine, green (E) diamond-extra fine
Surface: Interrupted diamond
MSRP: . . . . **$42–$75**

DMT® CERAMIC STEEL SHARPENER

DMT® DIAMOND VEE™ SHARPENER

DMT® DIAMOND STEEL™ SHARPENERS

DMT® DIASTRIKE™ DIAMOND BROADHEAD™ SHARPENERS E, F

SHARPENERS

DMT® Diamond Sharpening

www.dmtsharp.com

POCKET MODELS

4" DIAMOND WHETSTONE™ SHARPENER

Models: W4X, W4C, W4F, W4E, W4EE
Size: 4.33" x 0.875" x 0.1875"
Grits: Black (X) diamond-extra coarse, blue (C) diamond-coarse, red (F) diamond-fine, green (E) diamond-extra fine, tan (EE) diamond-extra, extra fine, silver (XX) diamond-extra, extra coarse
Surface: Interrupted diamond
MSRP: **$25.50**

4" MACHINIST STYLE DIAMOND WHETSTONE™ SHARPENER

Models: WMC, WMF, WME
Size: 4.33" x 0.875" x 0.1875"
Grist: Blue (C) diamond-coarse, red (F) diamond-fine, green (E) diamond-extra fine
Surface: Interrupted diamond; continuous diamond
MSRP: **$27.32**

70 MM MINI-STONE DIAMOND WHETSTONE™ SHARPENER

Models: W7C, W7F, W7E, W7EFC
Size: 2 ¹¹/₁₆" x ¹⁵/₁₆" x ³/₁₆"
Grist: Blue (C) diamond-coarse, red (F) diamond-fine, green (E) diamond-extra fine
Surface: Interrupted diamond
MSRP: . . . . **$9–$23**

DIA-SHARP® 4" MODEL

Models: D4C, D4F, D4E
Size: 4" x 0.875" x 0.1875"
Grist: Blue (C) diamond-coarse, red (F) diamond-fine, green (E) diamond-extra fine
Surface: Continuous diamond
MSRP: **$14.50**

DIA-SHARP® CREDIT CARD SHARPENER

Models: D3C, D3F, D3E, D3EFC
Size: 3 ¼"x 2" x 0.05"
Grist: Blue (C) diamond-coarse, red (F) diamond-fine, green (E) diamond-extra fine
Surface: Continuous diamond
MSRP: . . . .$13–$28.35

DMT® 4" DIAMOND WHETSTONE™ SHARPENER

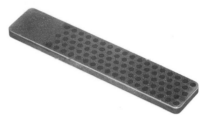

DMT® 4" MACHINIST STYLE DIAMOND WHETSTONE™ SHARPENER

DMT® 70 MM MINI-STONE DIAMOND WHETSTONE™ SHARPENER

DMT® DIA-SHARP® 4" MODELS E, F, C

DMT® DIA-SHARP® CREDIT CARD SHARPENERS

SHARPENERS

DMT® Diamond Sharpening

www.dmtsharp.com

DIA-SHARP® MINI-HONE® MODELS

Models: D2C, D2F, D2E, D2K, OD2C, OD2F, OD2E, OD2K
Stone Size: 2 ½" x ¾"
Overall Size Standard: 7" x ¾" x 0.19"
Overall Size Offset: 7" x ¾" x 0.375"
Grits: Blue (C) diamond-coarse, red (F) diamond-fine, green (E) diamond-extra fine
Surface: Continuous diamond
MSRP: . . . . $8–$24

MINI-SHARP® ANGLER SHARPENER

Models: FF70C, FF70F
Stone Size: 2 ¹¹⁄₁₆" x ¹⁵⁄₁₆" x ³⁄₁₆"
Size: 5 ½" opened
Grits: Blue (C) diamond-coarse, red (F) diamond-fine
Surface: Interrupted diamond; continuous diamond
MSRP: $14.50

MINI-SHARP® SHARPENER

Models: F70X, F70C, F70F, F70E
Stone Size: 2 ¹¹⁄₁₆" x ¹⁵⁄₁₆" x ³⁄₁₆"
Size: 5 ½" opened
Grits: Black (X) diamond-extra coarse, blue (C) diamond-coarse, red (F) diamond-fine, green (E) diamond-extra fine
Surface: Interrupted diamond
MSRP: $11.32

DMT® DIA-SHARP® MINI-HONE® MODELS

DMT® MINI-SHARP® ANGLER SHARPENER FINE

DMT® MINI-SHARP® SHARPENER COARSE

EdgeCraft Corporation

www.edgecraft.com

Founded in 1984, EdgeCraft Corporation is home to the Chef'sChoice® and Diamond Hone® brand sharpeners. The company offers a large selection of both electric and manual knife sharpeners for sporting and cooking enthusiasts.

CHEF'SCHOICE® ANGLE SELECT® DIAMOND HONE® KNIFE SHARPENER #1520

Features: 100% diamond abrasives and patented flexible stropping/polishing discs; three-year limited warranty
Options: Fine or serrated blades; available in white, black, or brushed metal; sports knives and pocket knives

CHEF'SCHOICE® DIAMOND HONE® EDGESELECT® #120

Features: Elastomeric angle guides; three year limited warranty
Options: Available in black, chrome, platinum, metal, red, white, or brushed metal

CHEF'SCHOICE® DIAMOND HONE® FLEXHONE/STROP® #320

Features: Electric; stropping/polishing technology; high precision angle guides; two year limited warranty

EdgeCraft Corporation

www.edgecraft.com

CHEF'SCHOICE® ANGLE SELECT® DIAMOND HONE® KNIFE
SHARPENER #1520

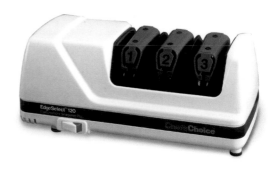

CHEF'SCHOICE® DIAMOND HONE® EDGESELECT® #120

CHEF'SCHOICE® DIAMOND HONE® FLEXHONE/STROP® #320

CHEF'SCHOICE® DIAMOND HONE® MULTI #110

CHEF'SCHOICE® DIAMOND HONE® HYBRID™ KNIFE SHARPENER #220

Features: Electric and manual Criss-Cross™ sharpening; brushed stainless steel knife guides; one year limited warranty

CHEF'SCHOICE® DIAMOND HONE® MULTI #110

Features: Electric; 100% diamond abrasives; BiLevel® magnetic guides; Trizor® edges; two year limited warranty

CHEF'SCHOICE® DIAMOND HONE® MULTI-STAGE #310

Features: Electric; orbiting 100% diamond abrasives; Bi-Level® magnetic guides; one year limited warranty

CHEF'SCHOICE® DIAMOND ULTRAHONE™ #112

Features: 100% diamond abrasive disks; powerful A.C. motor; two year limited warranty

CHEF'SCHOICE® DIAMOND HONE® HYBRID™ KNIFE
SHARPENER #220

EdgeCraft Corporation

www.edgecraft.com

CHEF'SCHOICE® DIAMOND HONE® MULTI-STAGE #310

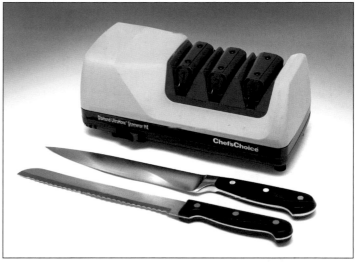

CHEF'SCHOICE® DIAMOND ULTRAHONE™ #112

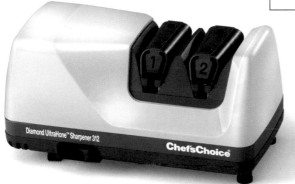

CHEF'SCHOICE® DIAMOND
ULTRAHONE™ SHARPENER #312

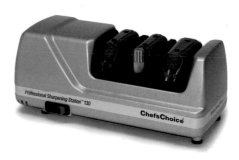

CHEF'SCHOICE® PROFESSIONAL SHARPENING STATION® #130

CHEF'SCHOICE® TRIZOR® XV™
SHARPENER EDGESELECT® #15

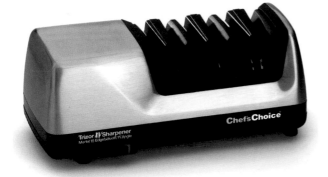

SHARPENERS

CHEF'SCHOICE® DIAMOND ULTRAHONE™ SHARPENER #312

Features: Conical diamond abrasive disks; knife guides; one year limited warranty

CHEF'SCHOICE® PROFESSIONAL SHARPENING STATION® #130

Features: Elastomeric angle guides; three year limited warranty
Options: Available in white, black, brushed metal, and platinum

CHEF'SCHOICE® TRIZOR® XV™ SHARPENER EDGESELECT® #15

Features: 3-stage sharpening process; 100% diamond abrasives; patented flexible stropping discs; flexible spring guides; three year limited warranty

EdgeCraft Corporation

www.edgecraft.com

Manual Sharpeners

CHEF'SCHOICE® CRYSTAL CRAFTER® #410

Features: 4-inch steel sharpening wand; 100% diamond abrasives; high-impact polymer handle
MSRP:$27

CHEF'SCHOICE® DIAMOND HONE® 2-STAGE #440

Features: 2-stage sharpening system; precision sharpening angle control; 100% diamond abrasives; dishwasher safe
MSRP:$27

CHEF'SCHOICE® DIAMOND HONE® 2-STAGE #450

Features: 2-stage sharpening system; precision angle guides; 100% diamond abrasives; dishwasher safe
MSRP:$35

CHEF'SCHOICE® DIAMOND HONE® EXACT-V® KNIFE SHARPENER #415

Features: "V-type" 2-stage sharpening system; precision spring-loaded angle guide; adjustable sharpening force; 100% diamond abrasives; limited one-year warranty; base converts into portable storage box to house rods and guides
MSRP:$55

CHEF'SCHOICE® DIAMOND HONE® KNIFE AND SCISSORS SHARPENER #480KS

Features: Manual sharpener for knives and scissors; 100% diamond abrasives; precision angle guides
MSRP:$40

CHEF'SCHOICE® DIAMOND HONE® MULTIEDGE™ #460

Features: Precision sharpening angle guides; 100% diamond abrasives; dust cover
MSRP:$35

CHEF'SCHOICE® CRYSTAL CRAFTER® #410

CHEF'SCHOICE® DIAMOND HONE® 2-STAGE #440

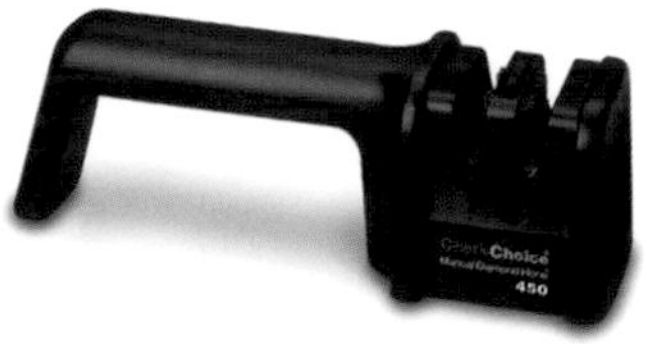

CHEF'SCHOICE® DIAMOND HONE® 2-STAGE #450

CHEF'SCHOICE® DIAMOND HONE® EXACT-V® KNIFE SHARPENER #415

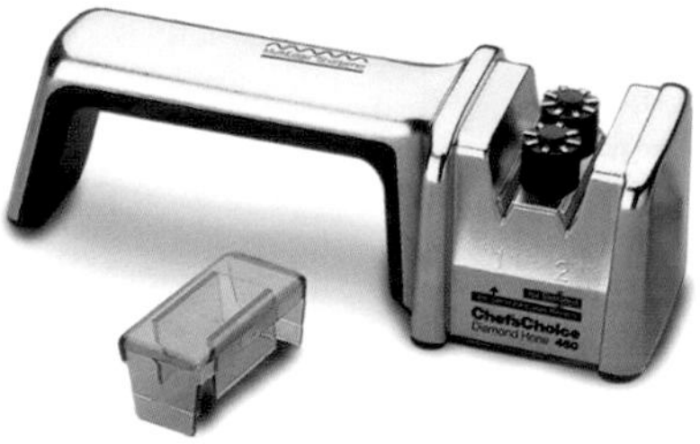

CHEF'SCHOICE® DIAMOND HONE® MULTIEDGE™ #460

CHEF'SCHOICE® DIAMOND HONE® KNIFE AND SCISSORS SHARPENER #480KS

SHARPENERS

EdgeCraft Corporation

www.edgecraft.com

CHEF'SCHOICE® DIAMOND HONE® POCKET SHARPENER #480

Features: 2-stage manual sharpener; precision guides; 100% diamond abrasives.

Options: Optional attachments include interchangeable handle-mounted auxiliary diamond abrasive pads, fishhook sharpeners, stropping pads, and storage hatch

MSRP: $14

CHEF'SCHOICE® DIAMOND HONE® SERRATED #430

Features: Manual; precision guides; 100% diamond abrasives

MSRP: $20

CHEF'SCHOICE® EDGECRAFTER® DIAMOND ROD SHARPENER #412

Features: Telescoping 100% diamond coated steel rod; pocket-size textured handle

Options: Solid brass or anodized aluminum handle

MSRP: $34

CHEF'SCHOICE® EDGECRAFTER® DIAMOND SHARPENER/FILE #420

Features: 100% diamond abrasives; files for pushing and pulling strokes

Options: Three 100% diamond abrasive pads are available: coarse, medium, and ultrafine

MSRP: $40

CHEF'SCHOICE® EDGECRAFTER® DIAMOND SHARPENING STEEL #416

Features: 100% diamond abrasives; easy-grip textured handle; dishwasher safe

Options: Available in three lengths: 8", 10", and 12"

MSRP: $62

CHEF'SCHOICE® EDGECRAFTER® DIAMOND STONES #400DS

Features: 100% diamond abrasives; ultra-flat steel plate; precision-built

solid hardwood box with cover; rubber feet

Options: Available in three sizes: 2" x 4", 2" x 6", or 2" x 8"

MSRP: $55

CHEF'SCHOICE® PRONTO™ DIAMOND HONE #464

Features: 2-stage manual sharpening system; "Soft Touch" handle; compact size

MSRP: $55

CHEF'SCHOICE® STEELPRO® #470

Features: Precise angle guides; handwashable; one year limited warranty

MSRP: $55

CHEF'SCHOICE® EDGECRAFTER® DIAMOND SHARPENER/FILE #420

CHEF'SCHOICE® EDGECRAFTER® DIAMOND SHARPENING STEEL #416

CHEF'SCHOICE® DIAMOND HONE® POCKET SHARPENER #480

CHEF'SCHOICE® EDGECRAFTER® DIAMOND STONES #400DS

CHEF'SCHOICE® DIAMOND HONE® SERRATED #430

CHEF'SCHOICE® PRONTO™ DIAMOND HONE #464

CHEF'SCHOICE® EDGECRAFTER® DIAMOND ROD SHARPENER #412

CHEF'SCHOICE® STEELPRO® #470

SHARPENERS

EZE-LAP Diamond Products

www.eze-lap.com

EZE-LAP is the originator of the diamond sharpener, starting business in the 1970s. Diamond stones can be used for hunting and fishing knives, woodworking tools, X-Acto blades, axes, and industrial use. No oil or water is necessary as the surface will remain true and flat. Many stones are available in super fine to extra coarse diamond and multiple shapes and sizes from 1" x 3" to 8" x 8".

1" X 3" DIAMOND STONES
Models: 21SF, 21F, 21M, 21C, 21XC, 22F, 22M, 22C, 24F, 24M, 24C, 26SF, 26F, 26M, 26C, 26XC
Length: 1" x 3"
MSRP: . . . . **$8.75–$17.95**

1" X 4" DIAMOND STONES
Models: 31SF, 31F, 31M, 31C, 31XC, 32F, 32M, 32C, 26SF, 36F, 36M, 36C, 36XC
Length: 1" x 4"
MSRP: . . . . **$9.85–$25.25**

1" X 6" DIAMOND STONES
Models: 41SF, 41F, 41M, 41C, 41XC, 42F, 42M, 42C, 46SF, 46F, 46M, 46C, 46XC
Length: 1" x 6"
MSRP: . . . . **$13.15–$32.95**

2" X 4" DIAMOND STONES
Models: 51SF, 51F, 51M, 51C, 51XC, 52F, 52M, 52C, 56SF, 56F, 56M, 56C, 56XC
Length: 2" x 4"
MSRP: . . . . **$17.55–$49.12**

2" X 6" DIAMOND STONES
Models: 61SF, 61F, 61M, 61C, 61XC, 62F, 62M, 62C, 66SF, 66F, 66M, 66C, 66XC
Length: 2" x 6"
MSRP: . . . . **$26.35–$64.35**

2" X 8" DIAMOND STONES
Models: 71SF, 71F, 71M, 71C, 71XC, 72F, 72M, 72C, 76SF, 76F, 76M, 76C, 76XC
Length: 2" x 8"
MSRP: . . . . **$35.15–$85.25**

3" X 8" DIAMOND STONES
Models: 81SF, 81F, 81M, 81C, 81XC, 86SF, 86F, 86M, 86C, 86XC
Length: 3" x 8"
MSRP: . . . . **$51.65–$127.45**

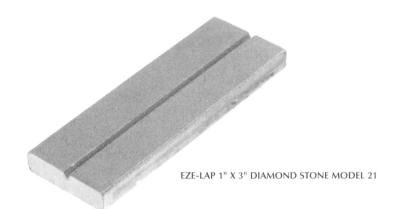

EZE-LAP 1" X 3" DIAMOND STONE MODEL 21

EZE-LAP 2" X 6" DIAMOND STONE

EZE-LAP 3" X 8" DIAMOND STONE

EZE-LAP Diamond Products

www.eze-lap.com

2-½" X 11-³⁄₈"
DIAMOND STONES
Models: 91SF, 91F, 91M, 91C, 91XC, 92F, 92M, 92C, 96SF, 96F, 96M, 96C, 96XC
Length: 2 ½" x 11 ³⁄₈"
MSRP: . . . . **$61.55–$151.75**

2-½" X 11-³⁄₈" X ³⁄₈"
DIAMOND STONES
Models: 121SF, 121F, 121M, 121C, 121XC
Length: 2 ½" x 11 ³⁄₈" x ³⁄₈"
MSRP: . . . .**$65.96–$151.75**

8" X 8" X ³⁄₈" DIAMOND
STONES
Models: 151SF, 151F, 151M, 151C, 151XC
Length: 8" x 8" x ³⁄₈"
MSRP: . . . . **$181.50–$434.50**

CREDIT CARD STONE
Length: 2" x 3 ¼"
Options: Available in individual stones or two stone sets; superfine grit (1200) or extra coarse grit (150)
MSRP: . . . . **$11.95–$24.95**

DIAMOND HONE & STONE

DOUBLE-SIDED STONE
Models: DD6SF/F, DD6SF/M, DD6SF/C, DD6F/M, DD5F/C, DD6M/C, DD8SF/F, DD8SF/M, DD8SF/C, DD8F/M, DD8F/C, DD8M/C
Grit: Combination of super fine/fine; superfine/medium; super fine/coarse; fine/medium; fine/coarse; medium/coarse
Options: Available in sizes 2" x 6" and 3" x 8"
MSRP: . . . . **$54.95–$87.95**

KNIFE SHARPENING KIT
Grit: Super fine, fine, and medium
Features: Includes knife clamp; angle guides; guide rods; and roll pouch
MSRP: **$44.95**

EZE-LAP 2 1/2" X 11 3/8" X 3/8: DIAMOND STONE MODEL 121

CREDIT CARD STONE

EZE-LAP KNIFE SHARPENING KIT

EZE-LAP Diamond Products

www.eze-lap.com

EZE-LAP OVAL DIAMOND SHARPENER MODEL D12

EZE-LAP ROUND DIAMOND SHARPENER MODEL G

EZE-LAP LPAK, LPAK 4, AND LPACK 5

LC
Grit: Coarse (250)
Length: ¾" x 2"
Handle Length: 6" x ¾"
Features: Black plastic handle; diamond pat blade
MSRP: **$8.95**

LF
Grit: Fine (600)
Length: ¾" x 2"
Handle Length: 6" x ¾"
Features: Red plastic handle; diamond pat blade
MSRP: **$5.95**

LM
Grit: Medium (400)
Length: ¾" x 2"
Handle Length: 6" x ¾"
Features: Purple plastic handle; diamond pat blade
MSRP: **$7.45**

L PAK
Grit: One super fine (1200), one fine (600), and one medium (400)
Length: ¾" x 2"
Handle Length: 6" x ¾"

Features: Plastic handle; diamond pat blade
MSRP: **$18.95**

L PAK 4
Grit: One super fine (1200), one fine (600), one medium (400), and one coarse grit (250)
Length: ¾" x 2"
Handle Length: 6" x ¾"
Features: Plastic handle; diamond pads
MSRP: **$26.95**

L PAK 5
Grit: One super fine (1200), one fine (600), one medium (400), one coarse (250), and one extra coarse (150)
Length: ¾" x 2"
Handle Length: 6" x ¾"
Features: Plastic handle; diamond pads
MSRP: **$34.95**

LSF
Grit: Super fine (1200)
Length: ¾" x 2"
Handle Length: 6" x ¾"
Features: Blue plastic handle; diamond pat blade
MSRP: **$5.95**

LXC
Grit: Extra coarse (150)
Length: ¾" x 2"
Handle Length: 6" x ¾"
Features: Green plastic handle; diamond pat blade
MSRP: **$10.95**

OVAL DIAMOND SHARPENER
Models: D5SF, D5F, D10SF, D10F, D122F, D12, 590, 591, 591/K
Blade Type: Oval shaft
Blade Size (length x width x thickness): 4" x ¾" x ¼"
Size (length x width x thickness): 10" x ¾" x ¼"; 12" x ¾" x ¼"; 5" x ¾" x ¼"
Options: Super fine grit and fine grit
MSRP: . . . . **$16.95–$34.95**

ROUND DIAMOND SHARPENER
Models: M, M/K, B, S, S/K, P, PGO, PGW, G, GGE, GGO, GGW
Grit: Fine (600)
Handle Material: Plastic
Handle Length: 8" x ⅜"; 10" x ⁷/₁₆"
MSRP: **$31.95 $39.95**

EZE-LAP Diamond Products

www.eze-lap.com

SPECIAL HOOK & KNIFE DIAMOND SHARPENERS

MODEL C
Blade Length: 3 ½ in.
Features: Retractable; plastic handle; small and large grooves for fishhooks
Options: Available handle colors are red, green, black, and orange.
MSRP: $11.95

MODEL H
Length: ¾" x 2 ½"
Features: Clip provided to attach to vest, belt loop, or keychain; groove for fishhooks
MSRP: $5.95

MODEL SD
Blade Length: 2 ½ in.
Features: Groove for fishhooks; d-shaped shaft; hook disgorger
MSRP: $6.95

MODEL ST
Features: Tapered shaft for serrated blades
MSRP: $7.99

MODEL ST/K
Features: Tapered shaft for serrated blades
MSRP: $10.95

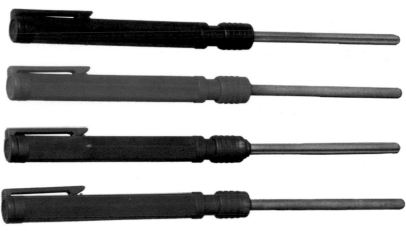

EZE-LAP MODEL

EZE-LAP MODEL

Lansky Sharpeners

www.lansky.com

Lansky offers a wide array of sharpeners and sharpening kits for outdoor and kitchen knives. Lansky's sharpeners come in a variety of materials including: ceramic, steel, diamond, tungsten carbide, pocket size, and benchstones.

3-STONE STANDARD DIAMOND SYSTEM PART # LK3DM

Grit: Coarse (120), medium (280), and fine (600)
Features: Flip-over knife clamp; sharpening hones on color-coated, finger-grooved safety holders; one guide rod for each honing stone; specially formulated honing oil; extra-long knife clamp screws; storage case; multilingual instructions
MSRP: $84.99

LANSKY 3-STONE STANDARD DIAMOND SYSTEM PART # LK3DM

SHARPENERS

Lansky Sharpeners

www.lansky.com

4-STONE DELUXE DIAMOND SYSTEM PART # LKDMD

Grit: Extra coarse (70), coarse (120), medium (280), and fine (600)

Features: Flip-over knife clamp; sharpening hones on color-coated, finger-grooved safety holders; one guide rod for each honing stone; specially formulated honing oil; extra-long knife clamp screws; storage case; multi-lingual instructions

MSRP: **$99.99**

DELUXE 5-STONE SYSTEM PART # LKCLX

Grit: Extra coarse (70), coarse (120), medium (280), fine (600), extra fine ceramic (1,000)

Features: Flip-over knife clamp; alumina oxide sharpening hones on color-coated, finger-grooved safety holders; one guide rod for each honing stone; specially formulated honing oil; extra-long knife clamp screws; storage case; multi-lingual instructions

MSRP: **$49.99**

NATURAL ARKANSAS SYSTEM PART # LKNAT

Grit: Soft stone (300), hard stone (650), black hard stone (1,200)

Features: Flip-over knife clamp; sharpening hones on color-coated, finger-grooved safety holders; one guide rod for each honing stone; specially formulated honing oil; extra-long knife clamp screws; storage case; multi-lingual instructions

MSRP: **$49.99**

PROFESSIONAL SYSTEM PART # LKCPR

Features: Flip-over knife clamp; sharpening hones on color-coated, finger-grooved safety holders; one guide rod for each honing stone; specially formulated honing oil; extra-long knife clamp screws; storage case; multi-lingual instructions

MSRP: **$55.99**

STANDARD 3-STONE SYSTEM PART # LKC03

Grit: Coarse (120), medium (280), fine (600)

LANSKY 4-STONE DELUXE DIAMOND SYSTEM PART # LKDMD

LANSKY DELUXE 5-STONE SYSTEM PART # LKCLX

LANSKY NATURAL ARKANSAS SYSTEM PART # LKNAT

LANSKY PROFESSIONAL SYSTEM PART # LKCPR

LANSKY STANDARD 3-STONE SYSTEM PART # LKC03

Features: Flip-over knife clamp; alumina oxide and ceramic sharpening hones on color-coated, finger-grooved safety holders; one guide rod for each honing stone; specially formulated honing oil; extra-long knife clamp screws; storage case

MSRP: **$34.99**

UNIVERSAL SHARPENING SYSTEM PART # LKUNV

Grit: Coarse (120), medium (280), fine (600)

Features: Flip-over knife clamp; alumina oxide and medium triangle-shape hone; sharpening hones on color-coated, finger-grooved safety holders; one guide rod for each honing stone; specially formulated honing oil; extra-long knife clamp screws; storage case; multi-lingual instructions

MSRP: **$44.99**

BENCHSTONES

HARD ARKANSAS STONE PART # LBS6H

Length: 6" x 2"
MSRP: **$22.99**

SOFT ARKANSAS STONE PART # LBS6S

Length: 6" x 2"
MSRP: **$19.99**

SOFT ARKANSAS STONE PART # LBS8S

Length: 8" x 2"
MSRP: **$22.99**

COMBO BENCHSTONES

COMBOSTONE PART # LCB6FC

Length: 2" x 6"
Features: Two grits in one stone
MSRP: **$9.99**

COMBOSTONE PART # LCB8FC

Length: 2" x 8"
Features: Two grits in one stone
MSRP: **$11.99**

LANSKY HARD ARKANSAS STONE
PART # LBS6H

LANSKY UNIVERSAL SHARPENING SYSTEM
PART # LKUNV

LANSKY SOFT ARKANSAS STONE PART # LBS8S

LANSKY SOFT ARKANSAS STONE PART # LBS6S

LANSKY COMBOSTONE PART # LCB6FC

LANSKY COMBOSTONE PART # LCB8FC

SHARPENERS

Lansky Sharpeners

www.lansky.com

CERAMIC AND STEEL SHARPENERS

2 ROD DIAMOND TURN BOX PART # LDTB2

Features: Two 5" long fine grit diamond rods; hardwood turn box with internal rod storage

MSRP: **$24.99**

2-ROD TURN BOX PART # LCS5D

Features: Two 5" long medium alumina ceramic rods; hardwood turn box with internal rod storage

MSRP: **$11.99**

4 ROD GOURMET KNIFE SHARPENER PART # LCSGM4

Features: 2 medium grit and 2 fine grit (for a highly sharp edge) 9" alumina ceramic rods; solid hardwood base; permanent hand guard; snap-in rod storage

MSRP: **$39.99**

4-ROD TURN BOX PART # LCD5D

Features: Four 5" long alumina ceramic rods (2 medium grit, 2 fine grit); hardwood turn box with internal rod storage

MSRP: **$21.99**

8" CERAMIC SHARP STICK PART # LSS8CM

Features: Hand guard; over-molded rubber, non-slip, comfort-grip handle

MSRP: **$9.99**

9" DIAMOND SHARP STICK PART # LSS9D

Features: Fine diamond grit bonded to heavy-duty steel rod; hand guard; over-molded rubber, non-slip, comfort-grip handle

MSRP: **$29.99**

9" STEEL SHARP STICK PART # LSS9S

Features: Hand guard; over-molded rubber, non-slip, comfort-grip handle

MSRP: **$24.99**

13" DIAMOND SHARP STICK PART # LSS13D

Features: Fine diamond grit bonded to heavy-duty steel rod; hand guard; over-molded rubber, non-slip, comfort-grip handle

MSRP: **$34.99**

13" STEEL SHARP STICK PART # LSS13S

Features: Hand guard; over-molded rubber, non-slip, comfort-grip handle

MSRP: **$27.99**

ERASER BLOCK PART # LERAS

MSRP: **$4.99**

FOLD-A-VEE SHARPENER PART # LCSFV

MSRP: **$17.99**

LANSKY 4-ROD TURN BOX PART # LCD5D

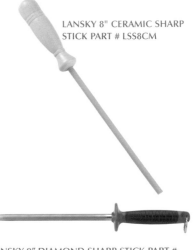

LANSKY 8" CERAMIC SHARP STICK PART # LSS8CM

LANSKY 2 ROD DIAMOND TURN BOX PART # LDTB2

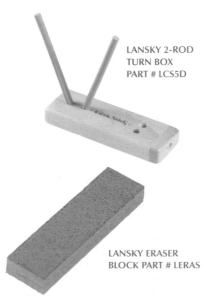

LANSKY 2-ROD TURN BOX PART # LCS5D

LANSKY ERASER BLOCK PART # LERAS

LANSKY 9" DIAMOND SHARP STICK PART # LSS9D

LANSKY 9" STEEL SHARP STICK PART # LSS9S

LANSKY 13" DIAMOND SHARP STICK PART # LSS13D

LANSKY 13" STEEL SHARP STICK PART # LSS13S

LANSKY FOLD-A-VEE SHARPENER PART # LCSFV

LANSKY DIAMOND BENCH STONE
PART # LBD6C

LANSKY DIAMOND BENCH STONE
PART # LDB6E

LANSKY DIAMOND BENCH STONE
PART # LDB6F

LANSKY DIAMOND BENCH STONE
PART # LDB6M

LANSKY DIAMOND BENCH STONE PART #
LDB6X

LANSKY DIAMOND BENCH STONE
PART # LDB8C

DIAMOND BENCH STONES

DIAMOND BENCH STONE PART # LDB6C

Grit: Coarse (120)
Length: 6″ x 2″
Features: Edge-to-edge diamond grit surface; high-impact plastic self-storing case; non-slip feet; overmolded rubber frame; two sizes and five grits available
MSRP: **$26.99**

DIAMOND BENCH STONE PART # LDB6E

Grit: Extra fine (1,000)
Length: 6″ x 2″
Features: Edge-to-edge diamond grit surface; high-impact plastic self-storing case; non-slip feet; overmolded rubber frame; two sizes and five grits available
MSRP: **$26.99**

DIAMOND BENCH STONE PART # LDB6F

Grit: Fine (600)
Length: 6″ x 2″
Features: Edge-to-edge diamond grit surface; high-impact plastic self-storing case; non-slip feet; overmolded rubber frame; two sizes and five grits available
MSRP: **$26.99**

DIAMOND BENCH STONE PART # LDB6M

Grit: Medium (280)
Length: 6″ x 2″
Features: Edge-to-edge diamond grit surface; high-impact plastic self-storing case; non-slip feet; overmolded rubber frame; two sizes and five grits available
MSRP: **$26.99**

DIAMOND BENCH STONE PART # LDB6X

Grit: Extra coarse (70)
Length: 6″ x 2″
Features: Edge-to-edge diamond grit surface; high-impact plastic self-storing case; non-slip feet; overmolded rubber frame; two sizes and five grits available
MSRP: **$26.99**

DIAMOND BENCH STONE PART # LDB8C

Grit: Coarse (120)
Length: 8″ x 2″
Features: Edge-to-edge diamond grit surface; high-impact plastic self-storing case; non-slip feet; overmolded rubber frame; two sizes and five grits available
MSRP: **$36.99**

SHARPENERS

Lansky Sharpeners
www.lansky.com

LANSKY DIAMOND BENCH STONE
PART # LDB8F

LANSKY DIAMOND BENCH STONE
PART # LDB8M

LANSKY DIAMOND BENCH STONE PART #
LBD8X

DIAMOND BENCH STONE PART # LDB8F
Grit: Fine (600)
Length: 8″ x 2″
Features: Edge-to-edge diamond grit surface; high-impact plastic self-storing case; non-slip feet; overmolded rubber frame; two sizes and five grits available
MSRP: **$36.99**

DIAMOND BENCH STONE PART # LDB8M
Grit: Medium (280)
Length: 8″ x 2″
Features: Edge-to-edge diamond grit surface; high-impact plastic self-storing case; non-slip feet; overmolded rubber frame; two sizes and five grits available
MSRP: **$36.99**

DIAMOND BENCH STONE PART # LDB8X
Grit: Extra coarse (70)
Length: 8″ x 2″
Features: Edge-to-edge diamond grit surface; high-impact plastic self-storing case; non-slip feet; overmolded rubber frame; two sizes and five grits available
MSRP: **$36.99**

LANSKY DIAMOND SHARPENING PAD PART # LDPMD

LANSKY/DIAMOND/CARBIDE TACTICAL
SHARPENING ROD PART # LCD02

LANSKY DOUBLE-FOLDING DIAMOND PADDLE PART # LDFPMF

DIAMOND SHARPENING RODS

DIAMOND/CARBIDE TACTICAL SHARPENING ROD PART # LCD02
Features: Tungsten carbide sharpeners; retractable diamond rod
MSRP: **$19.99**

DIAMOND SHARPENING PADS
Length: 6 in.
Features: Rubber over-molded handle
Options: Medium (Part # LDPMD); coarse (Part # LDPCR); extra fine (Part # LDPEF); extra coarse (Part # LDPXC); the sharpening pads are available in 5 color-coded 1.875″ x .75″ diamond grits
MSRP: **$6.99**

DOUBLE FOLDING DIAMOND PADDLE PART # LDFPMF / PART # LDFPCF
Features: Double-sided; rubber over-molded handles
Options: Medium/fine grit (Part # LDFPMF); fine/coarse grit (Part # LDFPCF)
MSRP: **$29.99**

LANSKY FOLDING DIAMOND PADDLE PART # LDFPM

LANSKY FOLDING DIAMOND RAT TAIL PART # LFRTF

LANSKY RETRACTABLE DIAMOND ROD PART # LRRDF

FOLDING DIAMOND PADDLES

Length: 3.5" x .75"
Features: Full diamond grit surface; comfort-grip; non-slip handles
Options: Fine (Part # LDFPF); medium (Part # LDFPM); coarse (Part # LDFPC); extra fine (Part # LDFPE); extra coarse (Part # LDFPX)
MSRP: $19.99

FOLDING DIAMOND RAT TAIL PART # LFRTF

Grit: Fine
Length: 3.5"
Features: Rubber-overmolded; comfort-grip; non-slip handles
MSRP: $14.99

RETRACTABLE DIAMOND ROD PART # LRRDF

Features: All-brass case with non-slip grip; sharpening rod can extend to 3.5 inches; grooved for sharpening fish hooks
MSRP: $18.99

POCKET SHARPENERS

COLD STEEL® KNIFE SHARPENER PART # LTRCS

Features: Pocket-sized; for the proprietary serrations used on Cold Steel® brand folding and fixed blade knives; safety thumb rests; keychain
MSRP: $7.99

DIAMOND POCKET STONE PART # LDPST

Features: 1" x 3" diamond grit; full diamond sharpening surface on both sides; sharpening groove for hooks; carrying pouch
MSRP: $12.99

DUAL GRIT SHARPENER / THE PUCK PART # LPUCK

Features: Easy-to-grip contoured shape; Dual-Grit design
MSRP: $7.99

MINI CROCK STICK PART # LCKEY

Features: Key chain; two removable alumina ceramic sharpening rods
MSRP: $4.99

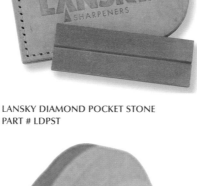

LANSKY DIAMOND POCKET STONE PART # LDPST

LANSKY COLD STEEL® KNIFE SHARPENER PART # LTRCS

DUAL GRIT SHARPENER/ THE PUCK PART # LPUCK

MINI CROCK STICK PART # LCKEY

SHARPENERS

Lansky Sharpeners

www.lansky.com

LANSKY MINI DOG BONE PART # LCDOG

LANSKY MULTIPSHARPENER PART # LTRIM

LANSKY SPYDER SHARPENER PART # LTRSP

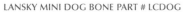

LANSKY POCKET ARKANSAS STONE PART # LSAPS

LANSKY SPEEDY SHARP PART # LSPED

MINI DOG BONE PART # LCDOG
Features: Keychain; colorful patented finger guards
MSRP: $3.99

MULTI SHARPENER PART # LTRIM
MSRP: $7.99

POCKET ARKANSAS STONE PART # LSAPS
Features: Two grooves; leather pouch
MSRP: $4.99

SPEEDY SHARP PART # LSPED
Features: Two ceramic crock sticks; recessed area for a comfortable grip
MSRP: $3.49

SPYDER SHARPENER PART # LTRSP
Features: Groove for sharpening fish hooks; non-slip thumb and finger rests; keychain
MSRP: $7.99

SHARPENING HONES

COARSE DIAMOND HONE PART # LDHCR
MSRP: $19.99

COARSE HONE PART # S0120
MSRP: $6.99

EXTRA COARSE DIAMOND HONE PART # LDHXC
MSRP: $19.99

EXTRA COARSE HONE PART # S0070
MSRP: $5.99

FINE DIAMOND HONE PART # LDHFN
MSRP: $19.99

FINE HONE PART # S0600
MSRP: $8.99

FINE SERRATED HONE PART # LSERT
MSRP: $9.99

LANSKY COARSE DIAMOND HONE PART # LDHCR

LANSKY COARSE HONE PART # S0120

LANSKY EXTRA COARSE DIAMOND HONE PART # LDHXC

LANSKY EXTRA COARSE PART # S0070

LANSKY FINE SERRATED HONE PART # LSERT

LANSKY FINE DIAMOND HOME PART # LDHFN

LANSKY FINE HONE PART # S0600

SHARPENERS

Lansky Sharpeners
www.lansky.com

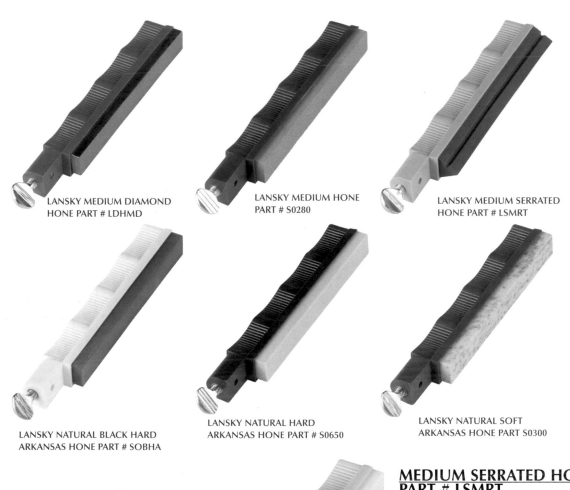

LANSKY MEDIUM DIAMOND HONE PART # LDHMD

LANSKY MEDIUM HONE PART # S0280

LANSKY MEDIUM SERRATED HONE PART # LSMRT

LANSKY NATURAL BLACK HARD ARKANSAS HONE PART # SOBHA

LANSKY NATURAL HARD ARKANSAS HONE PART # S0650

LANSKY NATURAL SOFT ARKANSAS HONE PART S0300

LANSKY SUPER SAPPHIRE HONE PART # S2000

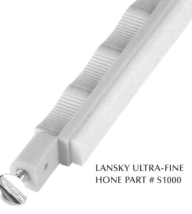

LANSKY ULTRA-FINE HONE PART # S1000

MEDIUM DIAMOND HONE PART # LDHMD
MSRP: $19.99

MEDIUM HONE PART # S0280
MSRP: $7.99

MEDIUM SERRATED HONE PART # LSMRT
MSRP: $9.99

NATURAL BLACK HARD ARKANSAS HONE PART # SOBHA
MSRP: $14.99

NATURAL HARD ARKANSAS HONE PART # S0650
MSRP: $10.99

NATURAL SOFT ARKANSAS HONE PART # S0300
MSRP: $9.99

SUPER SAPPHIRE HONE PART # S2000
MSRP: $14.99

ULTRA-FINE HONE PART # S1000
MSRP: $9.99

SHARPENERS

LANSKY AXE & MACHETE SHARPENER PART # LASH01

TUNGSTEN CARBIDE SHARPENERS

AXE & MACHETE SHARPENER PART # LASH01

Features: Comfort grip; built-in hand guard
MSRP:$19.99

DELUXE QUICK EDGE CAMO PART # LSTCN-CG

Features: Over-molded rubber non-slip grip; safety thumb rest; lanyard hole
MSRP:$9.99

DELUXE QUICK EDGE PART # LSTCN

Features: Over-molded rubber non-slip grip; safety thumb rest; lanyard hole
MSRP:$8.99

FILET & BAIT SHARPENER PART # LSTCF

Features: Tungsten carbide sharpening heads; ergonomic grip; finger guard; thumb rest
MSRP:$7.99

QUICK EDGE PART # LSTCS

Features: V-shaped tungsten carbide sharpening element; ergonomic grip; finger guard; thumb rest
MSRP:$7.99

QUICK FIX POCKET SHARPENER CAMO PART # LCSTC-CG

Features: Tungsten carbide blade; Crock Stick ceramic rods
MSRP:$6.99

QUICK FIX POCKET SHARPENER PART # LCSTC

Features: Tungsten carbide blade; Crock Stick ceramic rods
MSRP:$5.99

LANSKY DELUXE QUICK EDGE CAMO PART # LSTCN-CG

DELUXE QUICK EDGE PART # LSTCN

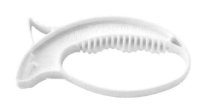

LANSKY FILET & BAIT SHARPENER PART # LSTCF

LANSKY QUICK EDGE PART # LSTCS

LANSKY QUICK FIX POCKET SHARPENER CAMO PART # LCSTC-CG

LANSKY QUICK FIX POCKET SHARPENER PART # LCSTC

SHARPENERS

Smith's
smithsedge.com

Smith's, in business since 1886, provides sharpeners for kitchen, home, sporting, and tools. Smith's provides electric sharpeners, manual sharpeners, and sharpening rods for knives and scissors, as well as fixed angle pull through sharpeners, precisions kits, and natural Arkansas stones.

3001 – 10" DIAMOND SHARPENING STEEL

Grit: Fine diamond (750)
Features: Layers of micron-sized monocrystalline diamonds; soft-grip rubber handle; oversized hand guard; hang-up ring; plastic sharpening tip
MSRP: **$29.99**

SMITH'S 3001 – 10" DIAMOND SHARPENING STEEL

50002 – 9" OVAL CERAMIC SHARPENING ROD

Grit: Fine ceramic (800)
Features: Oversized hand guard; hang-up ring; plastic sharpening tip
MSRP: **$14.99**

SMITH'S 50002 – 9" OVAL CERAMIC SHARPENING ROD

50005 - EDGE PRO COMPACT ELECTRIC & MANUAL KNIFE SHARPENER

Features: Electric; crossed ceramic rods for final edge honing; pre-set sharpening angles; soft-grip rubber handle; non-slip rubber feet; coarse wheel grade
MSRP: **$24.99**

50008 – 8" DIAMOND TRI-HONE SHARPENING SYSTEM

Grit: Coarse (325), fine (750), natural Arkansas (800–1,000)
Length: 8" x 2.5"
Features: Non-slip rubber feet; micro-tool sharpening pad for small tools; premium honing solution; sharpening angle guide
MSRP: **$99.99**

SMITH'S 50005 – EDGE PRO COMPACT ELECTRIC & MANUAL KNIFE SHARPENER

50023 – DIAMOND EDGE PRO ELECTRIC KNIFE & SCISSORS SHARPENER

Features: Interlocking diamond wheels with manual sharpening elements; low and high speeds; Pull 2 Lock scissors sharpener for both right- and left-handed scissors; edge alignment slot; honing/serrated edge slot; rubber hand grip; non-slip rubber feet; magnetic collection strip for metal filings; diamond wheel abrasive; medium grit wheel
MSRP: **$119.99**

SMITH'S 50008 – 8" DIAMOND TRI-HONE

SMITH'S 50023 – DIAMOND EDGE PRO ELECTRIC KNIFE & SCISSORS SHARPENER

SHARPENERS

50047 – EDGE STICK SHARPENER

Grit: Fine diamond (750)
Length: 0.375" x 2.875"
Features: Coarse carbide blades; fabric storage pouch; high quality abrasives; cast aluminum housing; reversible components
MSRP: $23.99

50090 – EDGE PRO PULL-THRU KNIFE SHARPENER

Features: Precision ground carbides; specially-shaped ceramic stones; soft-grip handle; non-slip rubber feet
MSRP: $14.99

50138 – DIAMOND EDGE 2000 ELECTRIC KNIFE SHARPENER

Features: 2-stage sharpening system; diamond coated sharpening wheel; blade guides; fixed angle ceramic stones
MSRP: $39.99

50139 – DIAMOND EDGE 3000 ELECTRIC KNIFE SHARPENER

Features: Electric; coarse and fine diamond sharpening wheels; crossed ceramic stones; blade guides; fixed angle ceramic stones
MSRP: $59.99

50185 – JIFFY-PRO HANDHELD SHARPENER

Features: Crossed carbide blades; scissors sharpening slot; patented "floating" carbide rod; soft-grip rubber handle
MSRP: $9.99

50245 – CERAMIC EDGE PRO ELECTRIC KNIFE SHARPENER

Features: Electric; interlocking, self-aligning ceramic sharpening wheels; initial edge setting slot with crossed premium carbide blades; two manual, pull-through sharpening slots; soft grip; non-slip rubber feet
MSRP: $99.99

SMITH'S 50047 - EDGE STICK SHARPENER

SMITH'S 50090 - EDGE PRO PULL-THRU KNIFE SHARPENER

SMITH'S 50138 - DIAMOND EDGE 2000 ELECTRIC KNIFE SHARPENER

SMITH'S 50139 - DIAMOND EDGE 3000 ELECTRIC KNIFE SHARPENER

SMITH'S 50185 - JIFFY-PRO HANDHELD SHARPENER

SMITH'S 50245 - CERAMIC EDGE PRO ELECTRIC KNIFE SHARPENER

SHARPENERS

Smith's

smithsedge.com

SMITH'S CCD4 - 3-IN-1 SHARPENING SYSTEM

SMITH'S CCKS - 2-STEP KNIFE SHARPENER

SMITH'S CSCS - 4-IN-1 KNIFE AND SCISSORS SHARPENER

CCD4 – 3-IN-1 SHARPENING SYSTEM

Grit: Fine interrupted surface diamond (750); two teardrop ceramic rods (800)
Length: 4″ x 1″ x ¼″
Features: 3-in-1 sharpener; pre-aligned carbide blades; protective storage lid; hand guard; compartment for rod storage; sharpening groove for hooks and small tools; non-slip rubber feet
MSRP:$19.99

CCKS – 2-STEP KNIFE SHARPENER

Grit: Coarse carbide/fine ceramic (800)
Features: Two tungsten carbide blades with pre-set angles; carbide sharpening slots; two crossed ceramic rods
MSRP:$5.99

CSCS – 4-IN-1 KNIFE AND SCISSORS SHARPENER

Grit: Coarse ceramic (600)
Features: Pre-set crossed carbide blades; scissors sharpener
MSRP:$9.99

DBSC – 6" X 2.5" COARSE DIAMOND BENCH STONE

Features: 325-grit; layers of micron-sized monocrystalline diamonds banded in nickel to a flat metal surface; molded plastic base with non-slip rubber feet; clear plastic lid; micro-tool sharpening pad for small tools
MSRP:$29.99

SMITH'S DBSC – 6" X 2.5" COARSE DIAMOND BENCH STONE

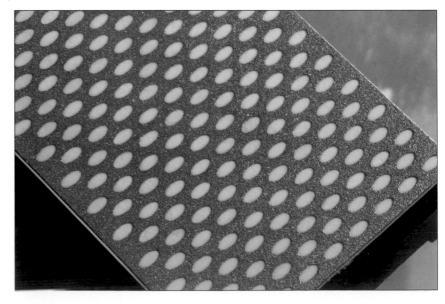

DBSC115 – 11.5" X 2.5" COARSE DIAMOND BENCH STONE

Features: 325-grit; layers of micro-sized monocrystalline diamonds banded in nickel to a flat metal surface; molded plastic base with non-slip rubber feet; clear plastic lid; micro-tool sharpening pad for small tools
MSRP: **$59.99**

DBSF – 6" X 2.5" FINE DIAMOND BENCH STONE

Features: 750-grit; layers of micron-sized monocrystalline diamonds banded in nickel to a flat metal surface; molded plastic base with non-slip rubber feet; clear plastic lid; micro-tool sharpening pad for small tools
MSRP: **$29.99**

DBSF115 – 11.5" X 2.5" FINE DIAMOND BENCH STONE

Features: 750-grit; layers of micron-sized monocrystalline diamonds banded in nickel to a flat metal surface; molded plastic base with non-slip rubber feet; clear plastic lid; micro-tool sharpening pad for small tools.
MSRP: **$59.99**

DCS4 – 4" DIAMOND COMBINATION

Features: Coarse 325- and fine 750-grit; layers of micron-sized monocrystalline diamonds; micro-tool sharpening pad; sharpening groove for fish hooks or pointed tools; soft-grip rubber handle; thumb guard; storage handle
MSRP: **$19.99**

DFPK – DIAMOND FIELD PRECISION KNIFE SHARPENING SYSTEM

Grit: Coarse (325), fine (750), fine Arkansas (1,000), medium triangular-shaped Arkansas (600)
Length: 4" x 1" x ¼"
Features: Fabric storage pouch; folding rod guides; diamond retractable sharpener; V-lock vise; premium honing solution
MSRP: **$49.99**

SMITH'S DBSC115 - 11.5" X 2.5" COARSE DIAMOND BENCH STONE

SMITH'S DBSF – 6" X 2.5" FINE DIAMOND BENCH STONE

SMITH'S DBSF115 - 11.5" X 2.5" FINE DIAMOND BENCH STONE

SMITH'S DCS4 – 4" DIAMOND COMBINATION

SMITH'S DPFK - DIAMOND FIELD PRECISION KNIFE SHARPENING SYSTEM

SHARPENERS

Smith's
smithsedge.com

SMITH'S DPSKP – DIAMOND PRECISION KNIFE SHARPENING SYSTEM

SMITH'S DRET – DIAMOND RETRACTABLE SHARPENER

SMITH'S MBS6 – 6" MEDIUM ARKANSAS BENCH STONE

SMITH'S DS3 – 3" DIAMOND STONE WITH POUCH

SMITH'S JIFF-S – "10 SECOND" KNIFE & SCISSORS SHARPENER

DPSKP – DIAMOND PRECISION KNIFE SHARPENING SYSTEM

Grit: Coarse (325), fine (750), medium triangular-shaped Arkansas (600)
Length: 4" x 1" x ¼"
Features: Fabric storage pouch; folding rod guides; V-lock vise; premium honing solution
MSRP: $39.99

DRET – DIAMOND RETRACTABLE SHARPENER

Features: Tapered diamond-coated reversible steel rod; layers of medium grit, monocrystalline diamonds; groove for sharpening hooks; shirt pocket slip; aluminum housing; handle storage
MSRP: $7.99

DS3 – 3" DIAMOND STONE WITH POUCH

Grit: Medium diamond (400)
Length: 3" x 1" x ¼"
Features: Groove for sharpening hooks; fabric storage pouch with fold-over flap and belt loop
MSRP: $7.99

JIFF-S – "10 SECOND" KNIFE & SCISSORS SHARPENER

Grit: Coarse (800)
Features: V-shaped sharpening slot; scissor sharpening feature with round ceramic rod
MSRP: $7.99

MBS6 – 6" MEDIUM ARKANSAS BENCH STONE

Grit: Medium Arkansas (600)
Length: 6" x 1 ⅝" x ⅜"
Features: Plastic lid; non-slip rubber feet; molded plastic base
MSRP: $17.99

MP4L – 4" ARKANSAS STONE WITH POUCH

Grit: Medium Arkansas (600)
Length: 4" x 1" x ⅜"
Features: Fabric pouch with fold-over flap and belt loop
MSRP: $6.49

PP1 – "POCKET PAL" KNIFE SHARPENER

Grit: Medium diamond (400), coarse ceramic (600)
Features: Pre-set, reversible, and replaceable crossed carbides and ceramic stones; fold out, tapered round, diamond coated rod; lanyard hole
MSRP: $9.99

SMITH'S MP4L – 4" ARKANSAS STONE WITH POUCH

SMITH'S PP1 – "POCKET PAL" KNIFE SHARPENER

SHARPENERS

SMITH'S SK2 – 2 STONE SHARPENING KIT

TRI-6 – 6" THREE STONE SHARPENING SYSTEM

SMITH'S SPSK – STANDARD PRECISION KNIFE SHARPENING SYSTEM

SHARPENERS

SK2 – 2 STONE SHARPENING KIT

Length: 5" x 1 ⅝" x ⅜" (medium stone); 4" x 1" x ⅜" (fine Arkansas stone)
Features: Built-in stone storage area on bottom of plastic base; premium honing solution; sharpening angle guide
MSRP: $15.99

SPSK – STANDARD PRECISION KNIFE SHARPENING SYSTEM

Grit: Coarse (325), medium triangular-shaped Arkansas (600), fine Arkansas (1000)
Length: 4" x ½" x ¼"
Features: Fabric storage pouch; folding rod guides; fine diamond stone; V-lock vise; diamond premium honing solution
MSRP: $26.99

TRI-6 – 6" THREE STONE SHARPENING SYSTEM

Grit: 6" medium Arkansas (600), 6" fine Arkansas (1000)
Length: 6" x 1 ⅝" x ⅜"
Features: Molded plastic base with nonskid rubber feet; "V" trough to catch the oil drippings; premium honing solution; sharpening angle guide; 6" coarse synthetic stone
MSRP: $29.99

Spyderco

www.spyderco.com

Spyderco, based in Golden, Colorado, makes and sells unusual knives, from one-hand opening to clips that attach knives to pockets. They also carry a full line of shaperners and accessories.

SLIP STONE FINE #307F

Grits: Fine
Size: 2" x 4"
Features: Tear-drop shape; Alumina Ceramic slip stone; suede carrying case
MSRP: $80

TRI-ANGLE SHARPMAKER #204MF

Grits: Medium (brown); fine (white)
Size: 7" x ½"
Features: Two sets of high alumina ceramic stones; triangular shape; brass safety rods; self-contained ABS plastic base
MSRP: $95

TRI-ANGLE SHARPMAKER

SLIP STONE FINE

Tandy

www.tandyleatherfactory.com

In 2000, Tandy Leather merged with The Leather Factory to provide a wide array of leatherworking supplies to businesses, individuals, and others. While Tandy focuses mainly on leather kits, the company does boast one sharpener for any honing needs.

CRAFTOOL KEEN EDGE SHARPENER

Description: This sharpener helps keep your swivel knife blade at the proper angle while honing.
MSRP: $14.99

TANDY CRAFTOOL KEEN
EDGE SHARPENER

SHARPENERS

Manufacturers

A. G. Russell Knives, Inc.
2900 S. 26th St.
Rogers, AR 72758
Tel: 479-631-0130
Fax: 479-631-8493
Toll free: 1-800-255-9034
Email: ag@agrussell.com
www.agrussell.com

Al Mar Knives
PO Box 2295
Tualatin, OR 97062
Tel: 503-670-9080
www.almarknives.com

Benchmade Knife Company
300 Beavercreek Road
Oregon City, OR 97045
Toll free: 1-800-800-7427
www.benchmade.com

Blackhawk! Products Group
6160 Commander Pkwy
Norfolk, VA 23502
Tel: 757-436-3101
Fax: 757-436-3088
Toll free: 1-800-694-5263
Email: cs@blackhawk.com
www.blackhawk.com

Blade-Tech Industries
5530 184th St E
Suite A
Puyallup, WA 98375
Tel: 253-655-8059
Fax: 253-655-8066
Toll free: 1-877-331-5793
www.blade-tech.com

Böker USA, Inc.
1550 Balsam Street
Lakewood, CO 80214
Toll free: 1-800-835-6433
Fax: 303-462-0668
www.boker.de/us/

A. G. RUSSELL™ SHOPMADE CALIFORNIA BOWIE

Browning
One Browning Place
Arnold, MO 63010
Toll free: 1-800-322-4626 x2860
www.browning.com

Buck Knives
660 S. Lochsa Street
Post Falls, ID 83852
Tel: 208-262-0500
Fax: 208-262-0738
Toll free: 1-800-326-2825
Email: pfstore@buckknives.com
www.buckknives.com

Busse Combat Knife Co.
11651 County Rd. 12
Wauseon, OH 43567
Tel: 419-923-6471
Fax: 419-923-2337
Email: info@bussecombat.com
www.bussecombat.com

Camillus
60 Round Hill Road
Fairfield, CT 06824
Toll free: 877-412-7467 (order information)
Toll free: 800-835-2263 (product information)
Email: info@camillusknives.com
www.camillusknives.com

Chris Reeve Knives
2949 S. Victory View Way
Boise, ID 83709
Tel: 208-375-0367
Fax: 208-375-0368
Email: crkinfo@chrisreeve.com
www.chrisreeve.com

Cold Steel, Inc.
6060 Nicolle Street
Ventura, CA 93003
Tel: 805-650-8481
Fax: 805-642-9727
Toll free: 1-800-255-4716
Email: customerservice@coldsteel.com
www.coldsteel.com

Columbia River Knife & Tool
18348 SW 126th Place
Tualatin, OR 97062
Tel: 503-685-5015
Fax: 503-682-9680
Toll free: 1-800-891-3100
Email: info@crkt.com
www.crkt.com

Dan's Whetstone Company, Inc.
418 Hilltop Road
Pearcy, AR 71964
Tel: 501-767-1616
Fax: 501-767-9598
www.danswhetstone.com

Dark Operations Fighting Knives, LLC
2231 W. Sunset St.
Springfield, MO 65807
Tel: 417-883-9444
Fax: 417-883-8636
Email: info@darkopsknives.com
www.darkopsknives.com

Diamond Machining Technology (DMT)
85 Hayes Memorial Drive
Marlborough, MA 01752
Tel: 508-481-5944
Fax: 508-485-3924
Toll free: 1-800-666-4368
www.dmtsharp.com

Camillus 8" Fixed

Edgecraft Corporation
825 Southwood Road
Avondale, PA 19311
Tel:610-268-0500
Toll free: 1-800-342-3255
www.edgecraft.com

Elishewitz Custom Knives
Allen and Valerie Elishewitz
3960 Lariat Ridge
New Braunfels, TX 78132
Tel: 830-899-5356
Email: allen@elishewitzknives.com
www.elishewitzknives.com

Emerson Knives, Inc.
1234 254th St.
Harbor City, Ca 90710
Tel: 310-539-5633
Fax: 310-539-5609
Email: Info@EmersonKnives.com
www.emersonknives.com

EZE-LAP Diamond Products
3572 Arrowhead Drive
Carson City, NV 89706
Tel: 775-888-9500
Fax: 775-888-9555
Toll free: 1-800-843-4815
http://eze-lap.com

Gerber Gear
14200 SW 72nd Avenue
Portland, OR 97224
Toll free: 1-800-950-6161
Email: sales@gerbergear.com
www.gerbergear.com

Grayman Knives
PO Box 50, PMB 132
Lake Arrowhead, CA 92352
Email: info@graymanknives.com
http://graymanknives.com

Havalon Knives
3726 Lonsdale Street
Cincinnati, OH 45227
Tel: 513-271-2117
Fax: 513-271-4714
Toll free: 1-800-638-4770
Email: customerserv@havalon.com
www.havalon.com

Havalon Piranta Original Stainless Steel Skinning Knife

KA-BAR Knives, Inc.
200 Homer Street
Olean, NY 14760
Tel: 716-372-5952
Fax: 716-790-7188
Toll free: 1-800-282-0130
Email: info@ka-bar.com
www.kabar.com

Kershaw Knives
KAI USA Ltd.
18600 SW Teton Avenue
Tualatin, OR 97062
Tel: 503-682-1966
Fax: 503-682-7168
www.kershawknives.com

Knives of Alaska
3100 Airport Drive
Denison, TX 75020
Tel: 903-786-7366
Fax: 903-786-7371
www.knivesofalaska.com

Lansky Sharpeners
PO Box 800
Buffalo, NY 14231
Tel: 716-877-7511
Fax: 716-877-6955
Toll free: 1-800-825-2675
www.lanskysharpeners.com

Remington Zulu Series I Civilian
Clip Point Fixed Blade

Ontario Knife Company
P. O. Box 222-5233
Franklinville, NY 14737
Tel: 716-676-5527
Fax: 800-299-2618
Toll free: 1-800-222-5233
www.ontarioknife.com

Puma Knife Company USA
13934 West 108th Street
Lenexa, KS 66215
Tel: 913-888-5524
Email: customerservice@pumaknifecompanyusa.com
http://pumaknifecompanyusa.com

Queen Cutlery
507 Chestnut Street
Titusville, PA 16354
Tel: 716-676-5527
Fax: 716-676-5535
Toll free: 1-800-222-5233
Email: sales@ontarioknife.com
www.queencutlery.com/

Remington Arms Company, LLC
870 Remington Drive
P. O. Box 700
Madison, NC 27025
Toll free: 1-800-243-9700
Fax: 336-548-7801
www.remington.com

Schrade Knives
Toll Free: 1-800-251-0254
Email: info@taylorbrandsllc.com
www.schradeknives.com

Smith's
747 Mid-America Boulevard
Hot Springs, AR 71913
Tel: 501-321-2244
Fax: 501-321-9232
Toll free: 1-800-221-4156
Email: sales@smithsedge.com
http://smithsedge.com

SOG Specialty Knives & Tools, LLC
6521 212th Street Southwest
Lynnwood, WA 98036
Tel: 425-771-6230
Fax: 425-771-7689
Toll free: 1-888-405-6433
Email: info@sogknives.com
http://sogknives.com

Spyderco Inc.
820 Spyderco Way
Golden, CO 80403
Tel: 303-279-8383
Fax: 303-278-2229
Toll free: 1-800-525-7770
www.spyderco.com

SureFire, LLC
18300 Mount Baldy Circle
Fountain Valley, CA 92708
Tel: 714-545-9444
Fax: 714-545-9537
Toll free: 1-800-828-8809
Email: helpyou@surefire.com
www.surefire.com

Tandy Leather Factory, Inc.
Attn: Sales
1900 SE Loop 820
Fort Worth, TX 76140
Toll free: 1-877-532-8437
Email: tlfhelp@tandyleather.com
www.tandyleatherfactory.com

TOPS Knives
Tactical Operational Products
P. O. Box 2544
Idaho Falls, ID 83403
Tel: 208-542-0113
Fax: 208-552-2945
www.topsknives.com

Victorinox Swiss Army Inc.
7 Victoria Drive
Monroe, CT 06468
Toll free: 1-800-442-2706
www.victorinox.com/us

W. R. Case & Sons Cutlery Co.
PO Box 4000, 50 Owens Way
Bradford, PA 16701
Toll free: 1-800-523-6350
Fax: 814-368-1736
Email: consumer-relations@wrcase.com
www.wrcase.com

Wenger North America
15 Corporate Drive
Orangeburg, NY 10962
Toll free: 1-800-267-3577
Email: customer@wengerna.com
www.wengerna.com

Zero Tolerance Knives
Sonoma Cutlery
130 Kentucky Street
Petauma, CA 94952
Tel: 707-766-6433
Toll free: 1-800-542-8854
www.ztknives.us

VICTORINOX RESCUE
TOOL LOCK KNIFE

Afterword

fter bundling so much information into one large package, it's time to reflect on the industry as a whole and take stock of where it's been and where it may be going. It's no secret that the firearms industry is not just healthy but a manufacturing juggernaut. For example, since becoming a publicly traded company stock, Sturm Ruger & Co. has outperformed gold. Can the knife industry be far behind? The dynamics of the knife industry share some common points both with the firearms industry and, oddly enough, with the music industry as well. In terms of its relationship to the firearms industries, advances in firearms design have been spurred primarily by needs of the military. In time, military weapons filtered down to the consumer level, supplying like technology to the hunter. We're seeing this today as the M16 morphs to the semi-automatic AR15 for civilian defense. For hunters, it has become the Modern Sporting Rifle.

Knives have a similar history, but the balance of flow between the development of hunting knives and military knives (or edged weapons in general) changed after the invention of gunpowder. Once firearms became the primary weapon, knives continued to develop but, until recently, were limited primarily to the needs of the hunter, farmer, and rancher. On the gun side, advancements were made by individual inventors such as John Browning. It behooves us to remember that huge companies such as Smith & Wesson and Ruger were once much smaller and ran on the hard work and creativity of just a few people, including the individuals for which the companies were named. Knife makers such as W.R. Case, Buck, Puma, Boker, and others have similar stories. Today, as it was back then, the success and growth of the knife industry continues to rely upon the efforts of individuals.

There are several ways for an individual to make it in today's knife industry. First, as reported in the feature article in the front of this book, Chris Reeve, a modern manufacturer, set up shop and remained his own boss with his own brand by growing his own means of production. That takes business acumen and financial savvy as well as manufacturing skill. But, some of the biggest names in today's knife business achieved success by applying organizational leadership, financial, skill and delegating the actual design work to others.

One of the most successful methods of delegation in the knife industry is to hire, consult, or contract with designers who are themselves custom knife makers or individuals who have special insights into field applications such as military trainers, first responders, and special operators.

The practice of working with individual designers, especially with custom knife makers, is where the parallel between big knife manufacturers and record companies comes into play. To illustrate, let's briefly track the career of Russ Kommer of Fargo, North Dakota and see if it is at all comparable to that of a recording artist. Russ is the custom knife maker who, along with input from edged weapon instructor extraordinaire Jared Wihongi, designed and developed Browning's Black Label Tactical knives. Did Russ Kommer play an endless string of one-nighters in towns large and small across the nation, learning how to entertain all types of people? No, but he did guide in Alaska for twenty-seven years and skin just about every animal that walked on four legs. Did Russ sell so many of the tapes he made in his own basement that fans urged him to contact a record mogul like Clive Davis? No, but he couldn't make enough of his Bear Claw knives for his friends and, on the advice of the legendary A.G. Russell, successfully "auditioned" the knife with Rod Bremer, President of Columbia River Knife and Tool (now known as CRKT).

Talented individuals such as Russ Kommer are brought on by manufacturers to provide not just expertise but, in Russ's opinion, to establish an identity for a brand or a specific line within a brand. Whereas most of the knives available from Browning were focused on hunting or collecting, advertising the Black Label knives as a collaboration of Kommer and Wihongi immediately gave Browning credibility to those interested in buying tactical knives. Other examples of hiring talent to project brand identity are the Crucible, by Kelly McCann for Blackhawk, or the Benchmade SOCP knife, designed by Greg Thompson to meet the needs of integrating a CQB knife with concealed carry or restrictive duty gear. In fact, defined expertise has always sold knives. In 1956, Puma brought out the White Hunter knife designed by the East African Hunter's Association to show the world that Puma was the maker of pre-eminent knives for the hunter. Just as big record companies signed the likes of Jimi

Hendrix and Janis Joplin in the 1960s to establish themselves as rock music knife makers have signed such name knife makers as Kommer, Elishewitz, McCann, Pardue, Jens Anso, Neil Blackwood, Tighe, Onion, and Hinderer. These are the rock stars of the knife world.

I have drawn on the analogy of the music business to the knife business and rock stars to custom knife makers to illustrate where the knife business might be headed. In the 1960s, the big record labels thrived because they were able to tap into what was popular, with rosters of talented and charismatic stars. The music itself was popular because it was organic. The younger generation picked up on what came before it and made it its own. In today's knife world, the threat of terrorism and the desire for self reliance have made civilians hungry for the tools and the knowledge made available to them from trainers such as Brian Hoffner, Michael Janich, Steve Tarani,

and a host of returning war veterans. This desire for defensive knife practices is just as organic as the music of the 60s, and what they teach is not strictly Escrima, nor the methods of Col. Applegate. The modern fighters have picked up on what came before them and made it their own.

What stopped the big music companies in the 1970s and caused them to fracture into smaller entities was a desire to come up with the next big thing without actually consulting their audience. The result was the rise in the number of independent labels. But, the independent knife makers are already here, en masse. If no single knife company ever profits in a boom like was experienced within the firearms industry, it won't matter. Knives and knife making will go on forever.

Roger Eckstine

Index